Fifty-Two Roughly True Short Stories

by

Pat Gillum

Other books by Pat Gillum:

Spreading Wing

The Truest Friend: Tooter of the Fourche La Fave

Forever Cry

Dead-Eye Samantha

These stories were put together over the past seven years. Many are related to other writings. Some are simply a product of what was rumbling around in my head that day. I hope you enjoy.

As with all my books, thanks to my wife Barbara, who helps me every day in so many different ways, I could never count them all.

TORNADO

THE BIG DAY FOR THE OBU Father-Son Golf Tournament had arrived. Corey, my son, (the OBU grad and a skilled golfer) and I, the novice, were entered as a team. Not *novice,* as in beginner, but the eternal type, as in *no good.*

We struggled through a dark, rainy morning. Fortunately, everyone else struggled too. It was March 1, 1997. A date seared into my brain forever. Not because it was the date I finally amazed everyone by suddenly becoming a good golfer. That didn't happen. Not by a long shot. Or by a short chipshot, or even by a putt. Not because Corey once again played well, which he did, Well enough to carry us to something close enough to victory to win us both a large umbrella. It is because weather straight from hell was on the way, weather that these umbrellas could not touch.

After lunch, bad weather predictions were coming in. I went down to our photography studio in downtown Arkadelphia. The tornado sirens started going off. I called my daughter Kinley. She was in her house, half a mile down Main street, already taking cover. Kinley has always had an unnatural fear of tornadoes. It had became a family joke. We said, "Kinley, think about it. How many people ever get hit by a tornado? What are the odds?" Still, she was always in a hidey hole at the first hint of a bad storm.

She told me she already had it figured out. In an interior closet, on the floor, her little dog Spanky in her lap, a pillow over her head. I told her that seemed about as good as any place.

I went outside. The sirens had stopped, then they started again, along with the report that a large tornado was on the way, scheduled to hit Arkadelphia at 2:20 PM. It was now 2:10. The electricity went off. I wondered for years if it went off because the coming storm hit a line somewhere, or because someone, somewhere, threw a switch, knowing what was about to happen to Arkadelphia, and what hot power lines could mean in the aftermath. Jim Burns, our Emergency Services Director, recently filled me in. The lines went down west of town, probably about the time he was getting help from Gurdon firemen clearing out his truck from downed trees so he could rush to town.

I went in and got our best camera, a Hasselblad. I loaded it, because if a tornado was about to hit, I wanted a good picture of it. I was standing on the sidewalk next to my door, and a man from the Honeycomb Restaurant next door was beside me. At 2:15 we began to hear a loud roar in the west.

"Sounds like a train." he said.

"No tracks over there," I replied.

The noise increased, and he went inside. I readied my camera. Then, a very strange thing happened. Clouds, from all over the sky, started rushing toward a single point, the point of the sound. I decided this thing might be about to form up right on top of me, and it was time to go inside.

I was playing chicken with an F-4, and I blinked. That blink saved my life. Twenty seconds later, a house trailer would be sitting where I stood.

I could not see anything that looked like a tornado, but I snapped a picture any way, and went inside. That would be my last picture for weeks. Afterwards, I could never justify to myself worrying about pictures, when so many people needed help. I don't have a single picture from that time.

The dressing room, in the middle of the building, looked like the best place. Just as I started in, the wind really picked up. *Aw, man, my awning is blowing away.* Then a house trailer, or what was left of it, mostly the frame, came through the front picture window. Windows at the back of the building were sucked in, the suspended ceiling around me was sucked down to the floor, and the two swinging doors behind me slammed with a loud bang. I went in the dressing room, lay the camera on the floor, and covered it with my body. My thought processes ran something like, *We've got to have something left to make a living with when this is all over.* I heard the most awful groaning sound I have ever heard, as my front brick wall, three bricks thick, moved forward a few inches at the top. My thoughts; *Damn! I can't believe this!*

I waited a few moments to make sure this was all over, then I headed for the phone to call Kinley. I was relieved for her. The tornado was moving across the street, I got hit full force, so I felt like there was no way it could have hit her too, *half a mile down the street.* Little did I know.

Just as I picked it up, it rang. It was my brother, Harry, in Yell County, saying he had just heard that downtown Arkadelphia was just blown off the map. I told him I was OK, but now I had to call Kinley. He hung up, and I was thinking, *We're OK, but he won't be OK.* Harry was worrying about me, yet he was dying of cancer. Before our lives and our business were put back together from this, he would be dead.

I tried a couple of times to reach Kinley, but I got a busy signal. I headed that way. When I got to the door, I saw a bright, sunny day outside. But Arkadelphia was pink. The town was covered with pink insulation. The trailer was also on my car out front, and the front door was a hard squeeze. A car in the street had a ton of bricks on top of it, but I could see nobody inside. I just cannot describe the town, and do it justice. Buildings everywhere were in rubble. Dazed, silent people were beginning to emerge. Screams from trapped individuals were coming from all directions. A couple of hundred yards down the street, the large brick shoe store was just a pile of rubble in the street, and amazingly, people were beginning to emerge from the rubble. I headed down the street toward Kinley's house.

Half a mile down the street when the tornado hit, Kinley was still in her closet, sitting cross legged on the floor, Spanky in her lap, a pillow on her head. Only that small portion of her wooden house she was in remained on site. The rest, except for scraps here and there, was blown to who knows where. Her wedding album would eventually be found a mile back up the track of the tornado, where it came into town. The girl who found it, one of my former students, lost her entire family. As the old, very heavy wooden walls collapsed on Kinley, and old chimney that we knew nothing about, that was in that wall, fell apart, bricks rained on her head, which was covered by her sofa cushion. A large chunk of the chimney fell beside her, and as the walls fell on her, forcing her face into the dirt, that chunk of the brick chimney held a small portion up slightly, just enough. As her adrenalin rush hit, she was able to rise up slightly. A woman she didn't know dug her out. The first thing she saw in her yard was our business sign, *Barbara's Photography*. She headed up to the studio, accompanied by the woman who helped her, and Spanky.

When I got a few blocks down the street, I saw her. She was coming up the street, Spanky in her arms, being escorted by *an angel*. No, I'm not speaking figuratively, I'm dead serious. This woman beside her had, I later found out, helped dig her out. She had told Kinley she lived across the street, but neither of us had ever seen her before. As Kinley and I ran to each other, hugged and cried, *the angel* was smiling. We looked around, and she was gone. We've never seen her again. To Kinley and me, she will forever be *her angel*.

Kinley seemed to be all right, and so was Spanky. I led her to a clear space in the street, and told her to not dare move from that spot. I had to try and help some of the screaming, trapped people.

I found a wrecked building with a woman inside. I talked to her. Yes, she was okay, but could not get out. I heard a scream nearby, different from the others. It was filled with total agony. I found out later it came from a young man who had just found his mother's body.

As I started moving boards, to try to help this trapped woman, a strange thing happened. A squad of fully dressed National Guardsmen, complete with camo on their faces, moved into my area. How could they be here already? We were 10 minutes into this thing, yet here they were. I later learned they were returning from a drill, and had to take cover on the edge of the tornado, just as it hit. Anyway, their leader told me to step aside, they would get the woman out. They formed a line, and started moving the boards, one by one. Later, I never had a chance to tell the trapped woman that I didn't just desert her. I've always felt badly about that. As I worked my way back toward Kinley, I saw a man. A merchant. He had cleared out a little spot beside his door, and was standing fast. He was later declared one of the heroes of the tornado, and maybe he was. I only saw him for a moment, and no telling how many people he rescued before or later. But when I saw him, at that moment in time, he was just guarding his stuff.

The alarms were going off at all the banks. I never knew if any unofficial withdrawals were made that day, but I do know of hundred dollar bills being found nearby.

When I got back to Kinley, the excitement was beginning to wear off, and she was not feeling good. I had to find help. I saw a police car in the distance, finally got him as close to Kinley as I could, and loaded her aboard. He said he would take her to the hospital. She was finally moved on to Hot Springs, because our hospital was overflowing. I later caught it, full force, from wife Barbara, for not going with her. I should have. But I reasoned at the time I was needed more here.

Walking up the street, I saw a strange thing. A unit of national guardsmen were marching down the streeet, in perfect order. At each intersection, the leader halted them, one went forward into the intersection, and held up his hand. First up the street, then down, to halt traffic. Well, the streets were full of wreckage, and there would be no traffic on them that day. Oh well, I guess if you ain't got discipline, you ain't got nothin'.

A renter, in one of my duplexes a mile away, called me. The front half of the building had been smashed to the floor. His mama was having a heart attack, and the lady from next door was out in the street, wandering about. I told him I was afoot, and could not get there. Call 911.

After a very long time, it seemed to me, rescue people began to arrive, and take over. I realize now, they got there very quickly, everything considered. But it seemed like forever at the time. I had no idea of the scope of this thing. Help was needed all over.

The police moved in, full force, and secured the buildings. I talked an officer into letting me go into our building and get our cameras and money, while he watched me like a hawk. About that time, Barbara and son Corey were arrriving. They told me Kinley had been moved to Hot Springs. Her back was injured. Since she was sitting cross legged, Indian style, the doc said if she had been pushed down another couple of inches, it would have done her in. The large chunk of chimney, holding the walls up a little, saved her. The monster F-4 (or F-5, depending on who's telling it) had to be at least a half mile wide. We went to where Kinley was.

The next day, it was raining. Mrs. Lois Barksdale, son-in-law Mickey's grandmother, along with my family, had mobilized a crew to help salvage what was left at their house. The town was shut down, tighter than a drum. We needed in, but only rescue personnel were allowed. I found an old Red Cross shirt, and led our caravan to the roadblock. "They're with me," I told the cop. He looked at my Red Cross shirt, and waved us in. Sometimes, you just do what you gotta do.

There was really not much to salvage, at Kinley and Mickey's house. While the others salvaged what larger items they could, I looked for little things. Kinley had always collected, and dearly loved, hundreds of little things. We were soon forced out of downtown by a gas leak.

I wish I could wrap my mind around this thing and tell you all of it. There were hundreds of stories in the making there, alongside mine. Many had a much worse ending. I just can't. All I can hope to do is tell you my family's story. Just one tiny ant in a very large anthill.

The next day, the rain stopped. My car was still trapped. I needed wheels. Officials were coming down the street, checking each building. Danger zones were being roped off. I knew my car would soon be inside a no-go zone, and I could forget about it for days. Trying to move it would tear it up worse, but I had to have it. I got in, started it up, and gunned it, and gunned it some more. With much scratching and screeching, it came out.

As soon as I got a chance, I went up on the roof of our building. The roofing was mostly still there, but it was all torn loose. I looked up and down the street. Every building that was still there had people on top that day.

Most of the old brick buildings, except one, were still standing, although badly damaged. Those old walls in the brick buildings were mostly three bricks thick. Almost all of the wooden buildings in the main path of the storm were just gone. If you ever have an F-5 swooping down on you, look for a brick hidey-hole. Not brick veneer, but the old fashioned type, three or four bricks thick. Or, concrete block with brick outside. Almost all of those buildings remained standing, some just barely.

The streets were littered with roofing nails. I got a lifetime supply of flats in the next two weeks.

I have a confession to make. The days following the tornado are sort of blurred together in my mind. Some of this story may very well be out of order. But it all happened.

I was in our building one morning, still checking the damage. Fortunately, our business equipment was still intact. The front wall had been pushed out six inches at the top, and would have to be replaced. The side walls were questionable. Heavy cables would have to be strung from one side to the other, then tightened, to hold it together.

A girl with a notepad wandered in. I warned her the building was still dangerous to be in at this point, but she didn't care. She was looking for a story for Dateline NBC. My son, Corey, a good writer in his own right, and a good a salesman to boot, came in. He started telling her about Kinley's experience, and about Mickey, her husband, a paramedic. Mickey, though he knew his neighborhood was hit, he was unable to check on Kinley because he was too busy pulling survivors out of the remains of a trailer park across town. Corey told her about Kinley, and about she and I finding each other afterwards. She wanted to meet her. He took her to Kinley at our house. She talked with her, noticing she spoke well, and frankly, is totally beautiful, which always helps. She called her boss. A story was in the works.

I went to check the damaged rent houses. The nearest one, on Crittenden Street, was on the very edge of the tonado's path. It was still standing. Everything across the street was rubble. In seconds, it went from being the worst house in the immediate neighborhood to being the best. Some roofing was off, trees were lying on it, the windows were all broken, the electrical service was torn off. Except for that, it seemed to be intact. The tenant, I found out later, was on the run from the law, and had left before the tornado hit. He never showed up to claim his stuff.

I went to the Clay Streeet house. While it was out of the main path of the tornado, the associated high winds had blown a huge oak tree across the street down and crushed the front one third of the house down to the floor. It also crushed a tenant's car in front. The lady who owned the car had already salvaged her things and moved out. The tenants of the other apartment consisted of an elderly lady and her son. She had suffered a heart attack during the storm, but was recovering. The son was still there salvaging when I arrived. He told me, "The living room furniture is brand new. We just paid $2,000. for it." It was totally intact, not even wet, though I don't know how. The store they had bought it from, not a downtown business, had offered to buy it back for $300. They were to pick it up the next day.

I told him, "You can get a lot more for it than that. Why sell? We can move it back into the protected part of the house and run it in the paper."

He answered, "We are living in Little Rock, and we need the money now." They were in a bad situation.

"All right," I said. "I will buy it from you right now for $300. I'll run it in the paper, and call you when it sells. Whatever I can get is yours." He agreed. I paid up in cash. Two days later, it sold for $1200. I called him, and two hours later, he was there to pick up the $900.

I didn't see the lady from the other apartment in that house again, until later, I ran across her uptown. I apologized for not being able to get there when she needed me, and gave her what money I had on me, $100.

President Clinton came to town. He was walking up the street toward our business, and a Secret Service dude was ranging out in front. I told him, "You better keep him away from my building. That front wall is going to come down at some point."

He looked at me. "Today?"

"Well, I hope not!" He looked me over good, then started going through my tool bag around my waist.

Our photography building would be unusable for a long time, but our equipment was intact. We were in the running for the job of photographing the Arkadelphia prom. We needed that money badly to help stay afloat. They decided to use the big city photog' from Little Rock. I try not to hold grudges for a long time, but I have to admit that bothered me for some time.

Dateline NBC was coming to our house that night to interview Barbara, Kinley, Mickey and I for their segment. Barbara always keeps her house very neat, and takes a lot of pride in it. It was spotless. Well, the Dateline crew descended upon our living room, and just changed everything around completely. They moved a couch, and there was a big pile of stuff under it. Mostly shoved there by me, I would imagine. Barbara was horrified! Oh well, at least the cameras weren't rolling yet. That pile got gone quickly.

The lights were on, cameras ready to roll, and Fredrica

Whitfield of NBC was sitting there, smiling, her notebook in hand. Now, me, I'm not always a good spontaneous speaker. Never, I would guess, with a national audience. I could not think of a single intelligent thing to say, the best being a few *uh's* and maybe a *duh*. I just knew I was about to become a major fool, on national TV.

Fortunately, Barbara interviewed first, and that gave me a chance to settle down some. Barbara did great, as we all knew she would. She's that way. But every word she said wound up on the cutting room floor, because she was not actually *in* the tornado. I did not say anything profound, but I stumbled through it. At least, the whole town was not laughing at me the next day. Not to my face, anyway.

Kinley interviewed well, as always, a little gift handed down to her from Barbara. Mickey told of being busy hauling injured people out on doors, etc. while knowing his house had been hit, not able to go there. Also, about the total loss of their house, the loss of a very large number of family antiques. But he jerked a lot of tears with his declaration, "But I got what I most wanted from that house!" Tears on his cheek really set it off, and he was instantly every woman's hero.

After the Dateline show aired, they also got a trip to New York to be on the Montel William's Show, where they got a new living room and bedroom suite out of the deal. Kinley's back was still bad, so Montel even upgraded them to a first class flight.

Insurance appraisers descended upon the town in droves one day. Before I knew they had even seen the house, they came to see me, bringing me a check for the total loss of the Crittenden Street house. I told them, "The contractor said he could repair it."

But for the amount of the policy?" he asked.

"Well, I don't know, I haven't got a bid on it yet." Finally realizing I was talking against myself, which is not uncommon for me, I shut up, thanked him, and gracefully accepted the check.

My banker had a good laugh when I told him. When he finished laughing, he told me that if the insurance people had just came down and looked in his files at a pic of that house before the tornado, they would never have paid me a dime.

Years passed. That house, which I have lovingly called Crittenden House for many years, sat right under the new City Manager's office window. I guess they finally got tired of looking at it, because the city finally bought that house from me, on a handshake, and it is now a nice new city hall secondary parking lot. The new city manager told me that I could salvage it, then bring him the keys. I did, but when I took the keys over to his office I had to tell him; "Here's the keys, but you see, Jimmy, it now has no doors. Or windows." My beloved Crittenden house passed on at the ripe old age of 106. Yet much of it lives on, spread all over Little Rock as antiques from the Blue Suede Shoes flea market.

I decided to repair it myself, after the tornado. I did, and three weeks later, it was leased again. One of those guys who makes a living off disasters came up from Florida. Told me he was short on cash, long on tools, and talked me into accepting a chain saw for a deposit. Said he would have a lot of money in a few days. But Arkadelphia had put in emergency rules to keep that kind of stuff down. He had no permit, so he must have been disappointed, because he called me a couple of days later from Hot Springs. Seems he had gone over there to drown his sorrows, got himself thrown in jail, and asked if I would bring his truck over to bond himself out of jail. I did, and he did. A week or so later, he went home. Later, he called and asked if I would send his chain saw to him. I told him that if he would send his rent money still due, and shipping charges for the saw to me, I would. I never heard from him again. His chain saw is still in my garage, but I have never been able to get it started.

One day, as I sat on top of that house putting shingles on, I sat awhile just looking over all that destruction with a bird's eye view. It still had a pink cast to it, from all the insulation lying around. FEMA was doing a great job, hauling off the waste. I had heard this town was the first one in which FEMA went onto private property, instead of requiring the landowners to haul it to the curb. This was back in the days when FEMA was still run by a good ole' Arkansas boy from Danville, James Lee Witt, and it was getting done right. Volunteers from everywhere were all over down there, chain saws going.

I looked down at the nice little lady, trudging along the street, pulling her little red wagon filled with cold water for the workers. She had been doing that for days and days now. I didn't know her, but I wished I did.

I just lost it, and sat on that roof bawling like a baby for my town.

The neighbors across Eighth Street were not as lucky as I. Their house was just a pile of rubble, along with two other small houses his dad owned. That was to be his inheritance, he said. His dad came to town, and they set in to rebuild it themselves. They worked endlessly, day after day, even the young children. Every plank was pulled out, the nails removed, stacked neatly. When I had finished my house, I asked the dad, a tough old man from the old school, if I could help. He thanked me, then said, "As sure as I do start letting people help, someone will get hurt, then they'll be sueing me, sure as the world."

They finally got ready to put the top on, but there was just no plywood to be had in town. They were stalled. Then I remembered. I had some plywood in a storage building, and I knew it would just about be the right amount for that small house. I told the old dad I would give it to him if he would let me help. The Dad was in a bind. No top for his house, and it was supposed to rain in a day or two, or risk getting sued.

I told him, "Now look! I've built three houses, almost completely by myself. I've worked on these rent houses of mine for years. I don't get hurt, and I wouldn't sue you if I did."

He just looked me over good for a long time, started shaking his head, grudgingly agreed, and walked off, muttering about getting his pants sued off.

We hauled the plywood from my storage building. I grabbed a piece of plywood, got up on the house, drove a nail, then took a step. My right foot slipped off a 2x4 down to another, only three inches or so, and my sometimes trick knee gave out, and when all of my weight came down on the toes of one foot, something went bad wrong with that foot. *Good grief! What could I tell that dad?* So I didn't tell him. Just said I had to run an errand, but he knew by the way I was hobbling what the problem was. I knew he thought I was headed for my lawyer's office. But, I drove to the emergency room. Seems my big toe had popped out of place.

The doc came in, gave me pain shots. But I had been wearing the same pair of tennis shoes every day since the tornado, three weeks, and my bare foot smelled really ripe. Rather that endure all that waiting for the pain shots to kick in, he just grabbed my toe and yanked it. Hard. I thought about screaming, but decided against it.

When I got back out to the old man's house, I was not going to be able to climb for a while, so I just had to confess to the old man, who was eyeing me hard. I again gave him another promise not to sue him.

They continued on with the house. A group of Mennonites came down from up north somewhere, and they helped finish it. How they ever talked the dad into letting them, I'll never know. Maybe since he had dodged one lawsuit bullet already, he was softening a bit. Just as they had put on the finishing touches and the last nail was driven, the city decided to use that land for the new City Hall. So, it was immediately torn down again.

But I guess the old man, (who reminded me of my Dad) his hard working son, wife and kids, came out better financially. When the city takes land, I've heard they pay by the square foot, which also means through the nose. I never did know their names, or what became of them. But I still think of them occasionally, with a lot of respect and a smile.

Much of this next segment is based on facts, as I

remember them. The rest is based upon the scuttlebutt around town about what was going on at City Hall. Scuttlebutt is not necessarily true, but it sure began to seem to me like it was. Some said City Hall was being transformed. Since so many were rebuilding, it was a really good time to toughen up the city building standards. The City Manager at that time seemed to me to be a bit of a gunslinger, and, as he came from Cut and Shoot, Texas, maybe he was.

Our Clay Street house was rebuilt, for about what the house cost me in the first place. This was the first rebuilt house to be finished since the tornado, I was told, and the scuttlebutt was, it was destined to become the test house for the new building policy.

The city inspector left about that time. In disgust, as the scuttlebutt went. Scuttlebutt had it he couldn't stomach what was about to happen to these poor people trying to rebuild. Three or so new, temporary building inspectors were brought in, from different parts of the country. I won't go so far as to say they were extreme hard cases, but in my dealings with them, I had every reason to believe they were.

When the contractor finished with the house, they would not approve it. They had me doing more and more little changes, call them to inspect it, then they would add another list of things. The house sat empty, for days and days. There was no shortage of people wanting to rent it, because there were tons of people without a house. I spent days sitting in city hall, waiting for an inspector to go look at the last batch of improvements I had been required to do.

A man from Catholic Relief Services came by. He had a family, he said, huddled in what was a piece of a house. A bulldozer sat in the front yard, ready to tear it down. They had no place to go. He wanted to rent my house. I told him I could not rent it to him, City Hall was not happy with it yet. He just said, "Let's go to City Hall." Well, when he got down there in front of those inspectors, I finally learned what a true hard case looked and sounded like.

The city eased up a little. An inspector came out. He finally said, "If you will build a wooden box around the breaker box on the front porch, I'll release the house."

I reminded him the breakers were already enclosed in a metal box. He looked at me hard awhile, then pointed to the front steps.

"You know, there really needs to be a rail there."

I shut up and started building a box.

Remember, that was 1997. This is much later. Today, we have a local guy as city manager, who turned out to be, in my opinion, our best. And, our new inspector, he's a firm but fair man. He still calls me to task, on occasion, and he holds my feet to the fire. But only when I deserve it. As a landlord, I have every reason to suck up to those guys. But what I have just said is true, nevertheless.

That was our last year in business. The tornado did not drive us out, we already had that planned. Our family was very lucky, all in all. But I sure would not want to go through it again.

Hundreds, and I mean hundreds, of volunteers stepped in and helped our recovery. I can't say enough about the University students. Kinley had stored what we salvaged in our garage, and a team of OBU students came out one day, went through each of the hundreds ot tiny things, and cleaned each one. They really came through for Arkadelphia when the chips were down.

During the time when the National Guard was deployed in Arkadelphia, two of them had planned on getting married. So, Arkadelphia threw them a free wedding. Business people chipped in to help out in their specialty areas. Barbara and I made the wedding pictures. It turned out to be a fun wedding for Arkadelphia, and them too, I think. It was a pleasant little respite during very hard, dark days.

We lost some of our best people. We all grieve for those families. They will never be forgotten. Many people lost a great deal. Arkadelphia has recovered, and the physical reminders of those dark days are gone, except for a blank space here and there. Kinley's homesite remains a nice, pretty, grassy lot in the midst of rebuilt houses. But March 1, 1997 will always be in the minds and hearts of all of us who were there that day.

Nowadays, our family tells Kinley when a storm comes up, "Kinley, think about it! Nobody, but nobody, ever gets hit by a tornado – twice!" It dosen't help her attitude about it much that she has twice had to be moved out into the hallway of a hospital when she was in labor, because a tornado was heading that way. So, don't expect to find Kinley when the dark clouds roll in. She will be in her hidey-hole. I will probably be there with her.

THE SUMMER OF MY BROKEN HEART

I SLUNK DOWN IN THE SEAT as I drove down Main Street in Watson, Arkansas. Well, actually, *the* street. It was dark, but not nearly dark enough. It was a well known fact at my college, Arkansas A&M, 25 miles away, that one just did not venture into Watson, alone, after dark. Watson had 3 or 4 really bad dudes. They loved to fight, and they were good at it. Stories were told of one average-looking guy who had mastered the art of getting in three running steps and throwing the first punch in a one-punch fight, usually against much larger guys. But I had a date with Barbara Dunnahoe, and nothing, or nobody, was going to stop me.

I had met Barbara two days earlier at the Delta Dip in Dumas, home of the Ding Dong Daddy. I didn't make that last part up, it's just what they say down there in the delta. I was finishing up my student teaching in Dumas, and I had just gotten my hamburger, and was walking back to my car. A guy I knew from Arkansas A&M was talking to a carload of high school girls. I saw a couple of nice looking girls in the car. But in the back seat, far side, I saw her. I almost dropped my hamburger. There, before my eyes, sat the most beautiful one-eyed girl I had ever seen. Her hair style covered one eye up, but a little later, I saw the other one too, and it was every bit as beautiful as the first one. This was it. This was the girl I wanted to marry.

But I had this problem. Every time I met a girl I really liked, I just froze up. I couldn't think of a single sensible thing to say. In college, when I found a girl I really liked, I called her up and said something like, "You wouldn't want to go out with me, would you?"

Then, if she hesitated, even for a second, I threw in the clincher. "I don't blame you. I wouldn't either if I were you. Bye."

Well, you can see my situation here, looking at this girl I wanted to marry. But this girl was so bubbly, so outgoing and friendly, she would just not allow me to freeze up. Before long, I had a date with her for Saturday night.

Following her directions, I headed for Watson that Saturday night and tried to be inconspicuous as I rolled down Main Street. I finally made it through town, breathing easier now, and headed out a winding gravel road 3 miles out through the cotton fields to her house.

When I arrived, Barbara invited me in. Her two squirmy little sisters whispered and laughed to each other about how tall I was, how big my hands were, and would you just look at those feet! Her brother, JD, about my age, was there with his wife and baby. He shook my hand and all, but the look in his eye was anything but friendly. It wasn't until years later, I began to piece it all together from his stories about his "three running steps" technique that I began to realize, JD was the one I had heard stories about. Little did I know, the *real* danger was not on the streets of Watson, but here, in this house, looking at me hard. But fortunately, his Mama and Daddy were there, and things went well that night.

We got to date a few times, then student teaching was over, and I was off to my new teaching job in St. Paul, Arkansas. I went to see Barbara every weekend I could, which meant when I was invited. But she was busy finishing up her senior year in high school, St. Paul was a long way off, and I didn't get to see her as much as I wanted to that semester.

At the end of the school year, Barbara was headed off to Arkansas A&M to start college. I knew Barbara would be making a big splash there that summer, pretty girls like her always do. Rather than endure that, I decided to go to Oklahoma, work on a pipeline, make a little money. I knew Barbara still had ties to some guy in the Air Force, and was not ready to put all her eggs in one basket yet. But we parted on good terms, each having no hold on the other.

About mid summer, I stuck my gloved hand into a block and tackle on the pipeline job, and the last inch of my thumb just stayed in the glove. I went over and told the foreman, who had caused this accident in the first place, that I had lost a thumb. He cussed me out really good, for messing up his safety record. My Oklahoma adventure was over, and I was headed back to Arkansas.

I drove down to see Barbara, in summer school at A&M. As I expected, she was making a big splash. Pretty, personable girls just tend to do that. Well, she was dating a football star, the son of the new head football coach, who was making his own splash, and she still had ties to the Air Force dude, but she seemed, in talking with me, to be leaving the door open for us just a little bit.

I suddenly decided I had best go back to school that second summer term, pick up some chemistry, and try to improve my chemistry with Barbara. Right before I left to go back to A&M, I wrote Barbara. Told her I had met her football jock, and he seemed to think he was pretty wonderful. She wrote back and said she had decided he was pretty wonderful too, and another thing or two along that same line of thought.

That hit me hard. Here I was, already paid my tuition money, and I was getting the royal shaft. After a couple of my hardest days ever, I decided to go to school anyway, as hard as that would be. I never liked to just throw away money.

To make matters worse, I got a job working in the cafeteria where Barbara also worked. My old pals tried to cheer me up. Didn't work. My buddy Sam, a one legged guy, offered to fight him for me since I was thumb incapacitated. I was kinda hard to cheer up, seeing her all cozied up with him every day.

One day while we were working, Barbara asked me if I would take her to church that night. I thought awhile, maybe a second, and told her I didn't see why not. I saved my celebrating until I got back to the dorm. Things were looking up! I was in a really good mood, right up until I saw them, right out in front of my dorm, hugging and such. I think he brought her over there to put on a show for me.

That didn't help my mood much, and I was pretty cool to her at church. When I pulled up to her dorm after church, the jock was waiting. He came storming up. I knew I wasn't in good fighting trim, thumb cut off and all. Actually, I have never been a good fighter, thumb or no thumb. Turns out, he did all the fighting, with his words, all aimed right at her, right there in front of me. Barbara very nicely listened to everything he had to say, just ranted himself out, ending up with, "You either leave with me, right now, or it's over!" She just looked at him, and very nicely said, "It's already over."

They say the meek will inherit the earth. Well, that

night I began inheriting the part of it I most wanted, Barbara. We got married on December 26 of that year, and headed off to New Orleans. We got lost somewhere in South Louisiana. Well, I couldn't understand those Cajun's directions, and we never found New Orleans. But somehow, it just didn't seem to matter at the time. The most amazing thing of all is, 51 years later, she's just as beautiful as she was that first night, at the Delta Dip in Dumas, home of the Ding Dong Daddy.

OUR FRIEND THE SPY

BARBARA AND I HAVE TRAVELED MUCH OF THE WORLD, the poor man's way. We fly on flyer miles saved up on our credit card, rent a car, and just drive. We never make reservations ahead, we just start driving and take the world as it comes. We often eat peanut butter sandwiches until we discover where the locals eat. All countries have those places, usually away from the haunts of tourists.

Once we found a nice little guest house in a small village in the Austrian Alps. The nice lady could speak only German, but the only other guest stepped forward, interpreting her German into perfect, even Southern, English. Talking just like we talked.

Well, if one knows Barbara, one knows she was not about to just let that lie. She had to know what was going on.

He was soon our friend, and over a glass of orange juice, she grilled him good. Yes, he had been to America. Still goes reguarly. No, he had never been to the South. She would just not let him quit answering her questions. I went into my hillbilly mode, pulling out, "We shore are much obliged to you-all," throwing in a "feller" now and then, even reaching way back and coming up with a "youens'." He couldn't speak hillbilly, but that was about the only thing he couldn't speak. I think it finally helped him realize we were harmless.

Finally, he just sat there and looked us over good for a long time, poured another glass of orange juice, and began to tell us a fantastic story. His name was Rio. He is a citizen of the world, he said, claiming no country as his home. He was born in a middle eastern country, and his family moved from one country to another as he grew up, and he picked up one language after another. He was a little dark, a little white, and could pass for about any nationality.

After becoming a pilot in the Portugese Air Force, he was trained in regional dialects, for many countries. His job was to travel about, assuming the identity of anybody from anywhere, and gather information.

He asked us if we had a certain stamp on our car that was required for travel in Austria. Of course, we did not. Agreeing to show us where we could buy one, we all got in our car and headed out. We bought the sticker, and drove around for a long time, just seeing the village and talking. He explained that when you violated a traffic law in Europe, a flash would go off, and they had your picture. The fine would be waiting for us when we turned our rental car in.

Well, I could already remember a bunch of flashes going off, usually when we were confused and wandering about, which was most of the time. I dreaded seeing our rental car bill.

He was at the guest house, he said, to meet his buddies, climb the mountain. Then they would spend a day drinking beer and playing cards on top, then climb down. He currently lived with his wife in Germany.

After arriving back at our lodging, he offered to buy us dinner. Well, who can refuse that? And, Barbara was nowhere near through with him yet.

We sat down. He offered to buy me a beer. I didn't like beer, so I said no thanks. He looked at me hard. "You won't drink a beer with me, Pat?"

I could tell he took that personally. I drank beer.

After we had eaten a great meal and he had a bunch more beers, he began to really loosen up, and tell us more.

During the first Gulf War, He was recruited by the U. S. Air Force because he spoke perfect Arabic. He was sent to Colorado Springs for training. His most fearful moments ever, he said, was the night he and his buddies wandered into the wrong part of Colorado Springs by accident. Sounded a lot like stories we had heard all over the world about their visit to America.

When he got to Iraq, he assumed his Arabic identity. Those same buddies arrested him one night, and he smiled and said, "It's me, guys."

They wouldn't believe him, and he had to show them his USAF pants, on under his robe, before they would let him go.

Currently, he said, he makes regular trips to the eastern US near Washington, D.C. The CIA was never mentioned, but we understood..

The next morning, he walked us out to our car. He had a small lecture for Barbara. "You travel far too lightly about the world. People will entrap you. You should never have let me in your car yesterday."

Barbara just smiled. "We had you outnumbered." she replied.

He laughed. "I wasn't worried." He waved Barbara's camera away. No pictures, no address, no e-mail address. "But I will e-mail you."

We're still waiting.

We traveled on into Italy, and traveled west along the Italian Riveara. After buying a $4 coke in return for the opportunuity to use the bathroom, we found lodging. Then be bought train tickets for Monaco tomorrow. Had we gotten a glimpse into what lay ahead, we probably would have just stayed home and slept in.

The train gave us a glimpse at the many congested little towns that lined the Riveara, finally moving into France, then Monaco. We spent a good day touring. It was a fantastic place, but not meant for pore' people like us. They were setting up the Grand Prix along beside the water. Police were everywhere. One policeman for every 60 residents. Barbara tried to get a picture of a grand car so exclusive that we didn't even recognize the name, with me standing beside it at a car dealership. Before I was anywhere near close enough to touch it, a man ran out, screaming at us, and ran us off.

We caught our train back toward our house and our car, smooth as silk. We're world travelers now, and we know how to act the part. When the train got to the border, it stopped. An announcement that we couldn't understand was made, and people were starting to get off. There was no train change on the way in, so we sat tight. After a few minutes, we began to realize we were the only people left. That's a bad sign, and just as that was sinking in, the train started back toward Monaco.

When we got there, we ran back to the ticket agent, who spoke a little English. "You should have changed trains at the border."

"Any more trains out today?"

"One is leaving right now. You might catch it if you run.

That's the last one."

We ran. I quickly outdistanced Barbara. I was nearly there now. The train started to move. I was even with the engineer, and I waved frantically. The train slowed, and a door opened. Barbara was just now coming into sight, a long way back, huffing and puffing. I put one foot on the train, and kept one on the ground, and held my position. If they shut that door now, they would have to squeeze me in it. Once we got on, we found a British couple, (english speakers) who were going past our town, and stuck with them like glue. So much for being big world travelers.

As we realized we must be nearing our town, Barbara asked, "Now, what is the name of our village?"

I didn't have a clue. It was beginning to get dark now. We moved close to the door, and strained to see something familiar. As the train slowed for a village Barbara screamed, "There's our car!" She bolted for the door, ahead of me, and started pushing it open as soon as the train stopped. But she was on the wrong side, and she was about to step out onto a live track! Those trains run silently, are very fast, and are about a foot apart. Stepping out on the wrong side could mean instant, silent death. The way Barbara remembers what happened next, she quickly realized her mistake, and stepped back. The way I remember it, several people tackled her, and pulled her back. Memory can sure be a fickle thing.

We were sure glad to see our cute little red car. We almost hugged and kissed it.

A DIFFERENT KIND OF CHILD

HE'S NOT LIKE ANYBODY you have ever met. Not like anybody anyone has ever met. The first sign that something was amiss came with the first ultrasound. He was grinning. His mischievous grin, I now know so well. The same one I have seen dozens of times, right before he does something little kids just do not do, and I go into panic mode, once again. Just biding his time. Just waiting to pop out and shock the world.

The day of his birth rolled around. A c-section. As soon as he was pulled out, he raised his head and looked around at the doctor and nurses, individually, as if in greeting. They were dumbfounded.

I watched him on my living room floor, when he was entering that stage were babies lie on their stomach and wiggle around. He put his hands on the floor and tried to push up, again and again.

Finally, he raised his upper body off the floor, held, his arms started to quiver, then collapse. Nothing abnormal here. But he did it again, held a little longer, arms shook more, tears started to flow. Collapse. Up again – tears – a little longer – Collapse. This was repeated, again, again, and again. Tears, hard sweat now. Finally, total exhaustion. Temporarily delayed, never defeated.

A healthy respect started to grow within me. How could his tiny body contain so much determination?

Winter came. It was cold in that house. His family lives like North Pole people. He was put into a sleeper, zipped up. The next morning, he was naked in his crib. Though he was far too small to leave that crib, little signs of mystery began to show up here and there. He had wandered at will about that house, naked.

I put a couple of rounds of duct tape around his chest, to keep that sleeper on. No luck. Next, a safety pin was fastened to the inside of the zipper, near the top. The next morning he was naked in his crib, punching holes in the mattress with the open safety pin.

I went shopping. In the fishing department, I found a giant snap swivel, so strong I could barely open it. I substituted it for the safety pin the next night. The next morning, the sleeper was still on, but he must have found a tiny hole in the toe, worked it, worked it, and worked it until one whole leg was out, which he proudly displayed.

His father, worn out by this struggle, was beginning to fathom the depth of his determination. He asked, "Which sleeper do *you* want to wear?"

He pointed one out. "That one." End of the great sleeper struggle.

For a time, his parents kept him in his crib with an elaborate, tent like structure over the top. Then, they just had to give up. He wandered the house at will at night, still too small to get out of that crib, supposedly.

They had chocolate cake for supper, just as he was beginning to talk. He loved it. He asked for seconds.

"No, save it for tomorrow"

Our subject calmly stated, "Mom, while you are asleep, I will come in and get a second piece." Well, he was less than two years old now, small for his age. But mom placed the cake on top of the fridge, just in case. The next morning, the cake was on the kitchen floor, intact, except for a piece missing, and a chocolate trail leading to his crib.

After the scolding, they just had to ask: "How did you do that?"

He brought out a two-step ladder with a circle bar on top for a handle. "I stood on top," he explained, pointing to the handle.

They were on vacation in a condo. He slept on the folded up hide-a-bed. When morning came, he was just gone. Could not be found. After a time, he crawled out of the bowels of the folded up hide-a-bed. He always liked tight places, loved the challenge of going where it seemed impossible for him to go.

I took him for a walk in an athletic field. I always try to keep him in large, open spaces, out of trouble. We came to metal bleachers by the tennis court. He started climbing half way up, going to the end, jumping off, rolling out of it. He never hurts himself when he falls. I was distracted for a moment, a very bad thing. When I looked around, he was at the top level, about to jump. My scream caused him to slip, and he fell down through the framework. He hit a bar that cartwheeled him. Hit another bar, another cartwheel. Finally, he hit the ground with a splat. I ran to him. The breath was knocked out of the boy. When he recovered from it somewhat, he said, "I need to sit down for a minute." No tears. We have an understanding in our family. If a hurt brings tears, call 911. At the end of that minute, almost exactly, that grin started to spread across his face as he jumped up. "I'm going to do that again!"

"No, you're not," I said. "We're going home."

My wife's family reunion rolled around. Later, we all visited the old farm home site. It was surrounded by hundreds of acres of plowed ground. The kids all romped and played. This one child, different than the rest, now two, started walking away. Farther and farther he went. Finally, a concerned adult asked, "When will he turn around?"

"He won't," I replied. "I will have to go get him eventually."

To make my point, I just watched. I decided I would just let him go, as long as he was in no danger. He became a speck in the distance. Finally, I started moving fast to catch up, before he had time to get to a road. He and I walked back, as the families watched. He tripped, falling face first in the dirt. A collective "oooooooooh!" arose from the onlookers. I paid no attention. He arose, wiped the dirt off his face, so he could see, and quickly caught up. He never hurts himself with his falls.

He was approaching three now, watching his brother's basketball practice. The coach was a hard case, ran his team with an iron hand. His teams almost never lost. Parents were afraid of him. When practice was over, our subject walked onto the court, shook the coach's pants leg, and said something.

The coach could not hear. The coach got down on a knee, face to face, and said, "What did you say, buddy?"

"I said, that was not nice of you, telling my brother to get his butt back on the court!" Everyone fell silent. The coach raised up, red faced. One or two of the coach's buddies laughed quietly momentarily, but they were quickly silenced by a red-faced glare.

At the next practice, the coach stated to a group of parents, "Well, I've never been dressed down like that by anyone that small! Then he laughed.

Then, everybody laughed.

Our subject was approaching five now. I have a two story tree house in my yard, for the children around me. To keep the small children below, and safe, a knotted rope must be climbed to reach the second floor. Well, it didn't work out right. The older children could not do it. Guess who did? You guessed it. Right to the top. When I arrived on the scene, he was on the second floor roof, singing a song to celebrate his accomplishment.

Time for the church fish fry. Our friends host this at their farm. Some of my wife's family were there, along with our subject. My wife has a large family, lots of kids, from five to twelve. A couple of the girls, twelve years old, ran the show. The older boys, ten and eleven, ran from these girls. For good reason.

Well, one of the older girls climbed up on a tractor. Our subject started up. She gently put her foot against his face, pushed him back. He needed to know his place. A major mistake. He came back, tiny fists flying. All night he pursued her. When he found her, he always attacked, fists flying. He finally graduated to a stick so he could do real damage. When a rescuing parent was finally brought to the scene, she was back peddling, "Get away from me, you little kid!"

On the way home, he was counseled wisely by his older brother. "You just can't do that," he said, "to older kids. They will beat you up!"

"They may beat me up," he replied, "But I will hurt them while they do."

He's at the top of the kid pecking order now. When

older kids see trouble with him on the horizon, they run tell us. They want no part of having to fight a small bundle of fury again, again, and again.

When kindergarten rolled around, his mother took him to preschool visitation. It was at the school his parent's badly wanted him to go to, as his older brother was there. But, the kindergarten classes were about filled up, and his chances were slim. We had all stressed to him about respecting and obeying the Principal. We had no idea what might happen in a school situation, because of his nature. When they signed in, he asked, "Is the Principal here?"

"Yes, she's over there."

"I would like to meet her."

When the secretary called her over, his mother told her, "I have a young man here who wants to meet you." And, she added, privately, "So, run with it!"

The principal, a very large, tall, stern lady, bent over to get her face next to his. Looked him right in the eye sternly, and said, "If you come here, and act like God and your mama want you to, you will have no trouble. But if you come here and cause problems, you will have lots of trouble!"

He looked her in the eye awhile, then that grin appeared. "Nah, you won't have any trouble from me. I can count to twenty! wanta' hear it?"

She burst out laughing, losing all her bluster. "I would *love* to hear you count to twenty!" Privately, she said to his mama, "I will see to it *personally* that he goes to school here!" Somehow, he managed to snag the very last kindergarten slot.

True to his word, she had no trouble with him. Nor did

his teacher. However, he was not good at obeying teachers whose class he was not in. Unquestioning obedience to an adult, just because they are bigger than him (almost everyone is) is just not a part of his makeup. But a logical, calm approach by his mother, about the "right thing to do" did the trick.

Millions for logic, not one single penny for intimidation.

In kindergarten, he quickly became a leader and protector of the weak. One large boy stomped on the foot of a small girl, who was injured and unable to wear a shoe. Our subject filed it away. Days later, he saw the boy with *his* shoe off. He stomped it, grinding it as much as his small body would allow. "You don't hurt little girls," he said, and walked away.

Summertime came. We all knew that swimming lessons were a requirement, again because of his nature. He really needed to be able to swim. His mother took him to his swimming teacher the first day. He was unable to swim a lick. He looked the situation over for a moment, grinned, then ran to the deep end of the pool, did a cannon ball, sank like a rock. The shocked teacher dove in behind him. As she was dragging him out, she was shaking her head. "He was grinning, all the way down, all the way back up!"

A neighbor gave him an old bicycle, when he turned six. Never rode a real one before. He ran to it, jumped on, and rode it to the top of the highest drive in the neighborhood, and flew down the drive, rounding a sharp curve at the bottom. After that, if he went out the door, he had a headgear on.

Razorback football came around. At one game, a redneck man, sitting up behind his family, spent the entire game shouting at the umpire, the other team's coach, and the other team, often with profanity. Finally, our subject stood up, turned around, pointed his finger at him. "Sir! Oh sir!" When he finally got the man's attention, said, "When I am a man, I won't talk like that!"

The shocked man turned red, then laughed. "Well, sonny, that would probably be a pretty good decision on your part!"

Soccer season came around. We had been waiting for the day, because of his natural ability. We just knew he would be great. That held true in the first game. He scored four goals, driving in and scoring at will. We were really excited, starting his second game. He just was not in the mood. When the game started, he bored quickly, would sometimes be wrestling a teammate to the ground while the other team scored on the opposite end. After a while, he walked over to a nearby field, lay down, chewing on a weed. The coach called him, no luck. Finally, the coach just went over and pulled him up.

Flag football was a mixed bag, also. He often thought it was just as much fun to pull his teammate's flag as an opponent's. About that time it hit me, remembering the sleeper caper.

It had to be his interest, his idea. Not his parent's, not mine.

He and his older brother both decided they would like to wrestle. His brother proved to be a coach's dream – listening to the coach, filled with effort and drive. His coach, a four time national wrestling champion in college, said the brother had more "heart" than any kid he had ever seen.

Our subject, however, was not a coach's dream. Often as not, when the coach instructed, he needed to go to the bathroom, or was at the back of the pack, in his own world.

After a few months, the State Wrestling Championship rolled around. Our subject became transformed, working his way up to the finals. He was seven, his opponent was ten. A much taller boy. The ninety pound division. He quickly pulled a very complex move the coach had been teaching all week, and pinned him. At seven, the state champ! The coach just walked away, shaking his head. "Now, where the heck did that come from? While I was teaching that, he was at the back, singing a song!"

Our subject has a very large heart for the homeless. Singlehandedly, he collected one hundred or more coats for the school "coats for the homeless."

Our subject is now 13. He makes reasonably good grades, but cannot stop talking to everybody around him. The teacher moved his seat right up beside her desk. He then leaned over on her desk, and said, " So, tell me about *your* family." She started doing so, then catching herself, moved him away from her too.

What kind of man will he become? One thing I know, it will be his decision. His area of interest. I just hope I'm around to see it.

BIG DAN

I LOST MY NEPHEW, Big Dan Gillum, just a short time back.

Dan was amazingly strong. When Dan was about 13, and I was a grown man, Dan challenged me to an arm wrestling contest. I knew Dan well, and I could see nothing to be gained except a lot of embarrassment by accepting that challenge, so I declined.

My dad talked a lot about Uncle Will, who was several generations back in my family. He told me a number of times that Uncle Will could wrap his big hand around the horn of a one hundred pound anvil, and hold it straight out.

Uncle Will bought a sawmill one day that the bank had taken away from another man. This man shot him in the back one day as Uncle Will rode his horse away from that sawmill.

Uncle Will's genes seem to have been strong also, because in each subsequent generation, that great strength seemed to be passed on to one or two lucky men. Big Dan had that great strength.

I was completely passed by. But I did have one strength when I was young. I could run a long way. I never had speed, but I discovered fear could add wings to my feet when trouble loomed. So, I made it through my younger years OK.

Years later, I was working on a gas well in Oklahoma. Big Dan roared up on his Harley one day, wanted a job. He was quickly hired.

One day a young, very small, very strong roughneck bragged that he could climb up a thirty foot drill pipe leaning up against the well. Nobody believed him, so he did. When he reached the top, he looked down to see how amazed we all were. What he saw was that Big Dan, who probably weighed 280 in those days, was right behind him. That took some of the shine off that roughneck's accomplishment.

Big Dan lived a hard life. Lots of trouble. Drug problems sent him to prison a couple of times. He ran with the Hell's Angels for a time.

But just a few years ago, he changed. No more trouble. But by then, he was having lots of health problems. He would get up very early, drain a couple of coffee pots, and disappear, working about half a day. Often he delivered groceries to people in need. Sometimes he just helped people who needed it. The rest of the day he spent hooked up to an oxygen tank.

He had found a Church, several miles away. Most of us knew few people in that church. But we all knew Dan was there every time the church doors were opened.

A couple of years ago, I spent the night at Dan's house. We talked late into the night. Dan was excited to tell me about his new-found life with The Lord. Finally I headed to bed. But I stopped, turned, caught Dan's eye, and said, "I'm proud of you, Dan. You're a good man."

"Thanks, Uncle Pat. You've always been a good man."

I slept well that night.

Dan died at fifty-eight. Partially because of his hard early life.

Dan's church wanted to do his memorial service. Our family agreed. The service was amazing to all in our family. I don't use that word lightly. I wanted to know more about how Dan's relationship with this Church came about. The pastor, a really top notch man, was glad to tell me.

Dan showed up there one day, and they welcomed him. Soon he was actively involved. Dan never tried to hide his past life, but was eager to tell them all about how the Lord had turned his life around. His great strength seemed to be that he was determined to be a better man with the Lord, and he never went back. His heart was set on becoming a better man, and spend the rest of his life working for the Lord. Dan prayed each morning that God would put someone in his path that day that he could help. And the Lord did. A lot.

The service was at 2:00 Sunday afternoon. Many people from the church fed my family a wonderful meal at 12:00. It seemed most all of the church members came back for the service.

The service just totally blew away all us Gillums. The pastor gave a great talk, a stage full of wonderful singers sang beautiful songs. The pastor asked if maybe one or two of the church members wished to speak. One man related to us that he heard a tractor in his field early one morning. When he investigated, Big Dan was bush hogging his field. Dan just said, "I thought you might need some help." Several other people stood up and related similar stories. When it was over, all the church, it seemed, came by, crying, expressing great love for Big Dan.

Afterwards, I told the pastor, "Well, I don't have an exact date yet, but I want to reserve a spot. I want a service like that!" My family all agreed. Everyone wanted a true Celebration of Life Service like Big Dan's.

All of us who are saved know we will find a wonderful life in Heaven someday. Big Dan has that life right now. But Dan showed us all: we do not have to die to find that wonderful life. Dan found his right here on earth in Arkansas.

I related this story to the men at Pine Bluff Prison. They really seemed to take it to heart. They even made a poster about Big Dan, which I later gave to his mother. Possibly, Big Dan's work for his Lord on this earth is not yet over.

GOBI

GOBI WAS AN INTERNATIONAL STUDENT at Henderson State University, majoring in business administration.

Barbara and I had just begun attending a small, new church in Arkadelphia, which is today Fellowship Church. Gobi was from another country, and he was not raised a Christian. He became friends with an instructor who was a leader in our church, and along the way he began reading the Bible.

One day, Gobi just showed up at our church. He became a regular. He told us, "When I was reading the Bible, I just could not get past the cross." Gobi was the first person baptized in our young church. Gobi had a full head of curly black hair, and was a very friendly and personable young man, liked by everyone.

He was only weeks away from receiving his Master's degree. He became ill, was having trouble breathing. He was soon diagnosed with cancer. A very large tumor was found in his chest. The doctor told Gobi he needed regular chemotherapy treatments at Hot Springs, 35 miles away, for a long time. Gobi was alone in America, had no car. He had a job he had been walking to, but he became too weak to do that. Kinley, our daughter, set up a schedule for our church members to drive Gobi to Hot Springs. Kinley's family soon moved to Little Rock, and Barbara took over the scheduling, and much of the driving. Many of the treatments lasted six hours, so it was a half day commitment to do that.

His beautiful hair soon became thin and ragged, and he and Barbara visited a barber, got it all cut off. We never saw Gobi with hair again. He became very weak at times, and during those hard times, he stayed with us. Sometimes, he became so weak from a treatment that Barbara had to help him get dressed so that he could go to yet another treatment. Barbara took over his laundry.

When the scheduled chemotherapy treatments ended, tests showed the tumor had shrunk, but not enough. The doctor told him he needed to go to M. D. Anderson Hospital in Houston to continue treatments. It was not clear what further treatments involved, possibly surgery, or radiation, or maybe both. Gobi did not want to go. He was asked why, with his life hanging in the balance, he would not go.

"I do not want to face surgery, and risk dying alone, so far from home," he replied.

Barbara and I assured him, if surgery came up, he would not be alone.

Barbara stood up in our tiny church that Sunday, and said, "Gobi needs to go to Houston, and I need $2000 by Friday." On Friday, she had $2000. And a plane ticket. And paid hotel reservations.

When Gobi got to Houston, surgery was soon ruled out. He began an intensive treatment with radiation. Someone from church had booked him a nice hotel. Gobi changed that to a bare bones hotel, so as not to waste other people's money, living better than he felt necessary.

When we talked to Gobi, he said he was doing fine, eating out of Target next door. "Target?" Barbara said.

"Who eats out of Target?" Barb and I left for Houston. Turned out, that Target had a very large grocery, and a deli.

Gobi finished his treatments, and he returned to Arkadelphia. HSU allowed him to live in the International House, for free, while he recovered. HSU friends gathered around him and helped.

Gobi's brother-in-law, Raj, the head of Gobi's family, flew to Arkadelphia to see about him, and ask about the possibilities of taking him home. Gobi emphasized to us, never speak to Raj about religion. He would wait for the right moment.

We had Gobi and Raj over for dinner, and took them on an outing to Hot Springs. Raj had a big laugh about the size of drinks at Wendy's. The doctor emphasized to Raj, it would be very risky for Gobi to leave his doctors, and travel home, now.

Raj prepared to return home. The last night, he lay awake in his bed, a long time. He said to Gobi, "Where does this kind of love come from? These strangers treat you like family. I have never seen this kind of love." Gobi's "right moment" had arrived, and he made the most of it. Raj carried a bible home with him.

Money for Gobi to live on was raised, by means of a few letters written to key people. He was pronounced free of cancer, and he finished up his degree.

Gobi was ready to return home. The scene at the airport was traumatic. He and Barbara hugged, cried, and Gobi started for the plane. He came back, they hugged and cried some more. Finally, he was on his way home.

Gobi left behind a pretty hefty bill at M. D. Anderson that his insurance did not pay for. He could have easily skipped out on that bill, leaving the country and all. But he insisted that the bills be forwarded to him. Out of his small income at the time, he paid every cent of that bill. He told Barbara, "How do you not pay people who saved your life?" That's just Gobi for you.

Gobi is now a professor, has a beautiful wife, Poova, and a wonderful child.

A few days ago, daughter Kinley made a nice little post on Facebook about her parent's love. A comment immediately popped up from a world away.

"I know all about that love. It saved my life."

Barbara and I had a good cry.

THE KING OF FAYETTEVILLE

THE YEAR WAS 1968 and I had just turned 24. I was flipping through the paper one day when I stopped on a picture of an old man with what looked to me like, at the time, an unbelievably large string of catfish. The caption under the picture was, "Dick Dyer does it again!" Seems Dick Dyer was about the best catfisherman around Fayetteville, Arkansas. I wished I could do that, but it seemed out of my reach.

When I was a kid, growing up in Wing, Arkansas, I caught lots of catfish, and we needed them. They sure tasted good, after a steady diet of salt pork. But they weren't real big, mostly mudcats. In the early days of Fayetteville, I had access to larger rivers, and I thought more and more about catfishing.

Well, as it happened, shortly after seeing that newspaper article, my wife Barbara and I moved over to a trailer park at Anderson Place. Would you care to guess who my neighbor, right across the street was? You guessed it. Dick Dyer. I befriended him, I cultivated him, I quizzed him. After a while, Dick's MO began to emerge. I studied his techniques. He even let me go fishing with him, once. Well, he began to see that I could be a competitor somewhere down the line, and Dick dearly relished being the best river catfish catcher around. Maintaining that status consumed his whole life. He pretty well cut me off from any more information.

But I knew enough. I began to catch more and more fish, emulating his methods. Dick was OK with that, he was catching more, and bigger fish. We went along there, him doing a bit better, for some time. Then I slowly began to catch as many fish as he did, and probably about the same in total weight. He still had the largest fish, 16 pounds. Every time he saw me, he told me about that 16 pound catfish... He never let me forget about that 16 pound catfish...

Barbara and I were coming into our last months at Fayetteville. One really deep hole I fished a time or two that spring, with my limb lines probably tied to limbs I know now were too solid, with very little give, just kept breaking. The lines were 120 pound test or so, and I couldn't understand it at the time.

Barbara and I were walking along the river bank, one day in June, on a picnic. I saw two old watermelon rinds lying on the bank, and they were just covered with hundreds of june bugs.

I had never heard of anyone using june bugs to catch catfish, but I knew that in the late summer, they often fed by just skimming along the surface, picking up floating bugs and whatever they could find. I had seen them doing that at night.

After Barbara had walked on toward the car, I went back, pitched the rinds in the river, and the june bugs all floated up. I just scooped them up, put them in a paper bag, and stuck them in the car. When we got home, I wrapped them up real tight in a freezer bag, and stuck them way back in the back of the freezer, out of sight. Barbara put no stock in mixing fish bait and food in the freezer.

Late in the summer, I was watching TV one day, and I heard Barbara scream. I ran to the kitchen. There she was, the bag in one hand, a handful of june bugs in the other.

Seems she had been going through freezer bags to find something to cook, stuck her hand in, and pulled out the june bugs. I caught it pretty good over that.

As Barbara settled down some, a little later, I said, " I've just got time for one more fishin' trip before we move, and no telling when I'll get to fish again. I'll get every one of those june bugs outta' here then." She agreed. Catch Barbara when she's not screaming with a handful of june bugs, and she's a great gal.

Next week rolled around. I asked John Philpott if he wanted to go with me. Said he guessed so, nothing better to do. We went back to that hole, where the White River and the west fork of the White River join, where my lines had been broken last spring.

This time, I had a new idea. We were fishing with cane poles, very limber, and we stuck them way, way back in that mud bank. I floated each hook right on top of the water, with a june bug on it. We ran the lines at midnight, and had a couple of ten pounders and a whole passel of smaller catfish. But, right where the two rivers join, that pole was going absolutely crazy! Ever tried to get a lively 25 pound catfish into a small landing net? We eventually did.

The next morning, we had a couple more ten pounders and another bunch of smaller catfish. Then, we approached that last pole, right where the two rivers join. The pole was completely pulled out of the bank, but it was still laying there, mostly out of the water. Lying in the water, either just too worn out for one more flip of the tail, or having learned from his struggles that was as far as he could go, was the brother to the last big one. He was also

25 pounds. Well, when I got home, the first thing I did was take them over to Dick Dyer. Dick came out, I held them up as well as I could. I didn't say a thing, I didn't have to. He never said a word to me. Just turned sorta sick looking, turned around, dropped his head, and walked back into the house. We moved to Hannibal, Missouri a couple of days later.

I never saw Dick again.

About two weeks after we got to Hannibal, a letter chock-full of pictures arrived. A 40 pound catfish, and a whole bunch in the 20 pound range. The letter just verified the weights, And in the picture an old man was smiling. Smiling right straight out at me. Thats all. Not another word. The return name on the envelope was Dick Dyer.

I knew Dick didn't have my address. But he managed to find it. And I knew he had found my Glory Hole. All I could figure out was, he must have ragged John Philpott into telling him. I was pretty put out by this whole thing for awhile, then after I settled down some, I began to think about it a little differently. I had used Dick's methods, developed through his many years of experience. He used me to locate the Glory hole. Fair's fair.

I've never been back to that Glory Hole, but someday I will. Over the years, I think I've figured it out. There's a dam on the White River, a quarter mile upstream. Catfish naturally swim upstream. Until they're stopped by a dam. The small fish stay there, in that shallow hole at the dam. The big fish must have deep water, and they go back downriver, only as far as they need to, stopping at the first very deep hole. Right where the two rivers join. In the Glory Hole.

And there they still lie. Year after year, just getting bigger and bigger. Just waiting for me to come back and challenge them again. But Dick Dyer passed away many years ago, and when he died, he was still the King of the Catfish Catchers in Fayetteville---and it just wouldn't be the same. Who else in the world could care as much about the size of the catfish I might catch there as Dick Dyer did? Nobody, that's who.

For all you fishermen out there, I know you can find my Glory hole from what I've told you here. But where will you be able to find a whole bag full of june bugs?

DIAMOND JAMES ARCHER

THE CRATER OF DIAMONDS STATE PARK in Murfreesboro, Arkansas is the only known diamond crater in North America. It's the only place in the world one can go in, pay a small fee, and keep what you find.

Back during my diamond mining days in the late 1970's, I was fortunate enough to buddy up with, and work alongside the most famous Arkansas diamond hunter of all time. A lot of what I learned by watching James Archer enabled me to find my first two diamonds during that first three-day trip, the first being my largest find ever, a beautiful 1.00 carat canary diamond. During those three days, I was determined to learn as much as possible from this legendary diamond hunter, and be just like James Archer. Alas, I failed miserably.

James Archer made his first trip to the Crater of Diamonds by horse and wagon, seventy some odd years ago. Later on in life, he and his wife came there again, determined to find a diamond. He failed, but his wife did find one.

This galvanized his determination to find a diamond.

He surface hunted for two years, off and on, and never found one, gently being teased about that by his wife the whole time. When he changed to digging deep holes, and washing the mud through screens, He quickly became successful, finding his first two, a 1.7 carat and a 1.71 carat brown diamond, all in the same day.

In the early 1970's, he worked at a sawmill, unloading railroad ties by hand, then going to the diamond mine to dig after work. At one point, he was not at the mine for two days. When he returned, his arm was in a sling. His hand had almost been severed at the saw mill. He should have been at home recuperating, but the hard working James was not the type to ever sit still. He could not stay away from the crater.

When he returned to the sawmill, he was told they no longer had a job for him. This was a turning point in his life. He decided to become a diamond hunter, six days a week, every week.

The number of diamonds found varies from one report to another, but the best estimate given by park officials was 5,000.

I met James and worked alongside him for three days in 1979. The characteristics I noticed about James that were not present in anyone else seemed to be that he worked very hard, very fast, all day long, every day. For thirty years. I did meet one other man who compared to James in some of these categories, except that he always kept a full time job otherwise, and he's still raising a family, so he does not get to go every day.

Henry Emison and his wife Lori were digging away when I met them. They were beginners at that time, but they quickly changed all that. Henry soon was recognized by all other diamond hunters on the field as a digging machine, a true man among men. He could work all day at his job landscaping, then drive to the mine and do as much work as we fully human diggers could do in a day. Of course, he quickly found a lot of diamonds. At one time, they moved to my rental house at Gurdon, Arkansas, partially because they loved that 130 year old, six bedroom brick house. But mostly because it was close to the diamonds.

What is it about rare, driven men like James and Henry that makes supermen of them when they step onto that diamond field? I wish I knew. I would buy up a few gallons of it and enhance my own diamond collection a bit.

Henry moved to the other side of Arkansas, because that was where his job was, a few years ago. But I know he's still not out of range of that diamond mine, so we still don't know how his lifetime collection will look.

He also differed from most people in another way. He told me at one point that he had given all his diamonds away to others who needed them more, except for one.

James told me the story of finding a very nice diamond on his screen just as two rough looking and talking men walked up. James, a black man, had been treated badly by such men in the past. Afraid they might try to take it away from him, he simply dropped it in the bucket of fine sand he would be taking home to look over closely that night. He was never able to find it again.

In 1994 James unearthed a very nice 5.25 carat diamond. This was, officially, his largest find. But, when a story came out about him in the National Enquirer, it was said he had found a 7.9 carat diamond. When asked about that later, he stated, "Well, they did get things sorta messed up in that story, all right. About my age and stuff. But I did find that 7.9 carat diamond." When pressed about this, James related this story.

"One morning several years back, I was out here in the parking lot getting ready to go in the park one morning when it opened. A man started talking to me, telling me he was here to find the largest diamond he could, and buy it for his girlfriend for her engagement ring."

"I told him I didn't have any diamonds on me now, but maybe we'll find one today." James went on to say, "A lot of folks talk big like that. But when it comes down to it, they don't have the money to back up their talk."

James continued his story.

"So the park opened its doors, and we both went in and bought our ticket, and went into the mine. When we got to the search area, he turned left and I turned right. I only went a couple of hundred feet before I saw something shining at me. I went over and picked it up. It was a big canary diamond, sitting right on top of the ground. I shouted, "Hey, mister! I got a big 'un for ya.""

The man came over, said he wanted to buy it as soon as he saw it. He asked, "How much ya' want for it?"

James said, "I didn't even know how much it weighed, and I usually set my price on that. So I just said, $7000. Then that fella reached in his pocket, and pulled out a huge roll of money. He counted out 70 100 dollar bills into my hand. When he was finished, that man's roll looked as big as it did when he started peeling bills off'a there. I said to myself, 'I shoulda' said $10,000.' But I didn't know he really had the money. The man took the diamond and never registered it at the park office. I heard from him later, and he'd had it cut and set in that ring. He said the jeweler weighed it before it was cut and it was 7.9 carats."

A lot of people have been wondering for a long time about just how well James has done. Tourists have been trying to pry that out of him six days a week for 30 years. Most people don't like having people trying to get information about their business, and James was no different. We do know he never lived in a mansion, or bought a new truck.

When tourists ask, "Is it true all your children graduated from college?"

"That's what they say."

When asked later how many children he had, he said, "Seven. And they all graduated college. And my wife will graduate college this year." Seems James did not invest his money in himself, but invested in his family's future.

On Wednesday, January 8, 2003, James Archer went into the Crater of Diamonds State Park as he had for thirty years. And, at the age of 77, he died there doing what he loved, digging for diamonds. The Crater will probably never see a more diligent, consistent, determined prospector than Diamond James Archer. And I feel fortunate to have had the opportunity to work alongside James, and learn much about diamond hunting, and about life, if only for three days.

Rest well, James. Your accomplishments at the Crater of Diamonds State Park will never be equaled. Nor will I ever find a nicer guy on that diamond field.

*Some info about James Archer for this story came from "A Thorough and Accurate History of Diamond Mining in Arkansas" written by Glen W. Worthington. Published by Mid America Prospecting, Murfreesboro, Ar. 71958

DECORATION DAY

I WENT TO DECORATION DAY at the Rover Cemetery this year. My son Corey and my grandson Carson went with me. They were short on time, so I took them around and reminded them where all the Gillum and Lazenby (my mother's family) graves were. As I started telling stories of some of those people, Corey could finish up many of them, because he had heard them before. My daughter Kinley had planned to come, like she always does, but she was waylaid by a stomach bug, and didn't make it this year. As I started putting out the flowers, they had to go on home, so I worked alone.

About the first time I bent over to place a flower, I heard the seat of my pants start to rip. Seems each time I placed a flower, they ripped a little farther. I never had realized before just how hard it was to keep everyone else in the cemetery in front of me each time I bent over. By the time I had the last flower placed, the seat was completely gone.

I had to go to a big church social immediately when I got home, but I managed to get Barbara to bring me a new pair of pants to Caddo Valley and meet me at a gas station on the way. I had planned to tie an extra shirt around my waist and just tell everyone I brought it along in case it got cold. As usual, Barbara again saved the day.

Decoration Day was a very big thing when I was a kid. We spent the whole day there, ate dinner on the grounds, and had a big singing. Then, the rest of the time, us kids spent the rest of the day playing in the cemetery. I realize now that was a part of our training, so that hopefully, we would continue to come to Decoration Day at Rover when we became adults, and train our kids to do likewise, so that the old Gillum's and Lazenby's would not be totally forgotten for a long, long time.

In the spring of 1997, my brother Harry, who had cancer, called me up in late April, and asked me if I would be at Decoration Day. That was the spring of our F4 tornado that wiped out a good bit of Arkadelphia. I told him no, I had a job to do that day, and would not be able to come. Our photography business was shut down then from the damage, and I was taking work anytime I could, to try to keep it afloat. Harry said, "You've got something else more important to do that day, do you?"

Ten days later, my wonderful brother was IN that cemetery.

Well, I haven't missed a decoration day at Rover since. Although, we did hit a deer on the way one year, tearing up our car, and were a week late.

Some months back, I got a letter from Ms. Perry Whitlow. She is one of my readers of my column in the Yell County Record. She had also grown up in Wing, and told me a lot about my Gillum relatives from the old days that I did not know. She finished up by telling me she would like to meet me, but I best hurry because she was about to turn 94. A week or so later, I was up that way, so I decided to look her up. All I knew was that she lived at Ola. I managed to find a nice lady that knew her, and gave me directions. It was several miles back out the Kingston road. When I finally found what I thought was her house, nobody was at home. We've been letter writing buddies since then, and I planned to make another attempt to find her.

Well, as I walked through the cemetery yesterday, a nice young lady approached me, asking me if I was Pat Gillum. I told her I was. She pointed to another lady a ways back, and said, "She's Perry Whitlow." Well, I was really glad to finally meet her, gave her a big hug, and we talked a long time. That made the whole trip up to the Valley worthwhile, I told her. She clued me in about the fact that her house was the next one down the road from the one I found. She is every bit as wonderful as I pictured her being.

I always make sure I locate every Gillum and Lazenby grave, and I think about each person a little, whatever I remember, good or bad. If my kids are along, I tell them a little about that person.

A Two Flower Man - There is one man in that cemetery who is not a Gillum or Lazenby at all, but he still commands so much respect in me that I always give him two flowers; R. L. Whitten. Back during WW II, he was a very close friend of Elbert Lazenby, my cousin. Elbert was a radio man on a bomber, his plane was shot down, and he became a casualty of war. R.L. continued to be almost a part of the Lazenby family. Elbert's sister, Delphia, was born with severe disabilities, and seemed to me to be bitter about her lot in life. This was back when cousins still kept a close association with cousins. R.L. and Delphia soon married, and he made her his princess, caring for her all their lives, very attentive and very tolerant of her mood swings. And, he single handedly raised her life up far above reasonable expectations. As a boy, I was around them a lot. I never knew what was in his heart, only what I saw. He was one of my best examples of what a man should be.

THAT'S JUST BARBARA

BARBARA, MY WIFE, HAS A PROBLEM with straight and crooked, something we worked very hard to control while we were in the photography business, with lots of cropping and tripods. When we were in Italy, and finally found the Leaning Tower of Pisa, Barbara took a picture. In the photo, it was standing straight up. She quickly deleted it, knowing I would get a lot of mileage out of that little jewel.

When we checked into a little villa in Austria, we could not communicate with the owner, who only spoke German. The only other guest there quickly started interpreting, speaking perfect, even southern, English, as well as perfect German. Barbara just had to know what was going on, and soon found out he could speak pretty well any language, and also regional dialects. Barbara made friends with him and quizzed him mercilessly. He offered to buy us dinner, and we accepted. We never pass up free food. After he had several beers, he finally decided we were harmless, and told us his story.

He was a citizen of the world, he said, claiming no country as his home. He was a free-lance spy. His specialty was, he could become anybody from anywhere. Starting with the first Gulf War, the United States has been the highest bidder, since he looked Arabic, and spoke it perfectly. He told of making a number of military friends while training in Colorado Springs. His scariest night ever, he said, was when he and his friends accidentally wound up on the wrong side of town in Colorado Springs. But then, that's another story.

Seems we had heard many similar stories from visitors to America, from countries all over the world. The good old USA was a great place to visit, the stories went, until you went to the wrong part of town. And they often did not know where those places were. Some said they had traveled all over the world, but would never dare go to the USA for that reason.

When he went to work in Iraq, he was in his Arabic dress. His friends arrested him one night. He told them, "It's me, guys." They would not believe him, and he had to show his USAF pants on underneath his Arabic dress before they accepted his story.

He walked us out to our car as we were leaving the next morning. He had a small lecture for Barbara. "You travel far too lightly about the world. People will entrap you. You should never have let me in your car yesterday. "

Barbara looked at him a moment, then said, "We had you out-numbered."

He laughed. "I wasn't worried." He waved Barbara's camera away, would give us no phone number, no address, no e-mail address. He said he would e-mail us. We're still waiting.

While visiting Kenya, we decided to ride a bus to Tanzania one weekend. Upon getting ready to return to Kenya, we were told our visa was a one-way thing. We would have to buy a new one, $200, to get back into Kenya. They would only take US dollars, and we didn't have enough. I was in the early stages of another panic attack, but Barbara said, "Don't worry. I'll handle it."

When we got to the border, she watched each of a dozen or so border agents carefully. She finally chose an agent who seemed to be friendly, and sometimes smiled. She chose his line. When we got up to the front, she started flirting with him shamelessly. Told him all about us being missionaries, laughed and joked. She passed the old visa, not valid now, over to him with a friendly smile. He was totally won over, and he stamped it, and smiling, said, "You have a good day."

We got gone quickly. Barbara just seems to have the ability to have her way with any man. Of course, she never uses that ability unless I am at her side. At least, I think so...

When we arrived in Australia, Barbara searched for a way to call home affordably. She found a way, if one did not mind having to dial 30 numbers, to call home all we wanted to that was cheaper than in-country.

Standing in a very long line at a toilet at a festival in Sweden, absolutely nobody spoke a word. Barbara, of course, did. "You Swedish people are an awfully quiet bunch."

An old man, way up the line, replied, "Yes, we have always been a very stoic people." That broke the ice, and by the time our turn came, Barbara knew each of them personally, and left dozens of new, smiling friends behind when we left that toilet.

Returning by train from Monaco to our car and motel in one of dozens of little towns on the Italian Riviera, we stopped at the France-Italy border. There was no stop there on the way in, so we sat tight. People were getting off. Soon, we realized we were the only passengers aboard. Just as that was beginning to soak in fully, the train started back toward France.

When we reached the station, we ran back, once more, to the ticket office, asking if there are any more trains out today for Italy.

"There's one more. If you run fast, you might catch it. You should have changed trains at the border." We ran. I quickly out distanced Barbara. I was even with the engine now. I waved wildly. The train slowed, and a door opened. I placed one foot on the train, kept the other on the ground. If they closed the door now, they would have to squeeze me in it. Barbara was just coming into sight, a long way back.

Once Barbara was aboard, we quickly found an English speaking couple, and stuck tight to them.

We knew we must be about there, and Barbara asked, "Now, what was the name of our village?" I didn't have a clue, and it was now getting dark.

We strained to see something familiar as the train slowed for a village. "There's our car!" Barbara screamed, and we bolted for the door. She was well ahead of me, and she had the door open before the train stopped. But she was on the wrong side, and she was about to step out onto a live track. Those trains are totally silent, very fast, and they run about a foot apart. Stepping out could quickly bring about an instant, silent death. The way Barbara remembers it, she instantly realized her mistake, and quickly shut the door. The way I remember it, half a dozen people grabbed her and dragged her back. Funny how each person has their own way of remembering things!

Driving through Australia, we noticed a nice clubhouse with a beautiful green lawn surrounding it. Dozens of old men, all dressed up fancy with broad brimmed hats, were rolling black balls around on the lawn. We had never seen anything like this. Barbara said, "Park the car. I'll go see what's going on." I stayed in the car, pretty well knowing what was about to happen. Barbara walked onto the lawn, and started asking questions. Every game stopped, and every man gathered around Barbara, all anxious to explain the game to her, many wanting to hold her hand to insure that she rolled the ball properly. Barbara quickly learned a little about lawn bowling, and a lot about old men.

If one just has to travel the world, Barbara is the kind of woman to travel with. Were it not for her, I would probably still be stranded in Italy, begging for pizza scraps to stay alive. Or in Australia, marking lambs for a living.

MOUNT IDA ADVENTURES

SOME TIME BACK, NEAL AND SCOTT, TWO OF MY PREACHERS, let me tag along on their spring fishing/turkey hunting trip. My friend Skeet was with us. "Skeet" is short for "Skeeter," which is short for "Mosquito," I guess.

The last time I tagged along, we were floating the last 17 miles of the Buffalo River. My partner and I didn't actually turn our boat over, we just took so much water in over the front in a rapids that it just sank part way. But we never abandoned ship, we were still paddling for the bank when we were chest deep in water. Neal, watching from above, shouted, "Hey! They made it!" then later, "But they sure look awfully short!" Using the term *rapids* sounds better, but with two preachers witnessing, I have to admit, it was more of a big riffle. A really big, wild riffle. I was glad to get to go along on this second trip. I needed to redeem myself.

This trip, Neal had gotten a really good deal on a very nice cabin on a branch of the upper Ouachita River near Mt. Ida, Arkansas.

Skeet is a really old man, two full months older than me. Skeet and I got there early in the afternoon and fished and sat around, catching lots of sunfish, while we watched what we felt like were three turkeys playing around up river. We had trouble convincing Neal of that though, since he felt like finding three turkeys that easily was just too simple. We also saw a lot of deer. Neal and Scott got there in the middle of the night, because Neal felt he should help wife Teresa get the kids to bed at home first.

When they arrived, with two canoes in tow, we got to

figuring out who was going to sleep where. Neal and Scott had bunk beds in their room, and the other room had a double bed. Trying to be helpful, I said, "I don't have any problem at all sleeping with Skeet. Sounds good!"

As a kid growing up in Wing, we kids often slept three to a bed. But Skeet, an only child, eyed me hard when I said that, and, deciding I was too agreeable, finally grabbed a couple of quilts, and headed for the couch. So, I had a big bed and a room to myself. Those things just seem to work themselves out better if one is agreeable enough.

Sometime in the middle of the night, I had to go to the bathroom. Quick. Standard fare for us old men. Once I stood up, the two minute warning sounded. I like to think that being old was not totally responsible for what happened next, because sometimes, my sleeping pill can make me a little crazy in the middle of the night.

I totally have my path to the bathroom at home memorized, right down to the last detail, and no light is needed. Can't wake Barbara up. This night, I seemed to think I was still at home. I knew right where the bathroom door was, and it was just where I remembered it, except the bathroom had shrunk, and clothes were hanging everywhere. Well, I didn't have time to move all those clothes, so I headed to the door into the rest of the house. Right where I remembered it. But now, someone had removed the doorknob, it seemed, and it was now shaped more like a window. I was beginning to get in a rush, and I ran back to my light stand to turn on my light. But, I felt all up and down that light, and the switch was gone! Time to move now, and I ran back to the first door, determined to search through all those clothes until I found that commode. Had to be here somewhere! No luck. As I headed back to that door that felt more like a window, The two minutes were up. Time for the last resort. I screamed for Barbara, maybe she could get her light on. No answer. Then, a tiny light of reality started to flicker on, and I found my light switch to my lamp way down on the cord. By then it was really getting ugly, so I will spare you the rest of the details, except to say that I had to convince Skeet the next morning why I already had clothes washed, and hanging out to dry, at daylight. "Just forgot to bring extra underwear," I said.

While Neal and Scott scouted for turkeys the next morning, Skeet and I fished some and sat a lot. We had to rest up for the big float trip. When the guys got back at lunch, they cooked up a meal. I had already eaten my meal, a peanut butter sandwich and three or four packages of peanut butter and crackers. I like to keep it simple, out in the woods.

We left Skeet's little red truck (Skeet only drives red automobiles, he has three or four of them. Red is the natural color of a truck, he says) at a bridge on the main Ouachita River. Neal led us to a spot upriver that would make for a four mile float, Neal says, and we launched our canoes. Neal and Scott, with pretty little seats (with a comfortable backrest) in their canoe, paddled a little, and fished a lot. Skeet and I, old men with no backrests in our canoe, (We forgot to bring them) fished a little and paddled a lot, so we were soon far ahead. Let's get this four miles in before our old backs give out, we decided, and we paddled on, fishing occasionally. Catching smallmouth bass was the main goal, and we did finally catch one, along with a largemouth bass and lots of perch and goggle eyes. We paddled past a dead smallmouth bass floating in the water, and I closed my fingers on it's tail momentarily. We had now caught two smallmouth. Two smallmouths sounded a lot better that one, which could be considered an accident. We just kept paddling on, and after Skeet and I figured we had gone six miles, no truck showed, and our old backs were worn out. Then we put our rods away, and paddled on, now just trying to survive this thing with a little dignity, and strained our eyes to see that pretty little red truck.

Helping a couple of other fishermen who had swamped their boat gather up their gear took our minds off our backs awhile, and we finally spotted our little red truck.

We cooked up a mess of steaks, and our tired backs were forgotten by the time that meal was over.

Neal said he sure got hot in his top bunk last night, and I told him he was welcome to share my double bed, but he didn't think that over very long, since I feel sure he had heard all the screaming for Barbara I had done the night before, and he did not wish to risk being mistaken for Barbara in the middle of the night. He allowed as to how he would just stick with his hot top bunk.

The hunters were long gone the next morning when Skeet and I arose. When they returned, no turkeys were in hand this time. As we ate lunch, I thought it was a shame I didn't bring a gun. I could probably have picked off one of those turkeys up river from my lawn chair.

As I headed home, just as I was coming into Caddo Valley, a big turkey gobbler flew right over my car. If I had only had my bow and arrow, I could probably have jumped out and bagged him right there. Next time, I'll have to bring it along, and help those young turkey hunters out a little. It never hurts to have a couple of woods-wise old men along, passing a bit of our vast storehouse of wilderness lore on down to the next generation. It's just the natural way with things.

THE DOUBLE BULLET DODGE

I HEARD THE SIREN, three hundred yards away, over on the Interstate highway. "Must be a wreck," I thought, then went back to work on my houseboat. Minutes later the phone rang. Barbara soon came running out to me with the phone. The police were calling. Our son, Corey and his family were involved in a wreck. Three in the car, one ejected. Come to the emergency room. Just the bare facts.

We arrived at the emergency room well ahead of the ambulance. We were anxiously awaiting when the ambulance showed up. Caylie came out first, just a baby, strapped tightly to a board, and screaming her head off. She looked around, within her limited field of vision, and saw Barbara and me. She stopped screaming, and smiled at us. We have never seen a smile quite so beautiful. Christi came next. She was also strapped down, but seemed alert, responsive, and, everything considered, remarkably calm. Corey was not in the ambulance.

He arrived moments later in a car. When he got out, he was beyond emotional. Way beyond that. As best he could, he was telling us he was driving behind Christi, in his car. A wheel had come off a trailer they were about to pass, hit her car in front, and the car did end over end flips, at least 12 rolls, then another flip, landing upside down. He reached through the broken back window, cutting his arm, and got Caylie out, but could not get Christi out. He was too racked by emotion to tell us more. Well, I knew Corey was totally distraught, probably in shock, far too upset for me to buy into all that. Nobody could have survived what he had just described to us.

It was determined that Caylie and Christi had only scratches and bruises, no broken bones, and as far as they could tell, no internal injuries, but Christi had a concussion, and both were cut up by flying objects in the car. Corey settled down enough that we began to get the whole story.

The family was driving home from church, driving both cars because Christi had early choir practice. They both stopped at Western Sizzlin', at mile marker seventy-three of I-30. Being Easter Sunday, it was closed, so they and their friends decided to drive on down to Wendy's, at exit seventy-eight. Corey buckled Caylie into her infant seat, strapped in the middle of the back seat. Starting to his car, for some reason, he stopped, turned around, went back to Caylie, and tightened up all the straps really good. Corey followed Christi in his car.

Approaching mile marker seventy-four, Christi started to pass a pickup pulling a horse trailer. A wheel came off the trailer, hit the front of the car. That broke the car's front axle, starting the series of end over end flips and rolls, ending upside down in the median, with one last end over end flip, right beside mile marker seventy four.

Corey pulled up behind. Later, a friend who happened to be nearby described the horrible sounds of anguish from Corey as he rushed to the car. Caylie was hanging upside down. The only way he could get to her was through the broken back window, which he did, cutting his arm. When Caylie emerged, he checked her over as quickly as he could, passed her off to a stranger standing beside him, saying, "Don't leave my sight with this baby," and rushed to Christi. As he tried to get her out, a fire started. A man from the interstate showed up with a fire extinguisher, and put it out. Christi was hanging upside down, and he could not get her out. About that time, the ambulance and police arrived. They had trouble getting her out, having to use the Jaws of Life.

Once Christi was out, and being strapped to a board, a paramedic tried to get Corey on a stretcher. Corey was bleeding more than anyone there, and the paramedic would just not believe he had not been in the car, and ejected.

Christi, not one to get unduly excited, later described her thought processes as the wreck progressed. "Well, that's one more flip, and I'm still alive!"

The car was a mess. Completely flattened on top, except for the two places where a human could have possibly survived. They just happened to match the two places where Christi and Caylie were.

The paramedics working the wreck said that upon arrival, they had no expectations of finding anybody alive, much less a four month old baby. They added that Caylie's car seat straps were so loose, one more roll and she would have flown. Good thing Corey had just tightened them up.

I went to the site the next day. Car parts were strewn along the road. From the location of the first car part thrown off, to the final destination of the wrecked car, one hundred yards. Twelve rolls and three flips? You be the judge. Our family dodged two major bullets that day.

We are always being told, wear your seat belts, all the time, most accidents are within one mile of home. Well, my family has been in seven accidents, mostly minor, none fatal. How many within one mile of home, as the crow flies? Five. For your own safety, please do as I say, but in all honesty, not necessarily as I do. I hate being hypocritical.

Caylie, early on, assumed the role of seat belt enforcer in our family. Nobody is perfect, but I sure haven't found any flaws in her yet.

However, just a few weeks ago, Jordan, our grandson four years younger than Caylie, approached Barbara and I with a serious question. "Do you think Caylie has ever sinned?" We all put our heads together, and tried to come up with a good solid sin.

Somebody remembered that her brother Christian, a few years younger than Caylie, used to like to aggravate Caylie. She usually countered with, "Christian, I'm going to pray for you tonight." Yet later, she had confessed she sometimes said that just to aggravate him.

So there ya are. A good, solid, sin.

At eighteen, she just got her first car, right after returning from the mission fields of Jamaica. God, it seems, had his reasons for sparing this girl.

If you live near Arkadelphia, judge this story for yourselves. The car came to rest even with mile marker seventy-four. The first car part thrown off was even with the brown sign just south of it. One hundred yards.

This story had been in my head nearly eighteen years. It automatically replays, in living color, every time I drive by those two signs. I now know the story very well. I needed no notes to write this.

My son-in-law, Mickey, a paramedic, described a roll over wreck they worked. A man was dead, but no marks were found on his body. Finally, a mark that looked just like the top of a coke bottle top was found on his temple. Every loose, even modestly heavy object becomes a deadly missile in a rollover wreck.

BUD

IN 1998, BARB AND I BOUGHT AN RV, leased our house out for a year (we took down our pics and personal stuff, locked it up in the attic, leased the house furnished as is, and walked out.)

We had bought several rental properties while working, so I looked for a property manager to look after them while we were on the road.

Bud Reeder had a large realty business in town, and managed dozens of rental units also, so he seemed to be the logical choice.

I had managed them myself up to that point, and I never really enjoyed that job. Seems every time I had listened to a hard luck story from a renter, and responded with a kind heart, I eventually got burned. Every single time. One of my last acts as my own property manager was to rent an apartment to a foreign framing crew which would be working in town a few months. A month or two down the road in our travels, we got an early morning call on our emergency phone. It was from our son in law, Mickey, who was then a paramedic. Seems he was the first responder to that rented apartment. A couple of the guys had gotten into a fight over a woman, spilling out into the back yard. One picked up a concrete block and bashed the other man's head in. Like I said. I never enjoyed managing rental property.

When we returned at the end of that year of travel, we decided to leave them all in Bud's hands. Let him deal with all those problems. He was doing a good job. If it ain't broken, don't try to fix it. Besides, Barbara and I still had a lot of world out there to see.

Bud's grandfather, Lon Reeder, brought his family to Arkadelphia from Colorado in the 1800's and built a farming and ranching operation where Turtle Point golf course is today. It later expanded out toward Old Military Road (The Trail of Tears) and farther.

Bud's father, Frank W, became a rodeo cowboy, participating in roping and bull dogging competitions in such places as Madison Square Garden in New York City, and at the World's Fair in Chicago. Many old western antiques still on display at the Burger Barn and Western Sizzlin' in Arkadelphia belongs to the Reeder family.

Bud's mother passed away when he was five, and he and his siblings were mostly raised by his grandmother. His means of transportation as he grew up was a Mexican burro.

Lon built a small, one room slaughter and packing house. Later, the government helped him build a much larger slaughter house on Country Club Road, to help control brucellosis, which was running wild in Arkansas at that time. Herds of cattle were brought in, and each animal was tested. Those showing no signs of the disease were run through a dipping vat, to control parasites, and taken back to their farm. Many cattle were slaughtered and buried. This was the beginning of the major push to rid our country of brucellosis, which took 76 years to do. It is still common in some other countries. Handling infected animals can cause undulant fever in humans, though not after it's cooked.

In 1934, the percentage of tested cattle affected was 11.5%. As of December 31 of 2000, no cattle herd in the United States, for the first time, was found to be affected. It was a long hard struggle, and the Reeder family were some of the pioneers.

The hides were salted, rolled up, and put in 55 gallon drums for a while, then spread out to dry flat. They were then sold to make leather.

Before refrigeration, animals were slaughtered on demand and hauled to stores.

John Wesley Davis raised his family nearby, in a house with plank walls covered with newspapers. John Wesley worked at the plant for many years, then gradually trained his family of large, strong boys, Dooster, Gyp, Man, and Sonny as butchers.

Man was employed at the plant throughout his working life. At 22, he married Gloria Smith, 20. They had a son, Randy, and a daughter, Teresa.

Man was once busy butchering a beef when a government inspector came in. The inspector soon came into the office, telling Bud, "These men can't touch that meat with bare hands. They have to wear gloves."

Bud said, "You go tell them that."

The inspector went out into the plant, then soon returned, headed out the door in a hurry, saying, "That man can do whatever he wants."

Bud later asked Man what happened. "Well," Man replied, "He came back there, right behind my shoulder, telling me I had to put on gloves. I just turned around and looked at him, forgetting that the bloody knife was still in my hand. I told him gloves slowed me down too much, I was being paid by the number of beeves I butchered. The next thing I knew, he left in a hurry." Sadly, Man died in a motorcycle accident at 32. Barbara hired Gloria to work for her a few years later. We all soon realized she was about the hardest working, most dependable and honest lady we have ever known. Thirty years later, we still see a lot of "Glo,", and she is now one of our dearest friends.

Bud started working in the plant when he was still in high school on a half day basis. Later, he married Ella Ruth, a very classy lady. She became the plant bookkeeper, and they ran that plant as a team for many years. They have currently been married for 59 years. They had two sons, John and Wes. Ten years later, they adopted Carol, 5 days old, in Dallas.

Bud once had a major shortage of bulls. He called his supplier in Paris, Texas, who told him he had plenty, but due to a major truck driver strike, he had no way to get them to Arkansas. Bud jumped in his truck, drove to Paris. When he arrived, he was surrounded by angry truckers. One bold man pulled his cab door open, only to find himself staring into the business end of Bud's double barrel sawed off shotgun lying across his lap, both hammers pulled back. The man backed up a few steps, now in a position where he would be impossible to miss. Bud introduced himself. "This is a Reeder truck, those are Reeder bulls in there, I'm Bud Reeder, and those bulls are going to Arkansas." With no more trouble from the truckers, he hauled his bulls to Arkansas.

Bud got in the real estate business more or less by accident, when somebody asked him to sell his houses. He got his papers in 1973. In 1980, son Wes designed a building for his business, and Harold Nix built it. Bud soon began managing properties, again by accident, when somebody asked him to look out for their three mobile homes. That business grew to around 400 units.

When I first got to know Bud, he always carried a sawed off shotgun around, displayed in the window of his automobile. If the local police ever felt they needed a little extra firepower, they dropped by and borrowed that sawed off shotgun. That was during a time when many loud and rowdy parties were held in his rental properties. Bud was called out late at night, maybe a couple of times a week, when the tenants got too wild. While the police could be held at bay if the tenants demanded a search warrant, the property manager can legally enter at any time, so they often called in Bud. Bud seems to be just enough of a cowboy that he relishes those occasions. While he's never had to fire a gun to protect himself or others, nobody ever doubted that he would, or could, if necessary. His current weapon of choice is a custom made .410 gauge shotgun pistol, revolver type. The first chambers are loaded with bird shot.

At 79, Bud is still on the job, and does not discourage his tough guy image, knowing that that next wild party may bust loose at any time. But actually, those of us who are around him a lot know the real Bud. He always looks after the needs of his owner's properties, on call 24 hours a day. If a renter is going to get mad at someone, Bud wants it to be at him, not the owner. Good cop, bad cop. He negotiates good prices with repair men, and passes that savings on. Bud is very civic minded, and willing to help all those around him at any time. I would guess that nobody in Arkadelphia has gone to more funerals than Bud Reeder, whether he really knows the family or not. He's always there to show respect. I read something on facebook today that made me immediately think of Bud Reeder. I think it speaks of Bud better than anyone I know.

"On a cold April night three years ago, my father died a quiet death from cancer. His funeral was on a Wednesday, middle of the work week. I had been numb for days when, for some reason, during the funeral, I turned and looked back at the folks in the church. The memory of it still takes my breath away. The most human, powerful and humbling thing I've ever seen was a church at 3:00 on a Wednesday full of inconvenienced people who believe in going to the funeral." – by Dierdre Sullivan

Bud never travels, fishes, or does anything else much, outside of his business, except playing with his tractors and dozers. He's in that business, ready to go, any morning at 6:30. When I started gathering info for this story, I went down to his office at 6:30 AM on Labor Day. I didn't call ahead. I knew he would be there.

Ever the loyal wife, Ella Ruth is there pretty well every day too. Just in case Bud forgets something. Ella Ruth just loves hearing about our travels. Some time back she won a free vacation. I know she would have loved to go. But Bud's not about to leave that business, and she's not about to leave Bud alone. It went to waste, as far as she was concerned.

A few years ago, Bud and Ella Ruth threw a big New Year's party. Barbara and I went, and, since they are leading citizens, I expected to see the elite crowd there. But no. Most people invited were a widow or a widower, or otherwise alone in life.

If our government ever decides to throw a big war, fought only by old men over 70, I guess I'll go if I'm drafted. (Come to think of it, maybe that's not such a bad idea. We've got a lot less to lose.) But I really won't feel very good about it, unless, maybe, Bud's the man I follow into battle.

HANGUPS AND STRANGE QUIRKS

SOMEWHERE AROUND 1947 OR SO, an enterprising businessman from Plainview, ten miles from Wing, came up with a good idea. Build a chicken hatchery at Plainview. He was a good salesman, and he sold a passel of farmers in Wing and the surrounding area on the idea of producing the eggs. Always searching for ways to bring in a little bit more money, Dad went into the egg business. This was along about the time cotton was on its way out in the valley as a money crop. That overworked land was playing out.

Dad built a long chicken house. It was up on the hill, just to the left of our house. Down under the hill, a couple of hundred yards away, was the huge barn that was built to house the Gillum/Compton/Turner super mule breeding project of the nineteen teens or so. The barn, by the way, was so large, it cost twice as much to build as the house we lived in, $1000. That business did well before the depression, but that business played out also, when tractors came into common use, also along about the time I was born. Old Murt, the only super mule alive when my memories began, successfully sidestepped the glue factory until the late forties. I rode him bareback many times, and an old, skinny mule without a saddle can be a hard ride. I'd about as soon walk.

My brother took a picture of our house, at the end of the lane by the barn in 1949 or so, after the chicken house was stocked and producing. I was just getting old enough to work the chickens. I was in that picture, close to the camera, with hundreds of chickens spread out between me and the house. Actually, I was placed in that pic later, though the time frame was about right. Looking at that picture, one fails to see a trusting, relaxed, laid back, self-confident soul in that face. I'll come back to that later.

That year, Dad needed a second generation of chickens coming on, to replace the six hundred some odd laying hens, along with a cranky, mean bunch of roosters. The hens in the house were playing out, and getting just too tired to produce an egg a day reliably. And the roosters, each with a very large flock of ladies to attend to, ensuring those eggs were fertile, were playing out too. So the next generation was housed in the barn. These young chickens were producing some eggs, but the eggs were too small for market value. Thus we ate a lot of eggs. During the day, they were turned loose to forage for themselves, cut down on the feed bill. I can count about two hundred in the picture, but there were six hundred or so out there somewhere.

I would like to tell you it was my job, every afternoon before dark, herding each of those six hundred chickens back into the barn to lock them up and protect them from the coyotes, coons, mink, foxes, etc. at night. Or, it might be an even better story if I told you I just started playing my little flute made out of a piece of fishing cane, marched down the lane to the barn, and they all just lined up and followed me in, a little trick I learned from the pied piper story. I just love to impress people.

Actually, though, I can't say either of those things, because this is a true story. And, it's awfully hard for a Gillum to just outright tell a bald faced lie, because of the Gillum Do Right Mechanism we're all infected with. So the actual truth is, we kept them shut up in the barn awhile until it became home. They came back in on their own at night.

My main job in the chicken house was gathering those eggs in a big, wire basket. Now, those chickens had big plans for those eggs. They planned to lay up about all the eggs they could sit on and keep warm, and eventually hatch out their own batch of baby chicks. Once they began to get the mindset to become a "settin' hen," they became protective of their eggs. I had to steal many of those eggs out from under that mad hen. She would flog, squawk, and peck me. Then I went on down the line to the next nest. Those cranky roosters didn't like me one bit, either. I was invading their territory, and messin' with their women folk. I never knew when one of those cranky old roosters would be on my back, scratching, biting, and floggin'. And, it was not unheard of for me to approach a nest, only to find it occupied by a really big black snake, containing several egg-sized lumps in his belly.

Carrying that heavy basket full of eggs to the house, I had to walk through the territory already staked out by Old Jersey, our mean-natured old milk cow. Every day, it seemed, she saw me going into the hen house with my empty basket, and when I came out, she was waiting. You ever tried to outrun a cranky ole' milk cow while carrying a basket full of eggs? Every day, again and again? But still yet, she never caught me, though my load of eggs sometimes were the worse for wear.

Is it any wonder I developed that angry but timid, distrustful look reflected in that face at a very early age?

Do you understand why I much preferred wandering the bottoms and the mountains alone?

The egg business played out in a few years. The scuttlebutt going around was, the main business was really selling a lot of chicken feed to the farmers. Lots and lots of chicken feed. The hatchery sorta took second fiddle. A plus was, all that chicken feed came in pretty cloth sacks, all decorated up to make shirts and dresses from. Mom and my sisters spent a lot of time on the old Singer sewing machine. It was not uncommon for Mom to give Dad a few scrap pieces of feed sack material for him to try and match when he headed to Plainview for yet another load of chicken feed. And, during that time, we ate lots and lots of eggs and chickens, enabling us to ease up on the salt pork awhile. Also, later in high school, I taught myself to pole vault with a well-seasoned pine pole I stole from the chicken roost. In addition, I learned to run fast at an early age. So, it would seem all's well that ends well.

Dad dispensed with the chickens. It seemed some of that chicken feed had gone bad, and we sometimes had to haul a tractor and wagon load of dead chickens off into the woods to feed all the hungry coyotes around. And that, along with the fact that the money making aspect of that enterprise was not too great to begin with for the farmer, did the chicken business in for Dad.

Uncle Franz, who was richer than us because he was a school teacher, once bought up a bunch of registered and double registered Polled Hereford cattle, and brought them up to us for Dad to raise and sell on the halves. That business enterprise did better, and Dad stuck with that business the rest of his life. He was growing up a pretty good herd of registered Polled Hereford cattle, concentrating on high quality young herd bulls for sale. And me, I began my stage in life as a cowboy without a horse. But I didn't fare a lot better than I did with the chickens. We had some mean cows there, too. And those big bulls just dared me to step into *THEIR* pasture. Once, one of those big bulls tried to get romantic with one of Aunt Lula's cows, through the barbed wire fence, and lost all his value as a herd bull. Another time, two of those big bulls got together and were fighting all over the pasture. Dad had gone to town, so I ran down and shot our double barrel shotgun, both barrels at once, over their heads, to try to scare them apart. It didn't impress them much, but it knocked me flat down. When Dad got home, one had a broken leg.

Those young bulls coming on were just beginning to strut their stuff, and they badly needed someone small enough to intimidate. I was the natural choice. A really good counselor could have had a field day, helping me get past all my hang ups and strange quirks I developed before I got big enough to look out for myself. But then, Wing didn't have any of those kind of people. I don't doubt that maybe a few of those strange quirks are still hanging around in my psyche today. Or maybe you have already noticed.

SAMMY LEADS ME INTO TROUBLE. AGAIN AND AGAIN

SAMMY TURNER WAS TWO YEARS OLDER THAN ME. We ran around together a lot in the 1950's. We had a call. "Whoo, Whoo, Whooie e ooo!" That call carried over the top of Whippoorwill Hill, between our houses, and pretty soon we would be on a great adventure. He was a leader, I was a great follower, and somehow I got into a lot of trouble following Sammy.

We decided to build a club house up on top of Whiporwill Hill. The small pines, chopped down, made a great frame. We went to an old barn, barely standing, and salvaged timbers and planks planks. One day we went back to the old barn, and it was flat on the ground. We must have removed a key plank the day before. When the clubhouse was just about built, we made up the club rules, wrote them down, folded up the rule sheet and stuck them in a crack. The next day, when we took out our rule sheet, I saw Dad had been there. Another rule had been added.

"Do not cut any more pines belonging to John Gillum."

Sometimes, after harvesting our peanuts, we would hang tow sacks (city people call them gunny sacks) full of peanuts up in the smokehouse. Sammy and Mack Carter, a cousin, finally got in the habit of coming by and manipulating me, two years younger, into sneaking into the smokehouse and getting them a good supply. I made a tiny hole in the bottom of a bag. After this happened a few times, I guess Dad caught on, because one day I snuck in, and Dad was in there, sewing the hole up with a needle and thread. One good glare from Dad was all I needed, and I hauled out of there and never tried that again. Dad never cared how many I ate, because he knew how hard I worked and I deserved them. But furnishing the neighborhood boys, who he knew did not work as hard, went against his grain.

As JR Turner once told me, "The Gillums were not like other people."

Once, Sammy decided we could catch perch in Stowe Creek by feeling under the rocks and grabbing them. That worked well, until we pulled out a big water moccasin! That was the end of that.

Sammy had another good idea. We stuck needles in the end of our arrows, put on an extra shirt for armor, and shot them at each other. Fortunately, we were not very accurate.

Another idea was to lay a .22 shell on the concrete, reach around the corner of their rock cellar, and hit it with a hammer. I nixed that one. Even I knew better than that.

Sammy and I spent a lot of time looking for arrowheads. One of our favorite places to look was down close to the river. There were plowed fields there then, but now they are covered with tall pines. One Sunday, as we started out, Dad said, "Don't get out of our pasture." Well, the good hunting was well past our pasture. When we got to the river, two miles out of our pasture, we decided to cross it and look on the other side. After we explored awhile, we tried to return to the Hale Ford, where we had crossed. Every time we reached the river, all we could find was wide and deep water. We could not cross. Well, we could have swam, but it was a little cold to relish that. We finally headed downriver and came out at Rover Bridge, a couple of miles downriver.

About sundown, we dragged in home. Dad said, "Sammy, maybe you need to stop coming over here so much." I had cows to feed and, since Dad was waiting for me, I got right to it. Finally Dad said, "I was down in the pasture today, and I didn't see you there."

"We decided to hunt arrowheads in the woods," I lied.

"No wonder you didn't find any," he knowingly said. I totally deserved a whipping that day, but he let me slide.

A different trip to the river with Sammy, which Mom had nixed, earned me my only real whipping Mom ever gave me. Mom took me out under the persimmon tree. She had a big limb. I was taller than her then, and I just kinda looked at that small woman headed toward me with that limb, and I sorta smirked. She got hold of me with one arm, and we went round and round with her working on me with that big limb. You could hear my screams all over that hill. I never doubted her abilities after that.

My older siblings filled me in early as to what Dad was capable of, so I never tested him much. A certain look over the top of his glasses and "put, put, put!" was all I usually needed to keep me in line. I never could figure out what that meant exactly, and I never wanted to know. If anybody knows what "put, put, put" means, I would now really like to know.

Sammy and I built two carts that we could sit on and steer. A piece of wood for a steering wheel with wires running to the front wheel area did the trick. We had trails made through the pines on the side of Whippoorwill hill, and it was great fun. One day Sammy showed up with a car steering wheel for his cart. I was jealous. Well, I went home and started going through my brother Harold's stuff he had stored. He was a mechanic in the Air Force at that time. I found something that looked like half a car steering wheel, so I got that. It worked great. By the time I totaled my cart against a tree at the bottom of Whippoorwill Hill, this cart thing was getting old anyway, so I left it there.

Some 50 years later, Ken Gillum, my brother Harold's son, called me up and said, "You would never believe what I found up on the hill. I can't figure it out! A B-29 steering wheel! Did you ever hear of a B-29 crashing up on the hill?"

I told him, "Ken, I think I can help you out on that one."

A year or two ago, one of Sammy's teachers at Fourche Valley School in the 1950's told me, "Sammy was the smartest student I ever had. He was so far ahead of everybody else, he was bored. He spent his time thinking of troublesome things to do. He helped me out a lot in deciding teaching was not for me."

THE SEVENTIES SURE ARE GRAND!

SOCIAL SECURITY! MEDICARE! AND ALL THAT GOES WITH IT! I can go to my doctor as often as I want, and it doesn't cost a penny! Those arm-and-a-leg health insurance premiums are mostly all gone! The rental property is all paid off! Just tinker around with them a little when they need it, keep them rented, and they will help support us well into old age!

Now, I can play golf any time I want, catfish all I want, and take long walks in the woods and mountains, to recharge, just for the fun of it!

I can go to the Recreation Center and run and walk with my friends, any time of day I want to. For as long as I want to! They say, lots of exercise gives me a good chance to live well up into my 80's.

And travel! Barb and I can travel all we want to, and can afford to. See the world! And I can write a lot!

Of course, for every action, there is an equal and opposite reaction. Got to look at the big picture. Both sides of the coin. Good vs. bad. Be realistic.

About those visits to the doc. Seventy is the year the doc says, "Maybe we should start doing those yearly physicals every six months. And, you know those questions you have stored up to ask the doc, those little things you want to ask the doc if he can fix? Well, seventy is the year when you have to start writing them down. Not on a small scrap of paper, but on a full-blown legal pad. And, it might be best if Barb went along too, to help remember his answers. Seventy is the year the doc's most shocking answer is, "Yeah, I can fix that, but you might want to consider just letting that problem slide, and live with that small inconvenience. I can fix it, or, you can keep on having sex."

My answer is, "That's not a big problem, doc. I can live with it," as I scratch it off my list.

Those free doctor visits. The paying through the nose starts at the Pharmacy. Maybe I should have opted for a little better supplemental prescription plan to help with that. But, when I signed up, I didn't take any prescription drugs. Back in the good old days.

Seventy is the year the daughter starts mentioning things like, "You know, Dad, they have really good ways to test your memory loss nowadays. And, if they catch it in time, they can slow it."

The rental property has a few leaky roofs. Sure, I can just climb up and smear some sealer around. I can fix that. But Barb keeps harping on me with, "Remember how many times you have fallen off that ladder, in just the last year? Let the property manager get someone to fix it." And that sagging floor. I can crawl under the house and fix that. But I keep rubbing all the belly buttons off my shirt to get under, then when I'm done, I can't turn around to get out. I know it's no big deal to replace a rotted bathroom floor, I've fixed a bunch of them. But why is it that now, when I finally get up off that floor, my knees and back are in such a shape that I get around like a 90 year old for some time?

Seventy is the year one realizes, "You know, my back sure does feel better when I just don't play golf." And fishing! My knees get all cramped up in my small boat, so that I have to put my cell phone in double zip locked bags. There's at least an even chance that I will stumble around in the boat when I finally do get up and I will find myself under water.

Long walks in the mountains are still a viable option at seventy. Better file a destination plan with Barb, though, in case I can't find my way back or fall and hurt myself.

Seventy is the year you always greet your friends at the recreation center with, "hey, man!" or hey, girl!" Why don't those names come to me anymore? And running. Works well for a day or two, until I pull some muscle somewhere. I can still walk fast, but if I walk fast too long, my back will be too sore to get out of bed tomorrow.

Traveling the world is still a viable option at seventy, unless I throw my back out carrying those heavy bags. And, if I can just fight back those panic attacks, when driving on the wrong side of the road, driving a car with the steering wheel on the wrong side, and just stop wishing I was home.

Those nice naps after lunch are great, until they start stretching out to supper time.

Writing at seventy is good. Does not require much physical exertion. Seventy is a good time to record my lifetime memories, if an old memory, once in my head, would just stay around long enough for me to find a pencil, considering I may have to interrupt my search for a quick trip to the bathroom when the two minute warning sounds.

I love those trips to the grocery store for Barbara. Milk and bread. Except that now I have to take a list, find the list when I get there, and finding my credit card on the way out complicates matters some.

You know, everything considered, the seventies can really suck!

SKEET

SKEET WAS BORN JESSE ADAMS IN PINE BLUFF, ARKANSAS in 1944. Somebody mentioned that day that he was no larger than a 'skeeter' when he was born, and that name seems to have stuck.

He and his wife of 45 years, Willene, a great lady who babies Skeet much as Skeet babies his boat, his cars and his truck, have lived their life in Pine Bluff until six years ago. Then they bought a house on Lake DeGray, partially to give Skeet's big, beautiful bass boat a home close to good fishing waters.

Skeet's big bass boat may very well be the most beautiful bass boat most of us have ever seen; bright red, with pretty sparklies all over it in typical Skeet fashion. He bought it many years ago, but also in typical Skeet fashion, it has been babied and cared for lovingly so that one would think it was bought brand new yesterday. I heard a dealer once tell Skeet that it was probably worth $80,000 today, though it only cost a small fraction of that new.

Skeet fondly recalls the Pine Bluff of his youth, when many people had no locks on their doors, and those who did seldom used them. "Everyone just seemed to get along," Skeet says. "A Pine Bluff youth of today, transported back to the 1950's, would think he had died and gone to heaven. Even a child, walking alone down a dark street where the beer joints abounded, with fist fights involving the patrons often going on nearby, was considered safe." However, some things were scary, such as accidentally falling into a shallow grave onto a pile of bones while running through the woods at night.

Pine Bluff night clubs of the fifties, such as the Trio club, were considered great stepping stones for Memphis by up and coming young musicians. Skeet regularly rubbed elbows with the likes of Elvis Presley, the Uniques, (he dated the drummer's sister) Jim Ed Brown, and Jerry Lee Lewis. They often played at area schools, also.

Riding his Cushman Eagle scooter back to school to pick up his grades, he accidentally collided with a 57 ford with yellow fender skirts, and his scooter hung up on a fender and the scooter was pulled out from under him. (Only Skeet would be admiring the color of the fender skirts in the midst of all this.) Skeet emerged with a broken leg. After lying up most of the summer, he went to Dr. Cunningham to have the cast taken off. When the doctor, who was their family doctor, realized his parents were not there with him, he asked Skeet how he got there. "Rode my scooter." The doctor took him to the back and gave him a spanking, and said, "I'm gonna tell your daddy!" He did, and Skeet got another spanking when he got home.

At Skeet's graduation ceremony at Watson Chapel High school, he was called up by the superintendent and recognized as the only student to ever graduate from Watson Chapel High School with straight F's in math his senior year.

Skeet and I both attended Arkansas A&M and lived in the same dorm, Sorrell's Hall, for two years. He lived upstairs and I lived down, and we never met. I do know many strange things occurred upstairs at Sorrell's Hall during Skeet's tenure, such as a trash can carrying a live skunk appearing in someone's room as a surprise gift, as well as a limb covered with honeybees arriving in much the same way. Blocking off the community shower with huge blocks of Styrofoam glued into place made a great swimming pool until the dam burst, sending a great waterfall of white water cascading down the stairs one night. Each of these incidents emptied the building for a time, and the culprit(s) were never caught. Skeet emphatically denies major participation in any of these dramatic events, but I do know things settled down up there when Skeet left to start working at the paper mill and signed up with the National Guard at Pine Bluff.

After 42 years working in maintenance at the paper mill, Skeet can fix any broken metal item, making it look new. He's an artist with a welder in his hand. He's also a gifted artist with a pencil in his hand. My grandchildren regularly fight over who gets to sit next to him in church. They know Skeet will draw a wonderful picture of a smokin' hot rod, or motorcycle, or some such vehicle during the service and the closest kid to him will proudly get to take it home. All the college kids flock to Skeet in droves. They know where to find him. He will always be occupying his accustomed place of honor on the back row.

Skeet and Willene have two children, five grandchildren, and one great-grandchild.

Life is never dull around Skeet. It becomes difficult, over time, to remember just exactly what his face looks like if he is not smiling, laughing, or telling a story. We need a lot more Skeets in this world. Provided, of course, that we keep them spread out a bit. I can just not imagine what a room full of Skeets would look like, or what could happen.

A VISIT BACK TO WING

I WENT BACK TO WING A WHILE BACK. I walked out and looked over the old farm. As I just stood, looking at that old farm, a large part of my childhood passed through my mind.

Right in front of me was where the huge barn had stood. Grandpa John Wesley Gillum used that barn to breed super mules. He bought a giant mammoth black male donkey to breed to everyone's mares. He paid a thousand dollars for King Leo, at the turn of the century. King Leo won first place at the Arkansas State Fair. Mares were brought from far and wide to King Leo.

Right over there, under that giant oak, my great grandpa, James LaFayette Gillum, built his blacksmith shop. That ground was just covered with iron scraps when I was a kid. I'll bet I could bring a metal detector up and dig up a ton of old horseshoes and other old Gillum treasures.

Right up on the hill, right there, the old home place stood, now long gone. It was a genuine kit house, ordered from Sears and Roebuck in the 1920's by my school teacher aunt, Hallie. She must not have ordered the entire kit, because it retailed at around $2300 dollars as a turnkey job in the 1920 Sears and Roebuck catalog, and this one cost between $500 and $800, depending on who was telling it. But she ran out of lumber, and lumber was taken off the old Gillum home place to finish it up. My aunt Lula

Bell had come over and thrown a royal fit when she found out, but the salvaging continued. By the time aunt Hallie's house was built, the old house was not fit to live in, so the whole family made the 20 foot move in with Hallie. Aunt Hallie never lived in her new house alone, dying early, in 1941. I was born in that house in 1944.

Fifty yards away is The Bluff, where ninety years of Gillum's threw ninety years of trash that wouldn't burn. The thick trees below now hide all those glorious piles of Gillum history. A thousand years from now, an archaeologist will dig into that spot, and be filled with wonder. Gillums always produced spectacular trash.

On out, between The Bluff and Stowe Creek is the field of stinging nettle. Sister Barbara Lou and I always had to walk through it to get to the swimming hole. That's the only place I've ever seen that particular plant. Touch it, and you itched for hours. Years later, I remembered this plant, and transplanted one to my biology class room, along with a big sign, DO NOT TOUCH THIS PLANT. But seems like most of my kids eventually just eased by and rubbed against it, just to spite me when I wasn't looking. But it never went unnoticed by me in the long run. The guilty party always scratched until the bell rang, then walked out scratching. Every kid needs to experience stinging nettle, once.

On the other side of the road is the big hill. My nine acres. As a kid, it had huge pines on it. It was cut over after I left Wing. Forty-two years ago, I bought it. Thirty-four years ago, son Corey and I planted those pines back. They're pretty big now, but nothing like they were when I was a kid. My brother Harold was a forester at the time. He kept on at me to thin them out, cut out the hardwoods. Maybe I could make some money off them someday.

But he never understood. I didn't want the money, I just wanted to see those pines like they were when Sammy Turner and I rode those carts we had made, with abandon, down that hill, dodging each big tree. Mine had a genuine B-29 steering wheel on it, and wheels off my little red wagon, removed when it was too tired to go any more. I hope I see those huge pines again before I die.

Whippoorwill Hill sits atop my nine acres, where large groups of that bird still gather each spring, just as they did when I was a child. My cabin now sits atop that hill, where I sit out for hours listening to them each spring night. Now, packs of yipping coyotes have joined them. That always gets the domesticated dogs to start howling, just like a wolf. That particular howl seems to have carried down through the eons when the coyotes yip, back to a time when the dogs, too, were truly wild.

Looking off the bridge over the little creek by Uncle Homer's house, I saw the little hole of water where I fished, using grasshoppers or wasp larvae for bait, as a boy. I could always count on catching four or five big perch or goggle eyes, string them up on a forked stick, and head for home to clean them for supper.

As I stood there and looked, two perfectly round black balls, the size of a basketball, each consisting of hundreds of tiny black animals, swam by. They were packed tightly, and they swam perfectly together, like synchronized swimmers, here and there. I had seen this before, once, as an 8 year old boy, not 100 yards from this very spot. My biology professor friend had no idea what I was talking about when I described them to him. Even tiny critters in Wing are just a little bit different.

The deer are back now. I had seen them today. They were almost totally absent during my childhood. Killed and eaten, in season or out. A couple of years ago, the bridge on Stowe creek, right beside my 9 acres was replaced. But this new bridge had no sides. Later, Harold noticed it had been caved off on one side, with the imprint of a pickup truck, lying on its side, mashed into the mud in the creek bottom. That mud had a bunch of shotgun shells, 12 gauge buckshot, lying here and there. One of those midnight spot lighters had a little problem here, it seems. Good enough for him. He had no business messing with my deer.

As I gazed over the old farm, I remembered back 60 years ago. Dad had me totally believing that the whole farm would go totally to hell if he was absent from it, even for a day. And he almost never left. Yet here it is, nearly 40 years after Dad had left it forever, looking much the same. New owners now, but they are keeping it up well. The woods have not reclaimed the fields where the cattle contentedly graze, as Dad had always feared. He pushed me to mow every square inch of it every summer. Even in 1954, when those fields were nothing much but dust and a few weeds. Then he always sent me out with a chopping ax, to walk the patches of persimmon sprouts, to make sure not a single one survived.

I went to see Elois Hunnicutt, now 94. Her sons Grady and Wayne were my good buddies as we grew up. They, Sammy Turner, Jack Larry Gillum and I often skinny dipped in that very cold, very deep hole in the creek down in our pasture. Some of the guys felt proud to walk the bank most of the time. I always called these show offs the *"Bank Walkers."* Personally, I tried to stay in the water nearly all the time.

Elois Hunnicutt and her husband Alja were always the hardest working people I ever knew. They did the same kind of work most everybody in Wing did, only they did twice as much, twice as fast. I worked for him one summer during college. I got to ride 40 miles in the back of his pickup to Dover and 40 miles back, every day. I totally wore out two good pair of work boots that summer, just trying to keep him in sight in those hard mountains. We lost him several years ago. A big loss to us all, and a very good man.

Elois still lives alone on their farm, still has a big garden. Some time back, she fell out there and broke a bone or two. Over several hours, she managed to crawl to her back door, but that's as far as she could get, alone. She had to lay out a good part of a day and night. Cell phones don't work well in Wing. But she's as lively as ever now, and gets around pretty good with her cane. I know I would be hard pressed to keep up with her now, much less when I'm 94.

I got to meet the Gillilands, the new store owners. There has been only one store in Wing, in my lifetime. I told them about sitting, cluelessly, reading the funnies, throughout the great robbery of that store, 56 years ago. That is the only sure-enough crime I ever remember happening in Wing. Effie Turner figured out she had been cleaned out when she came back from her supply room, called ahead, and they were caught before they could get out of the valley. The robbers got a year and a day. Effie was an older lady at that time, and she died at 100. During her lifetime, she rode in a covered wagon pulled by oxen, and saw men walk on the moon.

I told Mr. Gilliland I would like to place some of the copies of my book, Spreading Wing, there in November when it came out, as I wanted books available where it all happened. He said, "Sure, be glad to. And it won't cost you a thing." I told him I just never worked that way. He *would* get a commission. He said I was sounding like my brother Harold, who had come in for a three minute repair job on his car, and just insisted on paying him. I told him Harold and I had the same Daddy and Mama, who gave us both that same "Do Right

Mechanism." A Gillum always pays his own way in this world.

I went by and looked at the old church next door, where the Memorial Service for JR Turner, Effie's son, had just been held. JR died recently at 102. JR fired a wanderlust in me, as a child, telling me stories of his world travels, and showing me gold he had found "1000 miles off the pavement." Without him, all of my tales of *our* world travels might never have happened at all.

Scientists just really need to do a study in Wing, see why so many people live so long, far away from a major hospital. But actually, in my heart I already know. Folks in Little Rock would be amazed, living there in the hustle and bustle, and the rush, of big city life, at the lifestyle we at Wing lived, and how much longer many lived, just two hours away.

As I drove out of the hills of Wing, I knew, as I always know in my heart as I leave Wing, that, though I left those hills 50 years ago, and have never lived there again, I am forever a hillbilly, and proud to say it.

WINTER OF THE IVORY BILLED WOODPECKER

IN AUGUST OF 2006, I was walking out from fishing my favorite hole on the Fourche River when a very large woodpecker flew from a dead snag that had a large hole in it, near the top. I was struck by the bird's size, and its markings.

The ivory billed woodpecker had been considered extinct for 50+ years. It is similar in size and appearance to a pileated woodpecker. The ivory billed woodpecker is slightly larger, its back is solid white, while a pileated is dark on top with white feathers below. When this bird flew from me, it looked white on top of its back, and larger than any pileated woodpecker I had ever seen.

Barbara and I flew out for six weeks of wandering Europe aimlessly a day or so later, but I spent a lot of time, while there, thinking about that bird. I also spent a lot of time hobbling on my bum knee from wading that river so much. This was just after an ivory billed woodpecker had, in many people's minds, been spotted in Eastern Arkansas. Positive ID never happened in Eastern Arkansas, despite a long hard search by many scientists.

When we returned, there was a break between deer seasons that fall. The deer have returned to the valley in large numbers now. I knew deer season was about the only time anyone else ever went into that area and the split deer season was now closed, so I would be alone.

I left home at two AM, and arrived in those woods just before daylight. Immediately upon exiting my truck, I heard a drumming sound I had listened to on old tapes of the ivory billed woodpecker. "Bam, bam, bam, -- bam!"

This was one identifying characteristic of that bird. The sound seemed to come from the old snag I had seen before. It was immediately answered from the area of another large hollow snag I knew about.

I waited until dawn broke, and, with my camera ready, I eased toward that first snag. I began to hear woodpeckers working toward me. Suddenly, a very large one flew into my vision. It was much faster than I had ever seen a woodpecker fly before, flying more like a duck. As it exited my vision, I could hear its wing noises, also a characteristic of the ivory billed woodpecker. "Whoosh, whoosh, whoosh!" It was at least one hundred fifty feet from me, but the sounds were very distinct. It was still too early, and dark, for a flying picture.

I quickly set up a blind at the large snag, and I waited, camera ready. A pileated woodpecker flew in, stayed awhile, then left. The sun was just beginning to peek over Fourche Mountain, which arose sharply out of the far side of the river.

Then **IT** flew in, and changed my thinking forever.

It landed on the snag. I was, I must admit, too awestruck to even think about my camera. It was huge. The description fit. It hitched its neck, and turned it, looking behind. I was later told by one expert on that bird that even an ivory billed woodpecker probably could not do that. But then, he had never seen a living ivory billed woodpecker, and this bird did that. As it walked out a limb, certain distinguishing markings were very clear to me. Unfortunately, my forgotten camera sat idle in my hands, and I just gawked.

A piliated woodpecker has a white line running from

it's head to its wing, disappearing under its wing when the wings are folded, as this one was. The ivory billed woodpecker's white line goes up onto the wing, and down the length of it.

This bird had that white line, the full length of the wing.

That marking was very clear to me. The first rays of the morning sun spotlighted the bird as he reached the end of the limb. My camera suddenly came awake, and I shot again and again. The bird flew.

Afterwords, I went over what I saw and what I did not see in my mind carefully. The angle of my view was pretty steep. I had no memory of seeing the white shield on the back, characteristic of the ivory billed. I felt, at some point, though, I could have seen that. But, it was not in my memory afterwords.

I heard the "Bam, bam, bam, -- bam!" drumming sound, totally different from the pileated wood pecker, three more times that morning. Then it was time to go home. Deer season started up again the next day, and there would be hunters swarming this area, so I stayed away a few days.

I knew I would need all the help a great lab could give me with those pictures. From our professional days, I knew just the lab. I instructed them to "push" the film two stops. It was still very early in the morning for a film camera. I had no digital camera at that time. It was at about the time, 2006, when digital was beginning to take over, film was about to become a thing of the past.

It took several days, during which I knew I had the first

modern day photo of an ivory billed woodpecker. I was torn. Should I make it public, and risk an influx of people running the birds off? Or should I keep their secret, hopefully allowing them to make some sort of comeback in that very isolated place? The habitat was great. The Ouachita Mountains arose out of that river, with thousands of acres of pine timber. Down river about a mile, there was a very large plot of beetle-killed pines, very attractive to large woodpeckers. They simply strip the dead bark off the tree, and eat the beetles underneath. Hundreds of acres.

When the pictures arrived, I had the best books I could find in hand, showing all the markings. But, after studying the best photo, I knew it would not hold up. The bird had turned toward me, and the wing markings were indistinct. The best photo was not totally sharp.

I was still torn. I knew what I knew, but I had no real evidence. I decided to contact the man who was, it seemed, considered to be the world's expert on that bird. I discussed my situation several times with him, and I sent him my picture. After studying it, he said he needed a video. One questionable photo was not enough.

While I knew I was lacking in proof, I did see that bird well, and there was not a bit of doubt in my mind. I bought a good video camera, and went to work. I set up several blinds, some with bait stations. About fifteen mornings that winter, I left home at two AM, arriving in the river bottoms at daylight. But, to make a long story short, I never heard that particular drumming sound again, though I saw many pileated woodpeckers, and never another sighting.

I downloaded the actual sounds of the ivory billed

woodpecker, made over half a century ago, amplified and broadcast them out. The blue jays went crazy. Their sound is similar. I videoed several birds responding to that call, but they all turned out to be a dead end. One particular bird that responded seemed to sound a little different. I only saw it through my video viewfinder, and my video only showed a few flaps of its wings before it disappeared over the tree tops. Since my only view was through the video view finder, I could tell little about the real size of the bird. I could not stop the action at a point where I could see markings that would tell me something. I called the expert. I asked him, "If I send you a video I have, will you call me back and give me an opinion?"

He replied, "I'd be glad to, Pat." I sent it. A few hours later, I managed to stop the video at a critical point. Markings showed. I knew it was not what I had hoped. I waited to see if he was a man of his word. He never replied. Since he was not a man of his word, even to give me a negative answer, that told me a lot about this expert. That was our last communication.

What I saw, and heard, that one morning in November of 2006 just seemed to be there no longer.

The last morning I spent looking for the ivory billed woodpecker, the Corps of Engineers did a control burn on my plot, and the fire ran me out. My blinds and bait stations were destroyed. I knew by now the Corps of Engineers were curious about what I was doing there so often, and a local farmer was also, seeing me drive by his house so often. He sent word to me, "If there are ivory billed woodpeckers down there, I'll shoot every one of them."

I sent word back, "If you can find one down there, you're a better man than I am." I decided it was time to drop this search, and let that totally isolated spot become isolated again.

I knew I could never convience anybody else with my lack of evidence. But I know what I saw, that morning in November, 2006. And to my dying day, I will always remain convienced that the ivory billed woodpecker was alive and well in the Fourche River bottoms in 2006. Their secret is safe. Maybe, that's as it should be. That was one difficult decision I didn't have to make. Making such a claim as I have made here, without proof, makes one seem to be somewhat of a kook, so I have since been hesitant to talk about this, and I have told few people. I felt they may have raised young that year in that hollow tree I saw the one in. But if so, they have moved on. I pray they are making some sort of a comeback in those thousands of acres of the Ouachita National Forest near by. I won't bother them again. Six years have passed. I decided to tell it here.

The world needs to know.

Please do not ask for details about the location. I will not tell. That area is totally isolated, with no good reason for people to come in, except to deer hunt. It needs to stay that way.

THE MYSTERIOUS INTELLECTUAL PEST

A YEAR OR TWO AGO, I went back to Wing to see my big brother Harold.

Harold always kept a project going, and he thought through each step very carefully. This time, the project was to get rid of a very intellectual pest.

Harold's house has a small room off the porch where the cats sleep. But it had been invaded by some sort of mysterious animal, which continues to eat up all their cat food. He expelled the cats for the duration of this project, and came up with one idea after another for catching this unwelcome visitor. The room has access to the house underneath area, but closed off from the outside.

The first idea was to put out his homemade armadillo box trap, with lots of cat food as bait. The next morning, the bait was all gone, but the trap was not thrown.

Seeing this was not going to work, Harold got a wire box trap from Walmart. The next morning, all the bait was gone, the trap was thrown, but no animal inside. There had been enough cat food inside these traps to feed an army, and every bit of it was always gone.

This is where I came into the picture. We discussed this problem in great detail, for a good part of the day.

Since the animal had already defeated the two traps designed for relatively large animals, such as a stray cat, coon, or possum, we determined it must be smaller. And since it carried off tons of food, we decided it was carrying it off and hiding it. We put our heads together and came up with the logical solution, a pack rat! Once we agreed on this, we spent the rest of the day on strategy.

We got a rat trap, just a glorified wood and wire mouse trap, but much larger. We discussed bait. I recommended a chunk of cheese, as it would be harder to get it off the trap without throwing it. Harold wanted to stick some pieces of cat food around on the cheese, as this animal had already shown it was partial to cat food. I tried to convince Harold that everybody and everything just loves cheese, and a good round chunk of it, alone, would be sufficient. He finally gave in. We set the trap right beside the two useless traps already there, topped by a really nice chunk of ripe cheese.

Harold suggested we had to tie that trap down, because that animal might get a leg or something caught, and drag his only rat trap off. I said the trap didn't need that, because once a rat was securely in it, it was going nowhere anyway. We debated this for a good part of the afternoon, and by sundown, Harold had won out. It was his trap, and his house.

Big Dan, Harold's youngest son, was there, temporarily recovering from some medical issues, and he was not to be left out of this discussion. Dan allowed as how, in case it didn't get caught, it might circle the trap a time or two, to inspect the cheese, and we should sprinkle flour on the floor in the whole area, and that way, we might at least see a track or two, and get some idea about what we were up against. We discussed the merits and shortcomings of this idea, we each had our say, but in the end, nobody came up with a good reason why we should not do that, so we did.

As bed time approached, we were all anxious to see what the morning would bring. I wanted to peek in on the situation at bed time, but Harold said leave it alone. This animal never stirred before midnight, he said.

Now, I didn't really understand how Harold knew that, as he is always asleep by eight o'clock. But, I didn't mention that, because I knew it would only trigger a new round of discussions on that point, and we were all pretty well worn out from debating all day, as it was.

Big Dan has had a wild and adventure filled life. But Big Dan has now found the Lord, and was anxious to talk about it. He and I probably talked more that night at Harold's than we had ever talked before in our lives.

I lived for a time with Big Dan, in the Gas Fields of Western Oklahoma. I was working one summer on a large gas well, and Big Dan roared up one day on his Harley, and easily got a job there, when the boss saw how big and strong he was. He made my life there a lot easier. The other roughnecks stopped throwing large chunks of iron off the tower at me, just to see how well I could dodge, once Big Dan was on the scene. Those roughnecks were well named. Once, near the 4th of July, a bottle rocket war started up on the way to work, front seat against the back seat. Those rockets just continued to circle inside the car until it finally blew up.

Life was sure a lot simpler in that roughneck town, when I was hanging out with Big Dan. He was just a skinny kid then, about 280 pounds or so. Nobody messed with Big Dan.

When I headed for bed that night at Harold's, I turned and held Dan's eye for a moment across the room. "I'm proud of you, Dan. You're a good man." Dan flashed a smile. "Thanks, Uncle Pat. You've *always* been a good man." That was a good exchange to end that visit on. I slept well.

When I got up the next morning, Dan had already been up for a long time, and drained the coffee pot totally dry, maybe for the second or third time, because you can never tell about Big Dan. He was now long gone, off to see his girlfriends and boyfriends.

Harold was up too, waiting at his spot at the table while Lou cooked breakfast. He said, "Just go look for yourself, and see if you can pick a track out of that mess". Well, that told me we must not have been successful, but I rushed out there anyway. The bait was gone, the trap was thrown, and the trap was pulled to the end of the wire. There was a lot of claw and scratch marks where this animal pulled the trap around, but the flour was pretty much a mess, and using all my skills built up from my woodsman experiences, about all I could read from that was, he sure had some sharp claws.

Well, I sure did want to hang around until the end game of this mystery played out, but Barbara was expecting me home this morning, and looks like I would miss it. My last bit of advice to Harold was to remove all the cat food, sprinkle moth balls around in the room and under the house, leave the outside entrance open tonight to leave it room to get out, then close it back up tomorrow. Most pests I had experienced have no tolerance for moth balls. But I knew in my heart that Harold would not go with it, because by now, he just really had to get a look at this smart animal.

I wanted to grab that last piece of lemon pie, but there was just a tiny sliver left. Mom always frowned at us when we grabbed the very last bit. I always let Lou know when I'm coming, and I usually arrive at about meal time, and she has my favorite waiting. Coconut pie. This time she surprised me, and it was lemon pie. I now think my favorite kind of pie is lemon pie.

As I walked out the door, I could tell Harold was starting to plot his next move in his mind. I would like to tell you more, but another night has now passed, and I'm just dying to go call Harold. I can't wait to hear what happened last night.

Well, it's now a few hours later, and I have talked to Harold. He's had a change of heart. He feels sad and respectful toward this very worthy opponent, and he has decided to take all the cat food out of that room, open the outside opening to the underside of the house, and hopes, maybe when it has eaten up all the cat food it has stashed away, that it will move out and seek another life. Away from Harold's house. He wishes it well. We all would have liked to have gotten a look at this brilliant creature, though. Several people have mentioned getting a motion activated camera to help get a look at him, and everyone agreed it was a good idea, but no one stepped forward and offered to foot the bill. Goodbye, Einstein of the wild animal kingdom! We all wish you well. Sore nose and all.

Late news flash! Harold changed his mind, and did manage to catch the critter, using ladies' nylons and peanut butter. I'm not real sure about how all that played out. It was, indeed, a packrat! Now, why didn't I think of that! How simple it all seems now, ladies nylons and peanut butter. However, at last reports, the cat food still seems to be getting gone.

Some time later, I got the word. The creatures had made a move that would inevitably spell their doom. They chewed the coverings off the electrical wiring of my sweet sis-in-law's car. That put that look in Harold's eye that I haven't seen since I used and lost all of his steel traps while he was in the Air Force.

Now, it was all-out war, and many would not be returning from this final battle. I think I will just stay home and ask no more questions. This battle was about to get really ugly.

VERLA MAE

DURING THE EARLY DAYS OF OUR MARRIAGE when we lived at Fayetteville, and later, we spent a lot of time in Watson. Mostly, we just loved to be there, but also, Verla Mae, Barbara's mother, just had some mysterious hold on her large family. She seldom spoke, but when she did, they listened. Right up until the day she died. When she called our house, if I answered, all I ever heard was "Barbara there?" Then when she got Barbara on, she said her say, a few words, then just disappeared from the air waves. Never "bye" or "so long." just disappeared. If one of the things she said in that phone call was, "Y'all coming for Thanksgiving?" we went. We all did. She always prepared about twice as much food as we needed, and we ate it. By the time that food had just began the digestive process properly, she was at the living room door. "Supper." Then she was off to somewhere to eat hers alone.

Us prospective and actual in-laws never really knew where we stood with Verla Mae. She just never talked to us much. The only hint of where I stood with her occurred one day before we were married when another guy Barbara was dating for a time, the Jock, came home with Barbara to meet the family. (His idea, Barbara says.) She got Barbara alone, said, "Where's Pat?" A short time later, I was back in the fold, he was out. I've always had a warm place in my heart for Verla Mae about that.

Barbara tells of a little incident that happened when she was 12 years old, the one time Verla Mae used more than just THE LOOK on her. Barbara developed early, and at

12 she looked 16. Her brother brought a friend home with him. He was 16. He started paying Barbara a lot of attention, and Barbara was flattered. Barbara and the older boy were flirting away with each other in the back yard. Verla Mae called Barbara over to the back door. "Get away from him." Then Verla Mae turned and disappeared. Barbara did, pronto. Case closed.

I have never seen a large family so close. They pretty well all wound up living close together, but if some of us did venture off for a time to another state, Sport and Verla May just got in that old truck and came to us, regularly. Verla Mae worked very hard, and she was always very fast. If she was chopping cotton, and Sport dared to suggest she slow down a little, as she was chopping too many cotton plants, she didn't say a thing. Just threw the hoe down, went to the house. Sport seldom did that, by the time I came around. Throughout our married life, as we worked together, if Barbara or I got a little too bossy, we had only to say, "I'm gonna throw my hoe down."

If one of her children wanted/needed some new clothes, shoes, etc. badly, they never discussed it. Verla Mae just found a way to make it happen, it just showed up on their bed one day. There was never any family discussion about whether they could afford it or not, it just showed up. Never a word said later. But they always got by, money wise. Verla Mae just saw to that. Sometimes, after the girls got older, Verla Mae would buy them new shoes and she would wear their old ones. She made sure her children and grandchildren never missed celebrating a holiday. One rainy Easter, she hid a dishpan full of Easter eggs in the house. Took hours to find them all. She was a firecracker fanatic. I think she liked them more than the kids did.

Verla Mae loved to drive around, find an old house place, dig up some plants to put in her yard. When she got behind the wheel, she started humming church songs, then got to tapping her gas pedal foot to the beat of the music. That could be a hard ride. Phyllis said, they bobbed their heads long before head bobbing became the thing to do.

Verla Mae instilled an extremely strong sense of right and wrong in her children, similar to the old Gillum " Do Right Mechanism" I have already talked about. But somehow, she just brought it about, with no screaming at them, no constant reminding, no watching them with eagle eyes. However, they did get THE LOOK if they messed up. She expected it, therefore they did it. Maybe a "Stop messin' and gommin'" thrown in occasionally. Just generally speaking, some sort of magic.

A little word about THE LOOK. Barbara inherited THE LOOK. During the years Barbara was substitute teaching, she was always the first sub called to handle a difficult situation. Even in boy's PE, shop, whatever. They quickly learned, that soft spoken young lady could just put a rowdy kid on the floor with THE LOOK. Kinley was always especially vulnerable to it, and would do anything she could to avoid it. Oh, all right! I'll admit it. I was, and am, vulnerable to it too. I have changed more than one segment in my writing, when Barbara, while proofreading, gave me THE LOOK.

When Verla Mae's children got married, they always stayed married. None of that messing about stuff. The world needs a lot more mothers like Verla Mae Dunnahoe.

Verla Mae had a very hard time in her last years. Congestive heart failure dogged her for a long time. Once, in the hospital, daughter Patsy was helping her across the room. She just totally collapsed. Patsy ran to the hall, and there just happened to be a team of doctors with a defibrillator walking by. They hurried in. One doctor got to her side, while the other got the machine ready. Right after the first doctor pronounced her dead, the second doctor kicked a can out of the way to get the machine in place. "Do you want her back?" a doctor asked Patsy.

"Oh, yes! Yes!" After awhile, the machine brought her back to life. Later, she took Patsy aside. "You should have let me go. I was floating above that room. I saw the doctor kick something aside. I saw a bright warm light. It was pulling me to it. I wanted to go. Then I was pulled back, slowly, into my body. I wish I had been able to go." A year later, she finished that journey that she had started that day.

SCRABBLE WARS AND DOCTOR DEADLIFT

EARLY IN OUR MARRIED LIFE, Barbara and I were already playing Scrabble. I had played longer, all the way through college, and I had the edge. We realized quickly, we were both very competitive about it. Once I beat her pretty good, and she stormed out of the house, announced she was leaving, got in the car, and sprayed gravel all over that little box of a house. Well, I knew Barbara didn't even know how to get out of town yet, much less drive home to Mama. She drove a few laps around town, settled down some, and came home.

A marriage counselor would not have recommended it, I'm sure, but we both loved the game and just continued on playing. Pretty soon, Barbara was winning her share.

A year or two later, we had moved to Fayetteville, Arkansas. Late in March, we got a very unusual 17 inch snow fall. We had nothing else to do, so we played Scrabble. She beat me like a rented mule, and I stormed out, into the real storm. I plowed through that snow until I had a pretty good trail around and around that house, just gave out, then I, too, returned home. I'm sure people driving by wondered why I had a trail around the house in that deep snow, while my car would remain snowed in for days. I should have used all that energy to dig the car out, but Scrabble anger is not a sensible anger.

Jump ahead with me 40 years or so. Barbara, always a word freak and crossword guru, had taken command. After I had lost a very long string of games, the final loss galled me so, I lost it. I was now an old man, and that kind of rage is just not good for an old man. I grabbed the board, flung it far across the room. We didn't play for awhile, because I was digging tiles out of the far corners of that room for some time.

When I finally found a full set of tiles, old habits were hard to break, and we continued on. I finally accepted the fact that I was going to be the majority loser, and learned to relish my occasional victory. Barbara had learned so many new words, it was hard, but we played so often, I slowly began to learn them too, at a terrible price.

Finally, one glorious day, the Scrabble gods just started smiling at me, frowning at Barbara, and I won 7 games in a row. This juicy little tidbit has never been told before, It is just not a safe thing to talk about. Well, after that 7th loss, Barbara jumped up from the couch, grabbed the board, and just slammed it down, upside down, on the couch. Well, I knew it would take a long time to find all those tiles, and I was fine to rest on my laurels for some time, and just generally enjoy this current status. But Barbara would have nothing to do with that, dug them all out quickly, and stated she was ready to play. You just don't beat Barbara like a rented mule and walk away from it.

When Barbara got her magic phone, with internet-GPS-everything, she sought the best players she could find on the internet, and keeps a few games going all the time on Words with Friends.

When we went to bed, she would kiss me goodnight, I went to sleep, and she would play awhile with a couple of guys/girls until she went to sleep.

I've never been a jealous type husband, mainly because she never gave me any reason to be.

Things change.

Once she put her picture out on the internet to her personal friends, made a mistake somehow, and it went to the whole internet.

As anyone can plainly see, Barbara always looks good in a picture. She is totally beautiful, as well as being an expert poser, from her photography years, and always applies all her skill to her own pictures. Soon, Dr. Deadlift responded. Wanted to play some Scrabble. Said she looked like someone who could give him a good game. I wondered about that. He could tell all that from a picture? By way of introducing himself, he referred her to Facebook to explain his name. Barb called me up to look at it. At 56 or so, he was a world champion weight lifter, and worked in Homeland Security. Well, all that was too much for me. She was taking that picture off anyway, and she cut off Dr. Deadlift when she saw how much it bothered me. I soon came to realize, I was being silly. He never talked about anything except the game, always a perfect gentleman, and he *was* a top tier scrabble player. You either trust someone or you don't, and one of the things we had both always been happy about in our marriage was the fact that we never gave each other that kind of grief. I told her to put him back on, but don't be playing with Dr. Deadlift, in the bedroom, after I go to sleep.

I never play Barbara any more. With all her internet scrabble, she has left me behind. And scrabble is just something I cannot tolerate always losing at. The Scrabble gods just no longer have a role in it. Word to the wise: Don't challenge Barbara unless you are in the top tier. You remember what I told you about that rented mule?

One of our very smart college friends was about to move, and he asked Barbara if she would like to play Scrabble on the internet, by way of staying in touch. He told her he would make a point of taking it easy on her. She agreed, but specified she wanted him to do his best, because she could only learn more from a really good player.

He just smiled.

After they had played for some time, he came back for a visit. I asked him how the Scrabble was going. He turned really red, and stammered around a bit, then finally confessed he had not won a game yet. The life of a rented mule can be really hard.

THE SUMMER OF 1956

THE SUMMER OF 1956 brought a new friend and companion to the farm. Mike Ford, my city-boy cousin, arrived from California one morning in June. Mike had never been out of the Los Angeles area much, and even the routine occurrences on our hill farm became new adventures to him.

Soon after Mike's arrival, the raccoons attacked our corn patch, which was in the roasting ear stage, in force. Every coon in the bottoms seemed to show up at dark. Mike, my dog Tooter, and I were assigned the task of protecting our patch. The stage was set for one of our greatest adventures.

Early one warm summer night we headed for the patch. No sooner had we reached it than Tooter was on a hot trail. Mike and I ran down a corn middle. We could hear Tooter running toward us, knocking down corn stalks as he ran. A silent, furry shadow flashed in front of me, barely visible in the dim moonlight. Close behind came Tooter. Reason and common sense left me, and I joined the chase, momentarily not noticing that I was doing as much damage to the corn as the coons were, tearing and scattering stalks as I ran.

Suddenly, the game changed. The big coon turned to fight. Tooter, having better control of his senses than anyone else at the moment, jumped aside. I don't think I really made a decision to do what I did next, for I like to think my decision making process is a little better than this display. And I knew about coons. A coon like this can be a bundle of screaming and biting fury. They often whip a dog, and can kill them if they get on them in the water. I dived at the coon. I like to think I reconsidered in mid air, but I don't really think I did.

I sat on the coon, on my knees. I held the ringed tail tightly in both hands, while the masked face peered out from behind me. The coon was strangely quiet, giving me a moment to consider my situation. I asked myself, "How do I get off?" when no reasonable solution came to mind, I called, "Do something, Mike!" I don't remember exactly what he did, so I asked him when I visited him this past summer. He said he hit the coon on the head with a knife, and it just got mean.

I acted. I jumped up, holding the tail by the right hand, planning to slide my hunting knife out of its scabbard, and hit it over the head. Now, my knife was not just any hunting knife, certainly not one a 12 year old should be carrying. It was a US Marines combat knife, designed for hand to hand combat. Perfect for my needs now. But by the time I had began my draw, my fingers had just touched the handle when the coon went crazy. It was wrapped tightly around my right arm, biting and squalling, and my arm was turning into sausage. I shook it loose, only to have it latch onto my right leg, slightly above the knee. I was struck with a momentary flash of good sense, and I shook him loose. Tooter joined the chase then, for, still being a young dog, he liked it better when the coon was running from him. Myself, I was in the heat of battle now, and I stayed close behind. Again the coon turned to fight, raking Tooter with his claws. When I entered the fray this time, the knife was in my hand, and it was quickly over.

We proudly carried the big coon back to the house, and I basked in the attention and glory as everyone examined my wounds. We did not think much about things such as rabies in those days. Mike later confided, "I would sure like to have some scars like that to take back to California." A few days later, Mike went down to run the traps we sat out at the corn patch, got too close to a squirrel or coon or some such animal, and got his own battle wounds. For days, he pulled the scabs from the wounds, to promote scarring, and he proudly wore his scars back to California.

As the corn matured, the crows moved in. Life on our farm was a constant battle with assorted animals wanting our crops.

A few years before, I had seen a pure white crow, mounted, on Herbert Person's wall. Herbert was a next door neighbor a mile away. I assume he must have been genetically successful, for now many of the crows who preyed upon our corn had white wings. We were just never able to aim our shotgun toward one of them. They were too pretty. Only a few years ago, I told Herbert's grand daughter about that mounted white crow. She pulled a current photo out of her purse, taken recently. That mounted crow had turned completely black over the years. Now, he was just like his flockmates. He woulda been proud.

There being hundreds of crows, our focus turned to them. One who has never experienced the crow as an enemy cannot possibly appreciate the cunning intellect of a wild crow. Without a gun, we could get close, as we can with the tame golf course variety of today. But with a gun in our hand, they knew what that meant, and we could get almost within range before they abandoned the ear of corn and flew, laughing and calling to the others, or maybe at us, as they flew.

Mike and I built a blind in the patch. As we entered, one guard crow watched from the tree line. Even if we sat for hours in the blind, not a crow showed. When we finally gave up in disgust, heading for the house, the crows would always flog in and cover the patch when we got out of range.

One day Mike finally discovered a chink in their armor. A crow does not count well. We both entered the blind, one of us would leave, and the crows would flog in on top of the remaining shooter, discovering their error in math too late.

These crows also provided a source of spending money. The County had a fifty-cent bounty on crow heads, simply show them to the County Clerk and collect the reward. However, the first time we proudly sat a fruit jar full of aging crow heads on his desk, he suddenly decided, as he fled his desk with his nose covered, that he could trust us. From now on, we would only have to come in and TELL him how many we had.

Ticks and chiggers were also new to Mike. Me, I had gotten used to them over the years, just scratch it off when you got one. They also served as a good source of entertainment each night before I went to sleep, scratching all my bites good. For Mike, it was different. The first time he saw hundreds of seed ticks crawling up his leg, I thought he was going to throw a runaway.

The summer was drawing to a close. Mike was ready to ride the train three days back to Los Angeles. When he arrived, he got a dog, named him Tooter. He bought traps, and sat out a trap line in the concrete jungle of Los Angeles. All he could catch were cats and ground squirrels, though. He told me this year that the summer in Arkansas influenced the course of his life. He later made many trips into the wilds of the west.

I did not see Mike again until he returned from Vietnam as a demolitions expert, sporting a teflon orbit around one eye. We visited Wing a couple of days and talked about the old days. When he got back to California, he had a rude awakening. People there did not appreciate him and the other returning veterans. By the time he had completed college, he had had enough. He went to Australia, taught school a couple of years. Then he played basketball on a touring team of displaced American veterans awhile.

When he returned to California, pushing thirty, he applied for a teaching job. Remembering his earlier treatment, he did not mention to the Superintendent interviewing him about his war experience. But when the man asked him why, at near thirty, he was just now applying for a job, he came clean. The man, a veteran himself it turns out, stood up, shook his hand, and hired him on the spot. It turned out to be a 30-year job.

A BATH IN GOD'S LOVE

THE WORD KAIROS refers to a type of time. There is chronological time, as what our clock keeps, and there is kairos time. If the doctor tells a woman that the baby is due to be born on February 23, that's chronological time. If, however, severe and regular pains begin on February 15 at midnight, this might prompt her to wake up the husband, tell him it is time. He may tell her, "No. it's not due yet. Eight more days. Go back to sleep." He's dealing in chronological time. Yet she knows better. She is dealing with kairos time. God's perfect time.

Kairos is also a prison ministry. It was started in the early 1940's. For a time, it moved very slowly.

Two priests requested the opportunity to spend the last day and night with a condemned man who was to be executed the next morning. The prisoner agreed. "Sure. Why not." The men talked for a long time that day, yet the prisoner was unmoved. The talks continued into the night.

After midnight, things changed. The man cried. He became more and more emotional, as his time was growing near. Eventually, he asked the priests what he could do to help right all the wrongs he had done in his sordid life. This discussion continued for some time. Toward daylight, one priest approached the condemned man. "You are going to be seeing Jesus this morning. Will you ask him to bless our Kairos mission?"

The condemned man agreed.

From its humble beginning, Kairos has now grown into a worldwide organization with more than 18,000 volunteers, having only a handful of paid staff. Today, Kairos operates in eight countries.

I joined the Kairos group operating at Pine Bluff Prison five years ago. We go into prison for four days, twice each year. While it is difficult to recruit new Kairos men, almost all who stay the course for a year never seem to quit. They stay the course, and will die a Kairos man. My Kairos is made up of men from many different Christian denominations, and they come from all over Arkansas.

A man is allowed to lead a Kairos Weekend only once in a lifetime. *Lest he become prideful.* Many of the men in my Kairos have already led. Last spring, nobody stepped forward to lead our August weekend, and it was cancelled.

I am not a leader. I'm a great follower, always have been. The Kairos leader should be a skilled computer person, which I am not. And, it requires a major commitment in time. I was not ready to step forward. But God decided otherwise, and I agreed to lead Weekend 43 in February 2016.

Recruiting the team came first. The experienced men were easy to recruit. Since we had missed one weekend, everyone was ready. But, for Kairos to continue, we also needed new blood. My goal was seven new men. Initially, I thought it would happen. I had at least seven really good prospects. But, as the training commenced, that number dropped, for one reason or another. When we walked into Pine Bluff Prison months later, only two new men remained, with 28 experienced men.

The training came next. For five Saturdays leading up to the event, we met at my church, Fellowship Church of Arkadelphia. *Training* is not the best word here, for I had little to teach these men that they did not know. *Conditioning ourselves, and, maybe, training up a leader,* may be more applicable. We worked toward leaving all our denominational differences at the door, and worked toward *common ground*, our love for Jesus Christ. We worked toward becoming humble, vulnerable. Toward allowing us to let God use our bodies to model unconditional love and total forgiveness which is available only through God, and reflect God's love on the men in white. We worked toward making the entire weekend a bath in the love of Jesus Christ for our 24 men in white.

Two weeks out, I went to Pine Bluff Prison for a job I was not looking forward to. Picking 24 participants from the hundreds of applications. There are many reasons to want to be involved other than spiritual. Really good food, all the cookies anybody would ever want to eat, three days off work. Following prison guidelines, I did not meet the men before choosing, I simply looked at their records. Keeping a racial balance. Old men and young men. Their rating, from 1A, trusted men, to 4C, the other end of the scale. Represent each dorm equally. Then, a lot of praying.

In the end, there were twice as many 4C's as 1A's picked. Three Muslims. We do not look for the easy men to work with, but the leaders. Good and bad. Men who, once turned, could influence many others during their stay. On the way home, I had to cry. I had just given 24 men a great boost toward a more spiritual, and much better, life with Jesus in a very dark place, while rejecting dozens of others. Without even meeting them, or really knowing them. But I prayed to God about them, and God knows them well.

One week out, I went to Pine Bluff Prison again, to meet with the selected 24, along with 16 alternates. Telling the alternates they were on our list, and would receive a certificate, but they were *not invited to the party* was not easy. However, knowing they would be first on our list six months later for Weekend 44 helped. The 24 who were picked were elated. To the best of my ability, I started thinking in terms of their *bath in God's love* that day. And, I again had to cry for the alternates on the way home.

Our last training day ended with a ceremony to officially make us Kairos Priests for the duration of The Weekend, and the Foot Washing Ceremony. We were ready. We could hardly wait.

We use a church in Pine Bluff for our home base. Our first job was to bag up 1000 bags of cookies. Every Kairos man brings 50 dozen cookies, mostly donated by our outside team, church members and others who furnish agape and prayer for the duration. Every person inside those walls would receive 2 bags of cookies, delivered by Kairos men to their bunks; *Cookie Runs*. Each man with a laundry hamper filled with bagged cookies. New men seem to always be involved in the Cookie Runs. If God has not removed every last shred of fear from these men, this is where it will show up. But I've never seen it happen. A Kairos man cannot function with fear in his eyes. He can never reach these men. He might as well go home.

Thursday afternoon we went in. *The Bath in God's Love* was about to start. My job was now distilled down to making speeches. Speeches until my throat was sore. Yet, joyful speeches.

I wish I could tell you more. Take you along every step of the way. But I can't. I cannot risk spoiling the surprises for hundreds of other men in white at Pine Bluff Prison who may yet experience a wonderful Kairos weekend. Wonderful for the men in white, and wonderful for free world Kairos men as well.

Last week, on Sunday morning, I was back in my usual place in Fellowship church, on or near the back row. The pastor was giving a great sermon. At one point, the word muslim was mentioned, and a thought hit me hard. I sat there sobbing. I had just, at that moment, been struck by a realization. Though every one of our 24 men had hugged me and the other Kairos men long and hard at the end of our closing ceremony, I had no idea who the Muslims, the A1's, or the C4's were. At that point, they were all just 24 men who badly needed someone, or something more in their life, and many had found it. They had just experienced a Bath in God's Love.

WONDERGIRL AND THE SUPERMAN CLAN

MY WONDERFUL GRANDAUGHTER CAYLIE got married. Let me back up and explain to you that I *do not* use the word *wonderful* lightly. Read on.

Caylie has never been your average girl. At four months old, she, along with her mother Christi, survived the unsurvivable; a major car wreck involving multiple rolls and flips, with only scratches and bruises. I *measured* just how far that car flipped and rolled. *One hundred yards.*

God, I think, already had big plans for this baby. And, as a young teen, she was already in the mission fields; she began, early on, paying back God's investment in her during that *one hundred yards straight from Hell* event so many years ago. Ever since, she has always been a stern and demanding seat belt enforcer in our family.

At six, she always got up on her own, fixed her own hair, brushed her teeth, and dressed herself, usually allowing time to read her books before heading off to school. Her parents declared that she only needed adults around in her life to drive her to school and provide a little money. There was just no time in her early years to hold down a full time job, what with Kindergarten and all, but that does not mean she was not capable of it. She always had everything else pretty well under control all by herself. The turbulent teen years just passed her by. They just never happened. Her high standards she always set for herself were etched in stone early on.

But wait. That's not all. I've been saving the best for last.

I do not remember ever seeing Caylie angry. I'm sure I must have, common sense would tell you I have. But it's not in my memory pool. Of course, my memory pool is a bit shallow on both ends.

Her bubbly, bright, smiling, and loving personality just makes all around her love her.

Caylie was in no big hurry to start driving. When she finally did, she was always very slow, always very careful. We all call her our "Granny Driver." When her papa Corey was training her, one could often hear him saying, "Caylie, you need to speed up just a little." But when her younger brother Christian was being trained, one could hear a touch of panic edging into Corey's voice. "Slow this thing down! You just clipped a sign back there!"

Caylie and Tim have been hanging around together for a long time. After they had been together for a year or so, Tim had a question for his friend, who would later become his best man. "Do you think it would be too forward of me to hold her hand?"

When Caylie, one year older than Tim, was about to graduate from high school and go off to college, she decided it was time for her and Tim to have a talk. Tim should be free to fully enjoy his senior year. The prom, dating, and all that goes with it. Somewhere in the translation, it didn't come out just like she had envisioned.

Tim did not want to date anybody else. But he accepted her decision.

"If you're going to break up with me, Caylie, we should at least wait until after the prom." On the big night, it was difficult to determine who was breaking up with whom. Tim was heartbroken, but he took it like a man. Caylie was the one who cried all night. When Caylie got home afterwards, flowers were awaiting her in her room. As Tim later said, "I wanted to let her know I still wanted her, and I was not angry."

A few days later, Caylie graduated. As I walked through the parking lot afterwards, I saw a large bouquet of flowers on Caylie's car. I had to smile. *The battle was enjoined;* Tim's struggle to win her back had begun.

Long before she left for college, Caylie was having major second thoughts. Once she got to Ouachita Baptist University, she soon realized the boys around her did not measure up to Tim. Soon, she tentatively inquired how Tim felt about the two of them getting back together. She feared she had messed up; Tim may have found somebody else.

Tim thought about this for a long time, then replied, "I will need to pray about this for three days."

This was a long three days for Caylie, especially the third day. Walking to her dorm from classes, her head down, she got a call from Tim. "Where are you, Tim?"

"In a parking lot somewhere on campus. I don't really know where I'm at."

When she finally found him, he was by his car. He had a large bouquet of flowers, her favorite candy, and her favorite gum. He had one question. "Will you be my girlfriend again?" He handed her a card after she answered yes. Written on the card was one word; *always*.

Tim is a swimmer. Six years ago, he was a big time swimmer. He swam every day, five hours per day, with an elite swim team full of Olympic hopefuls. He had the second fastest time in the country in the mile, somewhere around fifteen minutes. (A fifteen minute mile is a pretty fast walking pace, in case you haven't tried that.) Also on Tim's elite swim team were two little girls, ages eight and nine. They were already, at their tender ages, showing great promise for the future, and have continued that grueling training pace to the present. I feel certain that six years ago, Tim was their hero.

The Olympic trials were looming. But as bad luck would have it, Tim had a serious allergic reaction to chlorine in swimming pool water, and had to drop out. Tim manages to stay in good shape, and swims when he can in lake competitions, but the world class level at which he had been swimming had to go by the wayside.

Last summer, Tim and Caylie borrowed my fourteen-foot aluminum boat. They floated from Lake DeGray to the Ouachita River Bridge near Arkadelphia, Arkansas. That's a pretty solid half day float. I drove down to pick them up, and when I was crossing the bridge, I could see they had missed the take-out ramp. They floated by on the far side of the river, and when they saw it, they were already well past.

The lakes were releasing a lot of water due to heavy spring rains, and the river was flowing swiftly. They were both paddling as hard as they could, but were steadily losing ground. I hollered for them to paddle to the bank, where Tim could walk along in shallower water and pull the boat up. They did, but immediately saw a large water moccasin on a limb, grinning at them, daring them to get *just a little bit closer*. They quickly headed back to deep water. Paddling was not the way to go, so Tim jumped into the river, put the rope around his shoulder, and started swimming. Now, for a normal person, considering Caylie was still in the boat, that would have been impossible. But Tim is not a normal man. He started gaining ground. It still took him a long time, but he got it done.

This past Saturday was a big day for me. For the first time, I was about to see Tim in action, swimming against strong competition. Hundreds of great swimmers from all over were competing at Degray Lake. Tim was entered in the one mile swim. Swimming in the women's division of that race were two teenage girls. Initially, this really didn't mean anything to me, I did not know them. But Tim did. They were the same two little girls from his old swim team of six years ago. He knew they had been swimming five or six hours daily all these years since Tim had to quit. He also knew they would be in top condition, and his chances against them would be slim. Not being in the know, I was concerned with the whole herd of musclemen Tim would be swimming against, and I paid little attention to the girls.

Halfway or so into the race, his shoulders began to give him great pain, but they soon went numb. Other than having to throw up a couple of times, everything was going smoothly. But Tim had been right. The two, no longer little, fourteen and fifteen, were first out of the water. Tim was next out, winning the men's division, at around twenty-four minutes. The musclemen I had been worried about were still specks far out in the lake.

Tim's father Joe is 55 years old. He owns a landscaping business, and he normally gets up very early, riding his bike totally unreasonably long distances. A one hundred mile ride is standard fare for Joe. He then works all day in his landscaping business. Then he goes out after work for a little exercise. Joe is a regular in iron man competitions.

Joe was once present at a one hundred mile run event in the mountains. He was not participating in this, so he had not been training for it. A friend who was entered knew Joe always stays in great shape, so he asked Joe to pace him during the last part of the race. Joe agreed. He paced him the last forty miles. That put both of them in the medical tent.

Joe hires several young men, twenty some-odd years old, in his business. Occasionally, they all gang up on Joe and attempt to pin him in wrestling, but have never yet been successful. Joe said recently, "I gotta stop doing that. I hurt one last time."

In the one mile swim – twenty five mile bike ride event at Lake Degray, Joe placed second. The one man who beat him in his age group also won first overall, and he is number four in the country in that event. Swimming was Joe's weakest area, but he made up for that once on the bike.

Joe's father David, Tim's grandfather, started his physical training early. At two, he was so active he was having trouble walking. The doctor determined he was too musclebound to walk properly. Later, his father Ray hitched David up to the plow to work the garden, instead of using a horse. He went on to become captain of the football team at The Citadel. The University of South Carolina was a major football power at that time, but David's team managed to beat them, the only time that has ever happened.

David was in the Korean War. He was a forward observer, maybe the most dangerous job in the army. Their job was to move into enemy territory, locate enemy forces, and call in artillery fire.

This was during a time of change and experimentation in the US army. Up to that point, the early 1950's, black soldiers were normally not highly trained in fighting, being usually assigned more domestic duties. That was changing. David was given a team of thirty men, mostly black, and he trained them up to a very high fighting level.

Also along about that time, the Chinese were flooding into North Korea to fight for North Korea against the South Koreans and Americans. They came in very large numbers. They fought with guns, pitchforks, hoes, etc. The large hordes of men more than made up for any shortage in equipment or training.

David's team, as forward observers, were spotted by one of these very large groups. The machine guns David's team were equipped with had two barrels. While one was firing, the other would be cooling off. Facing this vast hoard of Chinese, cooling the barrel was a luxury they could not afford. They had to keep both barrels firing constantly. Over time, both barrels melted.

Both groups were running out of ammunition.

Now, it was man to man, hand to hand. David realized they were about to be overrun, so he called in artillery fire right on top of the entire battlefield. That way, the enemy would be taken out also.

Officers, such as David, carried a pistol. They were trained to shoot themselves rather than be captured. David pulled his pistol, ready to do his duty. But he just could not bring himself to pull the trigger. The only other option was to fight to the end. David dimly remembers he and men around him beating each other with fists, and heads being slammed against the ground. After what seemed like forever, all was quiet on the field. There was no one left to fight. Only David and two of his men survived.

David's father Ray, Tim's great-grandfather, became a professional heavyweight boxer at an early age. He married at fourteen. He and his wife had eight children. His wife finally persuaded Ray to retire from boxing. He always regretted that decision.

Ray went on to become the ski jumping champion of West Virginia. At 55, he was the national skeet shooting champion. Even his bird dogs were national champions.

Ray became a state senator in West Virginia. When the presidential elections rolled around, he played a major role in helping John F. Kennedy get the presidential nomination. West Virginia became a key state in the election, and Ray campaigned tirelessly. Who woulda' guessed?

When West Virginia compiled a list of the one hundred greatest athletes in the last hundred years, both Ray and David were on that list.

Hopefully, Tim and Caylie will produce the next generation of supermen for the Barnett family. Who knows? Maybe a little of that super manhood will spill over into the Gillum clan.

Just look at me. As you can easily see, we need a little dab of that.

MY SWEET MOTHER

CONSIDERING THAT MY MOTHER was about the sweetest, nicest woman who ever lived, I really have not written a lot of material about her side of the family. She was quiet, and seldom told me stories of her family. Most of her sisters moved to the bright lights of California before I was born, and the others followed soon after, except for Mom. The few times I have carried on a conversation with her sisters, for the most part, was when I was very young. Her brother, Euriel, lived nearby, but he and most of his sons died early of heart problems. Mom's other brother died as a child. I never met Mom's parents. So there ya' are. My knowledge of Mom's family, for the most part, distills down to what transpired between my mother and I. She did tell me lots of stories, but most were funny, fictional and entertaining. They weren't about her family.

After Dad came back from WWI he went to the oilfields of Oklahoma. When his father died in 1922, he was called back to Wing to run the farm. He first became engaged to a Humphrey girl, (I was never told the first name.) She died soon after. From what everyone has told me, The Gillum family just loved that girl, totally had their heart set on her being Dad's wife. Dad had even built a house in the meadow for her. I'm not sure how much time elapsed after that happened before Dad and Mom married, but Dad was 33, Mom 21. Since there was no electricity in the Meadow House, Dad and Mom first lived with

Grandma Gillum. Hallie, Dad's school teacher sister lived there too. For a time, a picture of Dad's dead sweetheart continued to hang on the wall. After a while, a picture of mom's former sweetheart, Searce Pickens, appeared on the wall also. Well, Searce Pickens was now working for Dad, and both pictures soon came down.

My oldest brother Harry, the first born, told me that Grandma Gillum, and also Hallie, on occasion, did not treat Mom well. I don't know why, because my mother, when I knew her, was wonderful. Very kind, loving, and hard working. From what I have heard, my best guess is that Mom came from a family that was very different from the stern Gillums, and they were harsh in judging her. After three children were born, Mom wanted out of that house. They moved to the meadow house, even though there was no electricity, and Dad had to do without a radio. Jan was born there. Later, Dad bought the Marion Turner house, which was larger, and they moved there, where Barbara Lou was born. Both of these houses were within hollering distance of the house on the hill. After Grandma Gillum and Hallie both died in 1941, Dad and Mom moved their family back up on the hill. I was born there in 1944.

Mom was a very hard worker. Since the Gillums were determined to put up enough food for two or three years, just in case the dry years and The Depression returned, she sometimes canned as many as 800 quarts each summer over that hot wood stove. They were stored in the concrete cellar, dug underneath the potato house and smoke house.

The concrete floor was not very thick, and water often began to seep into that cellar in wet times. It had to get 3 feet deep or so before it reached the canned food, and before that happened, we often all worked most of a day, carrying it out bucket by bucket. Later, Dad figured out how to siphon it out, and he and I would do that.

Mom worked full time, while raising six children. Setting a bedpost on a dress tail of a toddler made a good baby sitter while Mom worked. Later, as the girls got old enough, they handled that.

This is a typical day for Mom on a summer day with no other major projects scheduled. She arose early, and had a full breakfast of hot biscuits, (made from scratch) sausages, oatmeal, coffee, etc. ready at daylight. After the kids were up and dressed, the entire house was swept. Our dogs entered our house only at great peril from Mom's broom. Mom might then work in the garden awhile, then it was time to start dinner (lunch). Always a full meal, always hot. After the dishes were washed, the dogs were fed the scraps. Dogs were only fed scraps. If there were none (but there almost always was) it was their responsibility to go catch a rabbit, or whatever, though Mom normally made a little extra cornbread for the dogs. So they seldom went hungry. Dishes and pots, skillets, etc. were washed, dried carefully, and put away.

Afterwards, Mom might have 30 minutes of down time, then she might head for the truck patch, a quarter of a mile or so down in the pasture. Most of the food growing took place there, a couple of acres or so. She would hoe weeds, or do whatever needed to be done, then she would head to the house, carrying with her a good part of what would become supper.

Time to milk both the cows. Mom always milked them alone, and they were so used to only her milking them, the cows would allow nobody else to touch them. Some of us could have helped, but I guess Mom figured it was just easier to do it all herself than to try to get the cows to tolerate us. Time to cook another hot meal, do the dishes, then maybe a little down time before bed time. Of course, as we grew older, we helped in all this. I helped Mom for several years before I graduated to helping Dad in the fields. Then, I was one of the MEN.

The girls, Barbara Lou, Jan, and Jonnie, worked very hard helping Mom, also. If it was a very busy time in the fields, one of the girls brought dinner to the men there.

This daily schedule varied, of course. One day per week, Mom would wash all the dirty clothes in the big black pots down by the creek, 200 yards down the hill using a rub board, lye soap, and bluing, whatever that is. The clothes were hung out on the fence or clothes line, and hauled in at night. On another day, all the clothes that needed it were ironed with flatirons heated on the stove. That always made the house very hot. Mom even ironed the sheets. The milk had to be hand churned to make butter and cottage cheese.

The winter time schedule varied from this, of course. There were clothes to be made, (mostly from chicken feed sacks) quilts to be made, etc. Mom was an expert at wringing a chicken's neck. I've seen four headless, bleeding chickens flopping about the yard at one time. Then they were scalded, feathers picked off, then dressed and cooked.

After we went into the egg business full time, that became a large part of the daily schedule. We kids knew nothing of allowances, pay for work, etc. It didn't exist on our farm.

In spite of all her hard work, Mom always found time for each of us, every day, though I don't know how. If Mom ever got a few dollars ahead, it was never spent on herself. She would tell me, "Well, I'll buy this for you now, then when you are grown and well off, you can buy nice things for me." Unfortunately, Mom died at 68, and that time never came.

Mom always found time for her neighbors. Edith Turner told me this year of Mom bringing her family loads of vegetables when they moved into Wing. We children never worked on Sunday, and officially Mom did not, either, but somehow, some way, all those great Sunday meals magically appeared. We were always in church on Sunday, Mom saw to it. We had a very large children's picture book, filled with bible stories. Mom saw to it we read every one, again and again. I fear I learned far more about the Bible under Mom's watch, that at any other time in my life.

Mom always loved having flowers in the yard. It was about the only extravagance Mom allowed herself. During dry times, we always found a way, somehow, to find enough time to haul water up from the creek and keep them alive.

One year, my oldest brother Harry came up with enough money for Mom to go to California and spend her birthday with her sisters. The well-oiled machine that was the Gillum farm went totally to ruin while Mom was gone. Dad trained me as the dishwasher. "Son," he said, "the open hand makes a great dish cloth." Barbara Lou and Jan took over the milking. The cows wanted no part of that. Early morning screams emanating from the cow barn became a regular thing. What with all the kicking going on with the cows, more milk dripped from the ceiling than wound up in the milk bucket. After a couple of weeks, Mom returned, and we all realized that in spite of the hard work by all the rest of us, Mom was the glue that held that well-oiled machine together.

Everybody in Wing and Rover just loved my mom. A very small handful of Mom's dear lady friends are still alive. My children, when they discover one of them, such as meeting Edith Turner at my book launching this year, just cannot seem to ever let her go. They are hearing, from a third party, just how wonderful my mother truly was;

they are realizing, it's not just me saying those things. It's the total truth.

After I graduated college and Barbara Sue and I lived at St. Paul or Fayetteville, I would slip by and see Mom when I could, surprise her. After I did that several times, she finally told me. "Pat, please let me know when you're coming by. Otherwise, I find myself sitting on the porch, looking down the road for you, every day."

Dad passed away, at 78, while Barbara and I lived at Fayetteville. When we decided to move to Hannibal, Mo., suddenly to a teaching job, Mom begged, "Let me go with you. I can cook and clean, and grow a garden." I knew Mom was not doing well, living alone. But we were moving with only a few days left until school started, and we didn't even have a place to live yet, and very little money. I told her, "When we get up there, get set up, and get a house, I'll come back for you." I could see the disappointment in her eyes. I have wished for many years that I had that decision to make over. But life does not work that way.

We had only been in Hannibal a short time when we got word that Mom was not doing well, Barbara Lou had taken her to Memphis to live with her, and she was now in the hospital. I rushed down. When I arrived, she was already in a coma. As I sat by her bed, I realized. I had seldom (or almost never) told her I loved her. Open expressions of love were just not normally said in our house as I grew up, or maybe that was just me. I started telling her over and over that I loved her, but in her coma state, I did not know if she heard me or not. She was moved to ICU, and I lived there in that waiting room for days. A couple of us could go in and see her every few hours.

The chairs in the ICU were very sleep resistant, unless one had one of the few recliners. One night, I did have one. About midnight, two young women and their mother came in. The older lady was in very bad shape. Her husband was in the ICU. I gave my recliner to the older lady, and moved over and answered the phone the rest of the night. The next day, I noticed that one of those three were always in that recliner. About 8 o'clock that night, one of the daughters called me over. She said, "You gave this recliner to my mother last night when she was in very bad shape. We've been saving it for you all day. You need to sleep tonight."

Harry arrived from California. I took Harry in, and told Mom, "Harry's here." She stirred noticeably. I now knew she had heard me. But way too little, way too late, for a mother like God blessed me with. I should have told her I loved her every day I lived with her, and I knew it.

Mom died shortly afterwards. I made a vow, then and there, that there would never again be a shortage of open expressions of love in my family. And I have kept that vow.

I did not set out to write a sad story. But, in writing of the older generations, it just seems to work out that way.

We can't change that. But we are given the opportunity many times to help improve the quality of life leading up to that ending. Once written, it can never be rewritten or erased. We just have to live with that.

MY DAD

I THINK EVERYONE in my branch of my family will agree, nobody shaped our branch of the Gillum clan like my dad, in my lifetime. My information about Dad's WWI experiences is incomplete. All he ever told me was that while riding the troop ship over, they had to sleep sitting up. It was too crowded to lie down. He also stated that he was close enough to the front to hear the guns when the armistice was declared at eleven o'clock AM on the eleventh day of the eleventh month of 1918. The main American force had just gotten fully into the war, and the Germans had been pushed back near the Germany-France border. They were well fortified there, and the generals in the field estimated it would cost 25,000 allied lives to defeat them. There were talks in progress about ending the hostilities, and the main question seemed to be, an armistice or unconditional surrender. General Pershing, the American commander, ordered that battle to commence. The field general, however, stalled, thinking of his men, and knowing the war could be over at any time. The battle was delayed, and in a few days, the fighting did cease. Had that attack order been quickly obeyed, would my dad have been one of those 25,000 casualties? Had Pershing's order to attack been obeyed immediately, with many, many more lives lost on both sides, would it have resulted in unconditional surrender eventually? Would that, as Pershing seemed to think, have prevented another world war in a few years, or at least delayed it? I really don't know. All I really know is, if that battle had been fought, and if Dad died that day, I would never have existed.

I learned recently that Dad was involved in the trenches in France, but he was in supply rather than actually shooting a gun. Often, he was so tired when he was finally allowed to sleep, that he could not pull his boots out of the mud, having to pull his feet out of his boots, and roll up in his blanket. I still have that blanket. Dad served during the occupation of Germany.

The Gillums were pretty well off, for the times, when grandpa Gillum died in 1922. Grandma Martha Jane called Dad back from the oilfields of Oklahoma to run the farm. Things went well, for a number of years. Dad bought a car, and spent more of his time overseeing the share croppers than actually planting crops. But 1930 brought not only the Depression, but also the onset of a number of very hot, dry years, when most all crops failed. The cattle had to be ranged out into the mountains for many miles to find forage, and Dad had to ride his horse many miles to find them. The sharecroppers could not get enough money to put in the crops, unless Dad signed the notes. He did, the crops failed, and the sharecroppers had to walk. It took many years to pay those notes off, extending the Depression for my family many years. Dad had to sell off much timberland to the government, at fifty cents to two dollars an acre just to be able to put in his own crop. Nimrod Dam was built, and the government took much of the prime farmland into that project. In addition to these problems, much of the topsoil in the valley was thin, and began to play out. Cotton and other row crops began to disappear, and cattle became the main crop, more and more.

As the Depression deepened and dry years persisted, it became difficult to feed a family. I remember Dad, many years later, showing me how to build rabbit gums, quail traps, etc. He also taught me little tricks for catching fish when the need was great. Dad once said, "If we saw a rabbit crossing the road, chased by less than two people, we knew things were getting better." After I arrived, I never knew of a Gillum eating a wild rabbit. Problems with rabbit fever during the Depression changed all that.

Once the unusually dry weather was past, Dad was able to grow plenty of food, with a lot of hard work and foresight. Just spend no money unless it was necessary, buy only staples like flour, sugar, a little coffee. Dad's solution to the problem was to just work harder and harder, longer and longer. But after the depression, Dad was never able to bring the farm back to the level it was pre-depression. Only I, the youngest and his helper in his older years, saw how hard he pushed himself.

Dad once planned a fairly long trip to find and buy the finest herd bull available. A neighbor got wind of it, and asked him to buy one for him, too. Dad did. When Dad got back, the neighbor told him he had changed his mind. Dad was now stuck with two expensive bulls. Dad never had any use for that man again. From this kind of experience, and others along the way, Dad began to get a general mistrust for a many people.

I think factors I mentioned above combined with the strong "do right mechanism" Dad had shaped him into the man I met when I came along in 1944. Work hard and long, every day except Sunday. Be careful about trusting people; don't buy food you can grow. Save up enough food for years, the dry years can return at any time; cut over every inch of cleared land, every year, or the woods will reclaim it. In the early 1950's, I was doing the pasture mowing. Those were very dry years, and grass and weeds didn't grow much. Dad insisted that I mow every square inch, even though it looked exactly the same afterwards. Don't think highly of lazy or wasteful people, lest you become like them; be honest, pay the bills first, before spending otherwise. If you feed a hobo, he will just come back the next day, and the next. Keep your daughters away from men, as long as they live in your house; Keep your sons away from honky tonks, no good can come from all that.

I know all this sounds extreme. However, if you look at the big picture, all six of his children, as adults, worked hard, were honest, fair, the do right mechanism strongly in place. Dad was hard, but it worked. Can one ask more from a parent than that?

I still have a lot of questions rolling around in my head. Most can never be answered in this world. My Dad and I spent much time together in his older years, with very little conversation passing between us. How could I have been so wasteful? There are so many of these questions I could have answered, had I only asked. If I had but one more afternoon with Dad, now, I could get an answer for them all.

IMPRESSING THE GRANDBOYS

I JUST SEEM TO HAVE THIS BURNING NEED, deep down in my soul, for my grand boys to remember me as being outstanding in some physical way, because boys are all about physical strengths. The problem is, I never did have many physical strengths to begin with, and what I did have are pretty well all gone. So I'm going to tell you my story about my search to implant this respect in my grand boys, over the years. Before it's too late.

Caylie is my oldest granddaughter. She's a married gal now. But Caylie is a lady, rarely impressed by an old man, trying to put on a show with his physical exploits. So, I just never felt the need try to impress her in that area. And, she runs half marathons, and is a skydiver. What could I do physically to impress a half marathoner, and a skydiver? Nothing, that's what. And Cati-Beth, the youngest of them all, is still too young to care one way or another.

The grand boys are totally different. All four of them. Christian is the oldest, weighing in at 230 with no fat, six feet tall, so I know better than to try to impress him with most physical things nowadays. Afraid he might impress me with his own physical things. But years ago when he was much younger, I did impress him with my ability to start a fire out in the woods under any weather conditions whether it be rain, sleet, or snow, using only one match and natural things available out in the woods. That impressed him. I also showed him how to start a campfire with flint and steel, and he just grabbed onto that one and worked and worked at it until he had mastered that too.

When he was much younger, he and I were sitting around a campfire one night. Now, sitting around a campfire just calls for a chew of tobacco. But I was still trying to conceal that from him. I didn't think he would be greatly impressed by that fact, and he never has been. Anyway, as we were sitting there spitting into the fire, as everyone worth their salt does in that situation, Christian just had to know. "Papaw, how come when I spit, it's clear. But you can spit brown. Now, why is that?"

Well, I wasn't ready yet to tell him that whole story, he would find out soon enough. "Son, you have to reach way down into your lungs and bring it up from real deep to get to the brown stuff." Christian started working at it. He just went deeper and deeper, just wore himself out. Couldn't do it. But he continued working on that for some time. He soon figured that whole thing out on his own.

Jordan and Jackson are brothers, and both are rough and tumble boys. They get a lot of experience at it, fighting like cats and dogs. All day. Every day. After coming home from two hours of wrestling practice.

I just feel like my grandsons should carry memories of me around when they are older, and I'm pushing up daisies, as a strong, fast, or tough old man. But it's too late. I can't impress them with my speed, I can barely get out of a good fast jog. On a good day. Strength, I never did have much of that. That just leaves tough.

We were sitting in their house one night, several years ago. I told them I would give them one shot each at pulling on the long hair on my forearm, as hard as they wanted to. I've got a lot of it. My "kids" at our orphanage we worked at in Africa often said, "Uncle Pat is like Esau."

They both pulled as hard as they could. Though I was screaming inside, I just sat there and took it, never changed my expression. After that, they often said, "Papaw is the strongest man in the world. He's even stronger than Daddy." Well, their father Mickey is about the strongest man I know. He could easily snap me like a twig, so I just wallowed in their admiration. Lately, the youngest boy, Carson, got his shot at my forearm hair. But he somehow had it figured out. He didn't pull straight out, as the older ones did. He just grabbed a good handful of hair, leveraged his fist some way against my arm to get an unfair advantage of me, and pulled out a whole handful of hair. I've decided it's about time to retire that one. But I kept a straight face the whole time. I'm proud about that.

Two or three years ago, they all got into a big gunfight with those air soft rifles (they shoot plastic BB's, unlike the metal kind) at my house, wearing goggles. I watched closely. Those plastic pellets went a long way, but you could follow the path of the pellet all the way out, so I knew they didn't pack a big punch. So I took advantage of that opportunity to impress. I put on goggles, and gave each of them five free shots at my face at about fifteen feet. When the pellet hit, I never blinked or moved. Only one, right on the ear, stung a long time, but they were all impressed. I worked very hard at never moving or blinking. That's the key to the whole thing.

Barbara and I looked after Jordan and Jackson this week, and our main job was to keep them from killing each other. They now had a new, up to date, and obviously, I soon found out, much improved model of the air soft gun, a pistol. Jordan was ragging Jackson about crying when he got shot in the back with it a few days ago. That impressed me, because our family motto for a long time had been, "If Jackson cries call 911." For good reason. He just almost never cries from pain.

Well, I saw a new way to impress the grand boys. I watched them shoot it a couple of times, and though I could never follow the pellet when they shot it, I just assumed it was because it would soon be dark. I backed off ten feet or so, turned my back, raised my shirt, told them to each shoot me in the back. Well, this turned out to be a whole different gun. Jack shot me, and the blood started flowing, I screamed and cried, but managed to keep it all inside. They were impressed.

Well, I still had one more shot I just had to take, and there was just no way I was going to destroy that image of being the world's toughest papaw that I had spent years building up in my grandsons. I turned around, told Jordan to take his best shot. He did, and it felt like it hit even harder, but at least no blood. Just a big bruise. I never reacted outwardly to either shot, though inwardly I was bawling like a baby. That's was enough of that for that day. My reputation was now reinforced in blood.

The boys went upstairs, and I went to the kitchen for a long, sharp knife. I called Jackson down, handed him the knife. Told him that bullet could still be in my back, possibly, and I couldn't reach my back to dig it out. I told him I was going to lie down, and, since he's the one who pulled the trigger, stick that knife in that hole about half an inch and dig that bullet out. Tough as he was, Jackson turned white as a sheet. While he was still in the white state, I took back the knife, told him I would let him off, as I could see he was a little nervous about doing that. I would just tough it out with that bullet in me. I told him that bullet would eventually work it's own way out, most likely. All those other bullets I've had in me did.

When we all go to the State Fair together, I let the boys pick out the baddest ride on the place, then ride that with one of them. That's all I ride. Always with a big smile on my face, flaunting the "no hands" thing. When I get off, I always get out of their sight as quickly as possible. In case I have to throw up.

Where carnival rides are concerned, Carson takes the cake. He's still very small, yet he begs to ride all of them. He managed to get on one this year that he should not have been on in the first place, and the bar did not fit tight enough to hold him. He got slung all over that cage.

So, all you Grandpa's out there, remember if you're weak and can't run, like me, you can still impress the grand boys in physical things. The key is to show absolutely no reaction to pain. Then you can go in the bathroom and have a good cry.

TRAPPED – AT THE WINDING STAIRS

MY DAUGHTER KINLEY'S FIRST CALL came in at about nine o'clock Friday morning. She was worried. "Mickey and Jordan are not back yet, and I expected them yesterday afternoon!" We talked awhile. Her husband and son, my grandson, had left for a hiking and camping trip on Wednesday, planning to walk up the Little Missouri River three miles or so to the Winding Stairs, a very scenic, remote, and rugged stretch of the river, located three miles or so down river from the Albert Pike campground. One could walk down river to the site from Albert Pike, or walk upriver from a commonly known parking site below, hiking up a trail along the river. They chose to approach from down river, Kinley said, and she did not think they were familiar with the Albert Pike approach, or possibly didn't know about it.

As we talked, I began to detect a bit of uncertainty on her part about how many nights they planned to stay, one night or two. "If you are not absolutely sure about how long they planned to stay, let's give them time to hike out to a point where their cell phone can reach today before we get too excited. Call me back at 11 AM," She reluctantly agreed.

I was headed to southeast Arkansas with another of my grandsons, Christian, for a few nights of catfishing with JD Dunnahoe, my brother in law. I knew the trail up river well. It was pretty well cut and dried. Just park the car and hike upriver along the trail. Although I knew heavy rains had fallen in that area Thursday night, the trail does not cross the river. Hard to get lost there, just follow the trail.

What I did not know was that landowners had fenced off the lower approach, so they would not be able to drive the car into the parking area. And, it would be two months yet before the unspeakable tragedy occurred at Albert Pike, where the suddenly rising river drowned twenty campers, and I did not know the horrible potential of the Little Missouri River to rise rapidly in those mountains, pushing the water far up against very steep cliffs, completely cutting off that trail out.

At 11 AM sharp, another call. "OK," I said. "Call the ranger headquarters at Glenwood." She called right back.

"All the rangers are at an in-service meeting today. Nobody is available to investigate."

"Call the Pike County Sheriff's office," I said.

We were now at JD Dunnahoe's house. His farm is beside the levee in far southeast Arkansas, near the confluence of the Arkansas and Mississippi rivers. There was only a couple of places on that farm where a cell phone could reach, and I waited at one of them for her calls.

Another call came in. "They have sent deputies in to investigate." Another call: "He found their car downriver. No sign of them. They are sending several men into the mountains to look for them." JD, his two grown sons Kevin and Mark, and Christian and I began to prepare for a dash to Pike County, and possibly a very long night. We were five hours away, and darkness would be closing in on that cold March night before we could possibly get there.

Another call from the Sheriff's office to Kinley – "We cannot reach Winding Stairs because of high flood waters. We've found no sign of them yet, but we have many men looking."

Kinley was losing it. "Send boats down from Albert Pike," she said.

"Ma'am, we cannot put a boat in that river unless it's life or death."

She totally lost it. "My ten year old son is out there, and it is life or death! Put boats on that river!"

Kinley called me, so distraught she was hard to understand. I told her, "Call Johnny Barksdale."

Johnny is Mickey's brother. He lives at Amity, only an hour away. He is an expert woodsman, is close, and knows that area like the back of his hand. He would be a major asset to the hunt. As we prepared to leave south Arkansas, I searched my mind for the best help possible, close enough to get there before dark. I got to thinking back to many years ago.

The year was 1985. I sat beside the campfire, looking at ten young faces in the firelight. This was a winter camping trip of the Arkadelphia High School Wildlife Club, which I sponsored. We were camped deep in the mountains ten miles or so behind Albert Pike. Johnny Barksdale and Greg Latsha were my stars. They were already expert woodsmen, even in high school. I knew they were destined to spend most of their lives in areas such as this. Greg could imitate the call of almost any bird or animal in these mountains. Sitting beside the fire, he gave a loud, long wolf call. Almost immediately, he was answered by a frightening call right across the creek. Everyone grew quiet, looking at each other with wide eyes. The fast thinkers, I could see, were counting heads, verifying that we were all here, at the fire, making sure one of us was not out in the woods, playing a trick. When the count reached ten, they bolted for the van. The others were right behind, including Greg Freeman, who had earlier just walked up to and kicked a skunk, to see how it would react. He found out, and he became pretty much a loner for the rest of that trip.

The next morning, I cooked eggs and bacon for the group, explaining to them I had seen only one baby chick in all those dozens of eggs I cracked, so they probably would not notice it at all, as I had fished most of it out of the skillet. I'll have to admit that, in the interest of being interesting, I may have fudged on truthful boundaries on that a little. Funny thing, though, most all the food we had left was eaten, except for the eggs. I got to eat all the eggs I wanted, with plenty left over. Even after I announced I had just been kidding, they would just never touch those eggs.

I knew these mountains had been Johnny Barksdale's home territory all his life, and if anyone could find them, it would be Johnny. Unless, possibly, I could find Greg Latsha, who grew into possibly the finest woodsman I know. However, I could not figure out how to go about finding Greg Latsha.

Greg is at times a duck hunting guide in season, calling those ducks in for the city guys flawlessly. At other times, he is a salt water fishing guide in Florida, and he had also been a professional wildlife film maker for the Game and Fish Department. In between, he often mows lawns for his brother in Hot Springs. But where in the world would he be in March?

Always very athletic, Greg was a very small but fast

pass receiver, with great hands, on his eighth grade football team. In the tenth grade, he was in my biology class, though he already knew more than I could teach him, when it came to wildlife and the wilderness. Once he brought me a photo he had taken, somewhere around Arkadelphia, of a black panther, as best we could tell. Although such an animal does not exist in Arkansas, Greg not only found, but photographed one. It was not unusual for him to leave a large covered bucket on my front porch. I came to realize the contents were going to be alive, wild, and very angry by now. It might contain the largest black snake I had ever seen, or some other exotic wild animal that always amazed me. I began to get really cautious about taking the cover off one of Greg's buckets. On our wildlife club trips, he never failed to set a very wild and uncontrolled example for the other, less woods-savvy guys. But he knew exactly how far he could push me, how far he could go before I kicked him out of the club in frustration. Actually, though I never allowed him to know, I could never have done that. He absolutely *made* the club, and, well, I just loved Greg Latsha. Headache though he sometimes could be.

Greg started growing. He grew into a tall, very muscular man, hitting home runs farther for the HSU baseball team than anybody ever had. His small waist gave way to huge biceps and shoulders. I had been told that he always mowed lawns for his brother Roger's landscaping business without a shirt. I had also been told that ladies just fought to get him to mow their yards, and always peeked out from behind their drapes to watch him, fanning themselves as their house just seemed to be getting warmer and warmer. But there just seemed to be no way to find Greg Latsha in March. But I knew if this turned into a night search, we would need him, as well as Johnny, badly.

Very excited about their camping trip, their first father-son adventure of this type, Micky and Jordan attempted to reach the parking area downriver from the Winding Stairs. However, landowners had fenced it off. They could not enter by the traditional route from below. Crossing to the far side of the river, they found another place to park. Mickey knew that a river crossing was required from this side, but Jordan was a tough boy who could handle it. They didn't let that dampen their spirits much, on this cold March day. They soon had to cross a rushing creek. Jordan slipped down, and got totally soaked, but climbing two mountains soon dried him out some, and warmed him back up. However, they now faced a river crossing, and it was much deeper than they expected.
 Jordan once told me when helping me dig for diamonds, "Papaw, nothing that's fun is ever this hard." He may have been thinking that now, but he kept quiet about it if he did. When they finally reached the Winding Stairs, they just stood and looked for a very long time – well worth getting wet for.
 They gathered up a lot of firewood. The night promised to be cold, and the situation was not helped much when Jordan got wet again, crossing a creek with a load of firewood. But the roaring fire soon fixed that problem. They set up the tent, and got a good night's sleep.
 The next day was great. They hiked, climbing a high mountain. A ledge near the top proved to be the winter

home of thousands of lady bugs. I had seen that before, at the old fire tower a couple of mountains away. They found bats in a cave. They finished out the day fishing. A great day. Seems Mickey had always planned on two nights, but didn't explain that to Kinley very well.

The rains moved in that night. It rained, and rained, and rained some more. Fortunately, Mickey picked a good spot on high ground, so they were not affected by the rapidly rising river. But the high winds somewhat blew down their tent. By the time that was fixed, Jordan's bag was wet. He finished the night out by sharing Mickey's sleeping bag.

By morning, the situation looked bad. The roaring river was very high now, rising quickly, hemmed in between two very steep mountains. Mickey knew trying to cross it to get to the car was out of the question. They would have to find another way out.

They headed down river, but soon came to a feeder creek that was a trickle yesterday, but was today a roaring torrent. They stopped, managed to build a fire with the wet wood, and made coffee. Mickey knew these mountain streams usually came up very fast, but once they passed the crest, they should also go down fast. Finally, though, Mickey came to realize that if anything, it was still rising. It had to be crossed, if they were to get out of here. The water edged up toward waist deep on Mickey. Jordan, with his pack, held on to Mickey in the swift current. He slipped, losing his grip on Mickey, and his pack. He was about to be swept down toward the roaring river. By the time Mickey chased him down and they recovered the pack, they were both soaked. It was getting colder by the hour. Jordan was proving to be a tough guy, though. He was hanging in there.

They ran into a very wet hiker. He said he had almost been swept away trying to cross the river, and he had decided to try to get out by going up river, to Albert Pike. Mickey knew that going in that direction would only take them farther and farther away from their car, and he worried about being trapped between the cliffs and the still-rising river.

They headed on down river. The water had overflowed much of the trail, however, pushing up against steep mountains. It was tough going. After many cold, hard hours, they reached the fenced off area where they had first planned to park the car. They knew they were still miles away from the highway, and many miles more from their car. They could probably get a phone signal now, but their cell phone was dead. Finally, they reached a dirt road. After they had walked down it a long time, they heard a noise. A car! Moments later, Johnny Barksdale pulled up.

Kinley's next call reached me on the highway. "They're out!" she shouted.

"Call the Pike County Sheriff's office right now." I said. She quickly called me right back.

"They were very glad they are out of there. They were about to call in many more searchers from surrounding counties. It's going to be a very cold night. Too cold for wet campers."

Christian and I headed back to the levee. Christian is my oldest grandson, and the only grandchild who inherited Grandma Martha Jane's red hair. He now seems to be getting a lot of mileage out of it. The girls at school just seem to love their "ginger," judging from the pics I see on

Facebook. He's a great fishing buddy, and now, at fifteen, he's showing signs that he could become the tallest Gillum in decades. He may well become one of the smartest Gillums in decades, also, if he makes maximum use of the tools he was born with. The jury is still out on that. Caylie, my oldest grandchild, was the first driver that son Corey trained. She's very cautious. She was constantly told by Corey that she "must drive faster." Now he's training Christian, and he now yells, with fear edging into his voice, "Christian, slow this thing down! You just clipped that sign back there!"

We still had time to catch a lot of catfish. And we did. We headed home two days later, with sixty pounds of catfish fillets from two hundred pounds of catfish. (There is no legal limit on catfish inside the main levees of the Mississippi River) And Mickey and Jordan headed home, still wet, but now for the first time all day, warm and no longer hungry. And, they have a great story to tell.

GOODBYE KILIMANJARO

WE LIVED IN THE SHADOW OF KILIMANJARO FOR SEVERAL DAYS. Yeen Lan, the Rafiki director at the orpanage we were working at, called us the last day before heading back to Kenya. We were able to tell her we had seen the top of Kilimanjaro every day, a rare event. This mountain is the tallest free standing mountain in the world, over 18,000 feet, standing right on the equator. It is a four day climb, the last day being through hellish arctic conditions. She told us she had prayed for us to see the mountain in all its glory. She said some people stay there for weeks without ever seeing the top. Don't doubt that Yeen Lan has those connections. I personally believe Yeen Lan is an African legend in the making. If we live long enough, many people will be enthralled to find we actually know her.

We got bad news just before heading back to Kenya. Deb, the director at Rafiki Tanzania, told us our visa was a one way thing, and we would have to buy another to cross the border back into Kenya, at $100 each. No way around it, that's just how it's done. We didn't have that much on us, and only cash could be used.

Deb insisted on cashing a personal check of ours before we left. Barb seemed confident we would never need that money. I wasn't so sure, and I took Deb up on her offer. But, as I well knew, its very easy to underestimate Barbara's abilities, when it comes to public relations.

On the bus headed out, we saw many small, circular compounds in the bush. Mud and cow manure huts were surrounded by a high fence of thorns. Most were unoccupied. The Masai, with their herds of cattle, mules and goats, just went wherever the grazing was in this dry, arid land that is East Africa. Donkeys were used to haul containers of muddy water from sources that might be many miles away.

Drinking water was a real problem there. The Masai often had to drink from the same source the cattle had been in, a very bad thing in Africa. Many people die because of the water. Modern water wells and filtering systems could save thousands of lives there.

Young boys herded the goats. "Isn't that dangerous?" I had asked.

"Yes, we do lose boys often." Those who survive and become a man are a very formidable force, with only a spear, in protecting their herds from lions.

Traditionally, a young Masai warrior-to-be has to draw first blood in the killing of a lion to become a man. One youngster showed me how this was done.

When a lion stalks their animals, four or five warriors track it down. They surround it, each with a spear and a cowhide shield. The young warrior seeking to become a man confronts it. When the lion charges, he braces the back of the spear with his foot, points the spear at the charging lion. If things go well, the lion will be impaled, and the warrior crouches behind the cowhide shield. But if things go bad...

Other warriors then move in and help. This is technically not legal now, but older men show many scars from the day they became a man.

Masai often open up a vein in a cow's neck, drink the blood, and close it back up. Safer than drinking muddy water, I guess.

When dry times hit, and the grazing dries up, they move the cattle into downtown Moshe, into the moist micro climate at the base of Kilimanjaro. They have been doing this for eons, long before the city of Moshe, and besides, who is going to stand up and tell these seven-foot-tall warriors no? Since they strongly believe that all the cattle and the grazing in the world belongs to them, they go where they wish, paying no attention to borders or city limits.

Barbara is the only woman I have ever known of who has held their hands, and danced with these warriors. *Their hands were sorta rough, she reported.* However, she had no spear, and her vertical jump was not impressive. I was not invited to dance, and I was not going to insist. Barbara's boldness has landed her in many unusual situations around the world. But she was well warned by our free lance spy friend in Austria – *You travel far too lightly about the world...people will entrap you... you should have never allow me into your car yesterday...*
Barbara's reply - *We had you out-numbered.*

When we reached the border, it was very congested. Barbara studied each line of border agents. She chose one man who seemed to be friendly, who smiled a lot. When we reached him, she started flirting with him shamelessly, telling him all about us being missionaries, etc. She handed over the expired visa with a nice smile. The man was completely won over. Smiling, he stamped it, and handed it back. We got gone quickly.

Barbara seems to be able to have her way with any man. But she never uses that ability unless I am at her side. At least, I think so...

WING – A TOWN THE WORLD FORGOT

SOME TIME BACK I WROTE about the beautiful old church at Wing, Arkansas. It was built in 1880, totally from virgin pine. I told you all I knew, at the time. But then I started wondering, how can it still be so solid, and so beautiful, after one hundred thirty three years? Are there no termites in Wing? I did a little more research about that. Seems the answer was right there, under my nose, the whole time, right in the back of my brother Harold's mind. Harold is eighty-two, does not get around much. He's told me a lot about Wing in my research for my book, Spreading Wing. But Harold's a private person. Some of his revelations were followed by, "But you can't put that in a book!" Anyway, I stopped in to say hi a couple of days ago, and Harold told me he had come up with one more memory. Well, I was due in Russellville in a short time, needed to go, but he said, "Sit down, and listen to this story!" I sat. And I listened.

Seems in the 1940s, Arthur Walden, reputed to be the best carpenter around, noticed the floor of the old church was infested with termites. He told the church, "I know of a certain type of oil to handle that problem." Well, the church folks listened. But the church operated on pennies in those days. The pastor was paid in produce from the gardens, and chickens. That oil was expensive. It seemed the church building was doomed.

Right about there was where Buford Compton, the legendary sheriff of Yell County for sixteen years, and a resident of Wing, stepped in, bought the oil, and put it on the floor. The termites just could not stomach that stuff. I remember my mother always told us, "If you're going to pray, don't kneel. Stand up." That seemed strange to me at the time. But apparently, she well knew what that black oil would do to our Sunday best. We stood. Actually, the most likely reason for me to be on the floor was when I was wrestling around with Sammy Charles Turner when I should have been sitting up and listening. I was two years younger, and I was usually the one on the bottom. But it sounds better when I put it in terms of how I was praying.

Many years later, a new floor was put down, right on top of that black floor. Kneeling was not only allowed now, but encouraged. Seems that old church would never have made it to the sixty's, when the Turners took over and completely renovated it, without Arthur Walden and Buford Compton's black oil.

My good friend Skeet, (short for Skeeter) decided to go to Wing recently, since I was always talking about it. But he came to me with a big handful of maps, said he had been going over all his maps with a magnifying glass, couldn't find it. I told him, "The map makers of Arkansas have forgotten Wing. Just go to Rover, turn west, drive two miles, only church on the right." He still headed out to Walmart, grumbling to himself, to get another map. Skeet just leaves nothing to chance. I knew going to Wing and back could be an all day trip for Skeet. He drives so politely, he told me one day it sometimes takes him up to an hour to get through a four way stop.

If you want to go see Wing, just remember those directions. When you get into Yell County, you start to notice that cars you meet will usually have a smiling face behind the wheel. And, they will wave at you. But about the time you leave Rover and head up the valley, put away your cell phones and your GPS. You are now entering a forty five mile dead zone. But I have found there is one place at Wing where you can get a good cell phone signal. Go two miles south of Wing, wade out to the middle of the Fourche La Fave River, and it will work wonderfully. Alhough one is often unable to hear, during a cold time of year, what with all the teeth chattering going on.

If you are there at night, you city folks might want to bring a pair of sunglasses. Those bright stars just jump right out at you in Fourche Valley. My friend Cindy Aikman, who seems to be a star gazer who knows about such things, says the valley has some of the darkest skies in the country. There are no large light sources in the valley, and those steep mountains on both sides shields other light sources out. I noticed the stars looked very dim in 1962 when I left Wing.

When you are arriving, you have to look closely for that tiny sign announcing Wing. Just remember, that old church is right in the geographical center of Wing. Just like it was the center of our world when I was a child.

Well, last fall, after three long years, I finished my book, Spreading Wing. I put it on Amazon, but Amazon seemed sorta hit or miss. One day right off, my friends and relatives, I guess, bought seven books, and I looked to see where I stood in the top one hundred. I was sitting right on number sixty nine thousandth. The next day I looked, nobody bought a book, and I was right around two hundred thousandth. After another day of bad sales, I had dropped to around four hundred thousandth. I've been afraid to look at those stats after that. I decided I had to step in, Amazon needed some help. This was no way to sell a book. Nobody seemed to know me, or Spreading Wing at Amazon, once we got past friends and relatives and readers of my blog, Forever a Hillbilly.

I mentioned to a friend in Fourche Valley the other day that some of my blog readers had heard so much from me about Wing and Fourche Valley, they just had to come see it. She said, "Tell them if they want to come, and don't have a place to stay, I've got a big house. Your friends can stay with us!" Wow. I thought that mindset played out along in the 1800's.

I have always wanted to have my book launching at Wing, in that old church of my childhood. I knew that was a big risk, since I had been gone from Wing fifty years. I wasn't sure very many would remember me. We cooked up six packages of salt pork and a ton of biscuits, since that was a staple at our house in the 1940's when I was a child. I knew I was running the risk of having to eat salt pork and biscuit sandwiches for the next few months if nobody showed up, and I had way more than my share of that fifty years ago.

Well, to make a long story short, (too late) those valley and mountain people of Yell County just seem to always support their own, even those fifty years removed, and when launching day arrived, they just kept coming. Sometimes, I had a stack of books half a dozen high waiting to be signed, and still they came. I've always dreamed about how great it would be, with a line of people coming to me to get my signature! But I didn't have time to fully enjoy it. Even so, it was one of my best days ever. I didn't even get a bite of that mountain of salt pork and biscuits. We sold seventy books that day.

Equally as important, they ate up every last scrap of that salt pork. Even more importantly, I had a chance to renew a lot of very old, wonderful relationships. Edith Turner was there. She was ninety, but not anywhere near the oldest person in Wing. My children, Corey and Kinley, found out she was a friend of my mothers. My mother passed away when they were at or near infancy, and they are now at or near forty years old. They just could not seem to let her go, just hung with her every word, until long after the big event was over. She told them story after story of my mother. Kinley said, "Holding her hand was like finally getting to hold the hand of my grandmother."

My son Corey and three others, at great risk to life and limb, climbed up to the old classroom above. The stairs were long gone. I started up the ladder, but at the top was a three or four foot wall, to keep people from climbing up, I guess. Well, I'm old, so I headed back down. But Cindy Turner Buford, whom I knew was at least eight years older than me, (maybe more, but who's counting) just upper middle aged by Wing standards, scrambled up and over that wall. When they were all about to come down, Corey came first, and I saw him standing under that ladder, panic in his eyes, already holding his arms out as if to catch someone. He told me, "There's a lady in her seventies about to come over that wall!" I didn't worry too much about that. Those normal age limitations don't always apply to Wing people.

I grew up with Cindy, just a tall ridge over. We often communicated with a loud holler, that went something like this: "Whoooo, Whoooo, Whoooo weeee ouhooooo! Of course, that was back at a time when I could still holler that loud. I well knew Cindy could have climbed that tallest mountain behind Wing again, if she set her mind to it. That hill up to her house was about as steep as any mountain around.

Anyway, in the old classroom, they found the name of my aunt, Leta Lazenby, who left Wing forever in 1930. It was on the chalkboard, still just like it had been written yesterday. It was just like it was when I saw it in 1950. That *chalkboard* was made, it appears, by painting or spraying something on those very wide, (1x20's) virgin pine boards. It also had a lot of newer names. Seems climbing up there has become a "rite of passage" for Wing children. Nephew Ken Gillum said, "It was just like stepping back in time." The old classroom had not been used in at least eighty years, maybe much longer. Nobody living knows for sure.

Effie Turner, an icon of Wing, ran the store next door all during my child hood. She died in 1979, at one hundred years of age. During her lifetime she rode to Wing in an oxcart, and saw men walking on the moon. Her son, JR, passed away last year at one hundred two.

Elois Hunnicutt, just across the road and down the lane, ninety four, still grows a large garden. But she fell, out in that garden last year, and broke some bones. She managed to crawl to her back door, but could not get in. She had to lay out most of a day and a night. Remember, cell phones don't work well in Wing. But she's back now, as lively as ever. I know I'd have a hard time keeping up with her now, doing the kind of day's work she does.

My sister Jonnie taught Sunday school classes in

Fourche Valley for many years. Once I visited her class. The best I remember, her youngest class member was in his ninety's.

Scientists should do a study of folks in the Valley. Try to figure out how they live so long and so well, here in a remote place far from a major hospital. But actually, I already know. People in Little Rock would be shocked to realize how quiet, peaceful, and wonderful life can be, only sixty miles away from the hustle, bustle, rush, and tension of life in a major city, with next door neighbors often a mile away. My Dad always said good fences make good neighbors. A little distance can do the same thing.

I'm learning some good life lessons along the way, though. I was scheduled to read one of my stories at a Senior Citizen's Center a few days ago. But as luck would have it, I was scheduled to start reading my story along about the time the food was passed out. I thought the story was one of my funniest, but I don't remember hearing many laughs. All I could hear was a hundred or so spoons hitting plates. I'm always a little nervous starting a reading, then when I hear a few laughs, (and it doesn't really seem to matter if they're laughing with me or at me) I just seem to feed off that and really enjoy the rest of it. But that day, I was nervous all the way through. Like I say, I'm learning some good life lessons along the way. But on the other hand, I did sell books as a result. Beats the heck out of hauling hay at a penny a bale, like I did as a kid at Wing. Now, I'm not saying my Dad ever paid a penny a bale for hauling *our* hay. That was when I hired out to someone else. My dad figured room and board was payment aplenty. Of course, hauling hay was not nearly as embarrassing.

    Like I said, it just seems that Wing is a town the world forgot. Wing was first named Mineral Springs, due to the large amount of fresh spring water produced right behind the old church. Wing was a thriving town around 1898, when the Gillums first arrived. At that time, there were said to be seventeen houses up Wing holler, right behind the old church, with every cleared spot as large as a wagon sheet growing cotton. There were none in my days at Wing, just old home sites.

    In 1898, the rich bottom land carved out by the river was dotted with small farmers rapidly clearing more land, more cotton and other row crops appearing. A cotton gin, a sawmill, and a grist mill sat at the mouth of Wing hollow, with the very large spring producing a sufficient amount of cold water year around for steam power.

    Wing and the surrounding area was then an educational mecca. In 1915, fifteen school teachers lived around Wing. The old school room above the church was only an overflow classroom. Mineral Springs Academy took in boarding students from many miles around, at $2 per month.

    Thousands of acres of prime, virgin forests covered the mountain sides. The walls of many of those old houses were made from 1x20 pine boards from that virgin timber. The mountains were free range land, with large numbers of cattle ranged out into those hills. My dad often had to ride horseback for many, many miles to locate his cattle. A bell cow, wearing a cowbell around its neck, was with each herd to help in locating the herd.

    But all this was not to last. By the time I came along in

1944, many changes had taken place in the valley. The thin rich topsoil was rapidly getting tired, and cotton and other row crops were becoming less productive. Cotton gins disappeared. Nimrod lake was built, taking much of the richest bottom land. Hundreds of acres of cropland were reclaimed by the forests. Most of the small landowners lived by grubbing out a living from the soil, and had to put the wagon sheet back on the wagon and move on.

The word was out. The delta land of southeast Arkansas was now a mecca for farmers, and the exodus from Yell County to the delta was in full swing. I met the love of my life at the Delta Dip in Dumas, home of the Ding Dong Daddy. I also learned while I hung around nearby Watson, trying to win her heart, that many, many farmers in that area came to the delta from Fourche Valley during that time period.

The larger landowners, including the Gillums, began to depend more and more upon cattle as a money source. The virgin timber was gone. In the 1920's, a rail line was built up in the South Fourche River Valley, to reach that virgin harvest. This brought about temporary prosperity. Saw mill towns sprang up, large bustling towns. Once the virgin timber was harvested, these towns disappeared, and were reclaimed by nature. The only signs remaining to show they ever existed is a rusting piece of metal or concrete lying here and there on the forest floor. In 1927, the harvesting was winding down in the south mountains. The flood of 1927 destroyed the rail line, wrapping rails around trees. Two of the large train engines were trapped at line's end. One was moved onto the railroad bridge during the height of the flood, to help keep it from washing out. Afterwards, the rail line had to be rebuilt to get the engines out, taking up the track behind the engines as they were moved out.

The government bought up much of this timberland for as little as fifty cents an acre during and after the Depression, which became part of the Ouachita National Forest. The free range mountains were no more. Without that free range land, many of the cattle farmers had to move on. Hundreds of old, deserted home sites dotted the valley.

But this is not the end of my story.

In our day and time, all of these factors, many of which seemed so negative when they were brought to bear, have come together to produce a valley which is an ideal place to be, whether it be living there or visiting. Of course living there would be a problem, for many. Options for making a living are few, and a child might have to ride a school bus two hours to get to a school, while never passing through a traffic light, probably not even a four way stop. I think that's why Skeet likes it so well. Those four way stops can be a booger for Skeet. He's just far too polite in his driving. If another car is in sight, he will always give them the right-of-way. The pollution problems of most of our world, whether it be air, sound, chemical, vast areas of concrete, an excessive number of large lights, or too many people crowded together in a small space, just do not exist in Wing or the valley. Having next door neighbors a mile away helps assure they stay good neighbors. Even in my day, Fourche Valley School was one of the largest school districts in the state, yet twelve students graduated with me. One year more recently, the senior class consisted of five girls. Even the old abandoned home sites that dotted the landscape in my day have been pretty well reclaimed by nature. It's hard to find one today. The river still runs clean and pure, without an excessive number of canoes or boats all crowded up on it, as with most of our beautiful rivers. The Fourche is a good river to float in the spring, but gets a little too shallow in the summer for a long float. The deer, which had mostly been chased down and eaten up in my time, are back in large numbers. Furry wild animals, no longer considered very valuable for their pretty fur as they were in my time, have returned. The squirrel, a prime choice for the dinner table in my day, can rest a little easier. The trees on the mountainside are large and beautiful once more.

Maybe I named this story wrong. Maybe, in this day and age, I should have named it, "The town the world has not discovered." Take a day sometime and make a slow drive up Highway 28 from Rover to Needmore, where Highway 28 hits 71. Stop along the way, and meet those friendly people of the valley. You will discover a world new to your experiences in Arkansas. Take a little time and explore, and get to know that long, narrow strip of land along the Fourche La Fave River. A place like no other, I can honestly say, and I've seen a very large chunk of the world. Once you've spent a full day in Fourche Valley, you will always want to return.

LATSHA

MY FIRST MEMORY OF GREG LATSHA was the year we moved to Arkadelphia. My son Corey was the eighth grade quarterback. At split end was a small, scrawny kid, who looked way too small to be out there with those bigger boys. But he knew how to catch a football, and he was Corey's favorite go-to guy when a passing situation came up. But when he was tackled, and Greg wound up on the bottom of a big pile of really large guys, we all kept our fingers crossed that Greg would soon emerge unhurt from that pile of meaty boys. Or, be able to emerge at all. But, when all the big kids had been peeled off, Greg always jumped up with a smile. That was Greg's last year of football. He was just too small.

Greg showed up in my tenth grade biology class a couple of years later. He was somewhat of a cutup, and could be a class disturbance on a regular basis. But he really loved biology class, and worked at it harder than anyone else. In spite of his disturbances, not counting the fact that he was sometimes a major headache, I began to like Greg Latsha.

One of the first projects we did that year was a fall wildflower collection. This was right down Greg's alley, and his collection was much superior to anyone else's. The same was true of his insect collection. He just put everybody else in the shade. Identifying all the local trees was a snap. He already knew them all, for the most part. I could tell he spent most all his time in the wilds, whether there was a project going on or not.

I thought organizing a school wildlife club would be a

great idea. Naturally, Greg was my star. (I knew he would be.) On club camping trips, I was amazed to learn that he could perfectly imitate the call of any bird out there, or any wild animal.

Camped far back in the Ouachita Mountains one night with ten youngsters, we had a good campfire going. Greg gave a long wolf howl. He was immediately answered, right across the creek from our fire. I looked at the ten kids around that fire. Many very big eyes. Everybody was perfectly quiet, and I could tell the smarter ones were busy counting heads around that fire, suspecting one of our campers was out in the woods, playing a trick. When they reached ten, they bolted for the van, nearly pulling the door off.

The next morning, I cooked up dozens of eggs for breakfast. "Dig in guys, these eggs will be great! I only found one baby chick when I cracked these eggs, and I was able to get a good part of it out, so that won't be much of a problem. Dig in!"

They would not touch these eggs. I confessed to them that I was just kiddin' around. But no luck. They still would not. I ate a lotta eggs that morning.

It was a good day. No other incidents of note, except one kid walked up to and kicked a skunk, just to see what it would do. He found out, and pretty much became a loner for the rest of the trip.

All day long, Greg was finding and showing us strange wild plants and animals. Though I considered myself a good woodsman, having spent much of my life in the wild, and after all, I am a biologist, I began to realize, Greg was *already* a really good woodsman.

As we cooked supper, a snowstorm moved in. Lee Lester finally said, "Uh, Mr. Gillum, I think I am getting a case of the sniffles. Maybe we should go home." Everybody laughed at that, but I was beginning to agree with Lee. At the rate snow was falling, we might have a hard time getting out of here soon, and we might be snowed in for days by morning. So, we headed home. We got out of the mountains ok, but we did have a little trouble getting over Amity Mountain. One of the major problems in going home was finding somebody who was willing to sit next to the skunk kicker.

We did other campouts deep in the mountains that year. Most of the guys were at least just a little bit nervous at being out there, and didn't react well when Greg would bring in a giant snake or a tarantula or some such animal, then "give" it off to somebody else, but we had fun. I finally found about the only way I could keep Greg under control was by threatening to kick him out of the club, not let him come along any more. But he soon learned just how far to push me. Actually, I could never have done that. He was the star, the one normal humans looked up to out in the woods, and he just *made* the club. And besides that, I just loved Greg Latsha.

Greg, of course, also took advanced biology. During those two years, Greg often brought me gifts he had found out in the woods. Something he wanted me to see. I began to get a little nervous about this, because they usually showed up in five gallon buckets, top on, with air holes cut in it – meaning, there's something alive, wild, and very angry inside. The first one held the largest black snake I have ever seen, as large as my forearm. I became very careful about opening one of Greg's little gifts – just pull the top off, and run.

Greg once left a very rare, large and strange looking beetle on my front porch, along with a note: "Mr. Gillum, I found this Rhino Beetle I thought you would want to see. It looked a little better before my brother stepped on it."

Greg's mother once bought a new mop she was very proud of. Greg was headed out on a snake catching trip, so he cut the handle out to make a snake catching stick. He caught a bucket of snakes – Moccasins, rattlers, black snakes. When he got home, he spread them all out on the basement floor for display. His dad got him good because of the house full of snakes, while Mom got him even better because of her ruined new mop.

One of our Wildlife Club field trips was to Degray lake. We were all asleep at daylight the next morning, except for Latsha. He excitedly woke us all up, telling us all he had located a school of white bass, right up at the edge of the water. We sleepily caught 115 large white bass.

On another field trip, I set up a Woodsman contest, involving tree climbing, wood splitting, and wood chopping. Guess who won all events.

Greg has a spectacular collection of Indian relics. He walked about every creek bottom around Arkadelphia to find them. I called Greg yesterday on my cell phone. Guess what – Greg had discovered a new spot to hunt Indian relics, and he and his sweet loving wife were on their way to search it out. The years have not changed Latsha. Or, his loyal wife.

Greg figures he has fished about every pond within sight of a road around Arkadelphia. His largest black bass caught is 8 lbs. 4 ounces.

Greg once brought me a photo he had taken in the woods of Arkansas, a black panther, even though they officially do not live in Arkansas. I asked Greg just a few days ago to show me that photo again. He said, "Ah, I don't know where that picture is anymore." Just par for the course for Greg Latsha, but it would have been the picture of a lifetime for me. I would still be showing it off to anybody who would look.

Toward the end of high school, Greg was still a small, skinny kid. His mother took him to the doctor, asked him why he was just not growing. After the doctor examined him thoroughly, the doc came in smiling. "Just sit back and watch. Something BIG is about to happen here!"

The doc was right. Late in high school, Latsha was 5' 10" and weighed 150 pounds. In the next two years, he grew six inches and gained 60 pounds – no fat.

Greg joined the baseball team at Henderson State University. At 17, he was hitting the baseball over the scoreboard at HSU. Soon, he set a school record by hitting a home run 600 feet. Many people began to take notice. The tennis courts are beyond the baseball field at Henderson. When Greg came up to bat, the tennis team just stopped practicing, and watched. In awe. And also, in case the ball lands in the tennis court. But if it was a good hit, it went over the courts, the path, the creek, and into the woods.

The pro baseball scouts soon heard of Greg. They began to show up at his games. They interviewed him. But that was not to be Greg's path.

In 1992, he played his last baseball game at HSU. A

scout from a super major softball team followed him to his car, and offered him the opportunity to play at the highest level of softball in the country.

Greg said, "Well, my buddies and I already have a softball team."

"Well, just let me tell you what we can give you. We'll send you a plane ticket each week, and fly you all over the country and Canada. This will give you an opportunity to play at softball's highest level." Then he went on to tell Greg what else they could give him. The list was impressive. He would be back to Arkansas, and the woods he loved, each Monday. So, Greg agreed to sign up to play in the super majors. This year, he was inducted into the State Super Majors Softball Hall of Fame. All indications are he will be inducted at the national level in a few years. They don't induct young guys, let them get a little age on them.

By 1999, softball was no longer fun. Four days later, he was in Destin, Florida, signing on as the mate on a deep sea fishing boat. Later, he signed onto a boat that goes after the largest fish. There he caught 600 pound blue marlins and sharks. He often hooked the monsters, then handed it off to a client to bring it in. The client takes home a trophy, Greg took home a very nice tip. He often made three hundred trips each year. He fished for 14 years, two trips per day.

Latsha is a top notch duck hunting guide. He stays booked solid each season, and can perfectly imitate every sound a duck makes. He has a wide range of calls, and demonstrated them for me – feeding, greeting, come back, hail, chuckles, and more. He can even play a song on a duck call. He has guided for 25 years.

Latsha has hunted a wide range of animals for many years. Now, he figures he has about shot his share, and just goes hunting to watch the animals, mostly.

Greg worked for the Arkansas Game and Fish videoing wildlife for a year. Then, it was no longer fun.

Though many around Greg have tried to change the path of his life, they are unsuccessful. He sticks to his own chosen path, doing what he loves, no matter what. Now who can ask for more than that in this one lifetime that we all are given?

Latsha's favorite bible verse is Matthew 7: 13-14: "Narrow is the gate that leads to life". Few find it. Greg has found the gate that leads to the life he wishes to lead; he sticks on that narrow path. No matter what.

His goal for each and every day is to make someone smile. And he reaches that goal, many times each day.

And, I still just love Greg Latsha.

THE INDIAN UPRISING, AND MY CHILDREN IN PERU

I PUSHED WITH RECKLESS ABANDON against that gate with every pound of my considerable weight, and every ounce of my inconsequential muscle, sweat running off me and fear running through me. My mind was a blur. This could just not be happening to me! This sort of thing does not happen anymore, Indians just didn't do things like this. Not for at least 150 years. But then, I'm thinking about back home, in the good old USA. I had not been in this remote corner of the world before. Apparently, these Indians didn't follow the new guidelines. No telling how many outraged Quechua Indians outside pushed back, screaming at me, trying to force their way in.....

Only a few days before, I was in my comfortable home in Arkadelphia, Arkansas, spending hours on end, praying that God would put the correct words in my mouth as I witnessed to the Quechua Indians of Peru, high in the remote Andes Mountains, near the headwaters of the mighty Amazon River. Well, I should have spent some time praying that none of my fellow mission trip members, even with the very best of intentions, would trigger an Indian uprising.

I had heard about the trip at a community group meeting of our church. It was planned as a backpacking trip, out of Cusco, Peru, pushing into the wilds of the Andes Mountains, hoping to reach previously unreached Indian villages for Christ. It was organized and carried out by Outdoor Discipleship Ministries, involving mostly Ouachita Baptist University students. The time was around 1999, and, I must confess, I was not really the strongest of Christians at the time. My motives for my sudden decision to go were suspect. It was spurred on more by the thought of joining a great adventure into one of the remaining truly wild places of the world, than about the thought of fulfilling the Great Commission. But, I must confess, I came back a changed person. The most noticeable outward change was, I am more emotional, unable to tell even a slightly stirring story without choking up. I had never been that way, but the change appears to have been permanent. The upside of it is, I now can write with true sensitivity and emotion, and I know when my writing is good, because tears begin to flow...

I didn't even think to pray about God giving me the ability to preach, or do dedication ceremonies, funerals, or anything like that. I had no idea how far my gray hair would take me, what kind of tight spots it would put me in, here in a land where few people ever reach the age of gray hair.

Anyway, when I heard about this trip, and that a spot remained unfilled, I just said "I'm going." Maybe I should have thought it over a little bit. But I didn't. I was the only older person. (In 1999, I was "older." Now, I'm just old.) My little group consisted of several girls and a few boys. As I say, this was billed as a backpacking trip, and during preparation, when I started hearing some of those little girls saying things like, "I've never slept on the *ground* before" I began having doubts about the whole thing. But those "little girls" soon proved it was myself I should have been worrying about, not them. Their oft-stated motto was, "I could have stayed at home and been comfortable. Or, I could come to these unsaved Indians and do God's work.

No complaining." And they didn't. Not one time.

As I said, I spent a lot of time in my room praying for the right words to come to me. At the very least, "words." I have never quite gotten over the time in college, in church one night, (This is another "first time ever told" story) the preacher asked me to pray. Well, I searched and searched for the words, but they just would never come. Finally I stuttered out an "Amen." As I glanced up at my girlfriend Marty's face, I saw it was red as a beet. She was embarassed about/for me. That always seems to hang in the back of my mind when I start to pray in public, or when I start to witness. Also, I dearly loathe hypocrites, and I often just feel unqualified to witness, feeling like I'm saying, "I sure do wish you guys could just be as perfect as me." It took many years for me to fully realize, witnessing is just one sinner talking to another. But it finally came, although witnessing ability is coming along somewhat slower.

I read Jeremiah a lot, concentrating on the part about "If you go, God will put the words in your mouth." Well, I went, and God did, mostly, to small groups. But He seemed to have some reservations about my preaching ability, and the like. (For some reason, I am learning, I can make confessions to this computer, and God, that I can never make to another person.)

Things were kinda tight for us then, having just sold our business and traveled for a solid year in our RV, and I began to feel guilty about going at all when I thought of that final payment I owed, $1500. A day or so later, I had to look about something in our old statements from out rental property manager. The statements are sent to me, the money sent to our bank. I pulled a two-year-old statement out, and guess what just fell out of it. A check! Well, guess the amount. Yes, you got it. $1500. Here was proof. God was in my corner in this adventure.

I knew I had to get into shape, if I was going to keep up with these kids on a backpacking trip at high altitude. Or at any altitude, for that matter. I put a heavy backpack on and walked the steepest and longest hills in Arkadelphia, daily. As it turned out, I was put into a group going to a village that could be driven to, and we only backpacked through the airport. But I was in shape, mostly, except for the knee I nearly ruined getting in shape.

We arrived in Lima early in the morning, and loaded onto a smaller plane for the flight to Cusco. That city is at 12,000 ft. altitude, the highest inhabited city in the world, and planes only go out and in during the morning. Has to do with thin air. Not enough lift. Well, If I'm going to fly over these mountains, I sure do want some lift!

A group of young women from Peru got on our plane at Lima, and I was totally relieved to see that they spoke perfectly good English. We had been told a lot about the language barrier problem, and it worried me, but listening to these young ladies made me feel better. "Hey, guys! These Peru people speak great English!"

One of our kids rolled his eyes. "Uh, Pat, they're our interpreters."

We had been told, in pre-trip planning, that these Indians who live at high altitude prevent altitude sickness by drinking coca tea every day. Well, since cocaine is made from that plant, we had quite a discussion about using that at all. After all, this *was* an OBU trip. Finally, our nurse who was going along just said, "I've done it both ways. Without coca tea, I got very sick. With it, I was fine. This is *not* Cocaine. It has to be refined, refined, and refined to get to that point." We drank coca tea.

That first day in Cusco, at 12,000 feet altitude, we just took it easy, to make the altitude adjustment. And, we drank coca Tea.

The next morning, we headed out to our Indian village, a couple of hours out. We traveled in a hired taxi, a van. All our stuff, mountains of it, was piled on top, and the driver found a little short piece of rope on the ground, and tied it down with that. I don't know how he did it, but he made it all stay on, over some of the roughest mountain roads I had ever seen. I'd heard the story of Jesus stretching the loaves and the fishes, and I think God must have stretched that rope a lot to handle the job that little piece of rope did.

The country was totally beautiful, with green fields sloping up to great mountain tops, speckled with fields of corn and potatoes, and villages of little mud houses with thorn fences around them, keeping the animals in.

Halfway out to our village, There was a major landslide across the road. A single set of car tracks told us that at least someone else had crossed it, so we followed. At the peak, we met another van. No way to pass, and nobody was anxious to back down. The driver and our taxi owner got out. A couple of men from the other van got out. They held a true *summit* conference, concerning which van was on the most important mission. Finally, our driver told them he was carrying a great team of missionaries, who came all the way from America. He pointed out that big man with gray hair, me, and I felt my first guilt attack. The other men could not argue with that. They had absolutely no grey hair in the van. They slowly backed down the landslide. Being *big* and *gray headed*, I began to learn, carried a lot of weight with the Indians, because they were very small, up to my chest, and very few of them lived long enough to ever have gray hair. I felt like the fake I was the whole time I was there, because I got a lot more respect, God knows, than I ever deserved, having impure motives for even starting this trip in the first place.

When we arrived at the village, we unloaded our gear, and stashed it in the church. It had been built years ago by another missionary group, and was a small wood and mud structure with very short benches inside, and with its two doors open, it was mostly being used now as a place for hogs and chickens to lounge in.

One of my first chores was to filter a supply of drinking water with a hand operated pump. Although we did have access to one of the few faucets in the village, the water had lots of specks in it, and, we were told earlier, 30% of us, at least, were destined to lose a lot of weight the quick and hard way, when their terrible stomach bug hit. A young boy, about eight, quickly latched onto me and was a great help in filtering water. I showed off some of my four or five Spanish words I had learned over the last 3 weeks by naming him, "Aqua Amigo." My water friend.

Sure enough, when I got in front of a small group of Indians, with my two interpreters ready, (first into Spanish, which the kids understood, then into Quechua, the only language the older Indians knew) God and Jeremiah came through for me, and the words just poured out. Partly, I guess, because I had lots of time to think up the next paragraph, while the interpreters did their thing. I think God just had it planned out that way, because it took every spare second to think up the next line.

I had proudly worn my Indiana Jones hat to Peru, thinking if I was going to be like him, I should look the part. But as it turned out, every Indian woman in the village had one on just like it. That sorta dulled the luster on my hat some.

After we had gotten settled and talked to the Indians awhile, we found out that today was a big celebration day in the village, celebrating the day it was first built. It was all taking place at the soccer field, and we went. The mayor and elders all sat in chairs along the edge of the field, and everyone else sat in the grass behind. Well, the Mayor took one look at my gray hair, told one of the elders to go sit in the grass, and with much fanfare escorted me down to his seat. Another guilt attack.

They were having guinea pig races, with each girl having a string attached to hers, and a little switch to spur him on. I had doubts about how fair these races were, because usually, the winner just dragged hers the last few feet.

Guinea Pigs were, I found out, in a class with llamas, etc. in that they did well at high altitude. They just ran free in their houses, a pet, until, one fateful day, there was a need, and they became a meal.

At church that night, the little Indian preacher from Cusco, Pastor Cirro, who was supposed to meet us there and preach, just did not show up. We sang a few hymns, then all the Indians turned and looked at me. After a couple of minutes, Lenore, the "mother" of the church, suggested we sing some more hymns. Then, they all turned and looked at me again. It finally hit me, they were expecting me to preach! Well, I had no sermon prepared, and I was, really, no sort of preacher. Not even a bad one. Witnessing to a small group was one thing, but I had not even thought to ask God to make me a preacher. That went back and forth awhile, then me and a student or two got up and told them how much we appreciated their hospitality, etc. We said a prayer, and they headed home.

The girls were to sleep in the church, which was right next to the church mother Lenore's house. The ground was rock hard, and had bumps the size of a baseball all over it, but those girls just took that all in stride, They even adjusted quickly to the toilet in that part of town, which consisted of a few bushes out by the creek. Ever since I really got to know these OBU kids, I was just totally blown away by them. I felt honored to be on this trip with them.

A man in the village donated his house to us men as sleeping quarters. The ground was just as hard and uneven as the church floor. There was a bed in there, but we all figured that was where the guinea pigs would all wind up, so we just spread our bags on the floor. When we got settled, and turned out our flashlights, we began to hear tiny feet scurrying about. We never could spot one, so we were never sure if they were guinea pigs or not – or worse.

Like I said earlier, I was deeply affected and changed greatly by this trip. I got to thinking about the terrible living conditions of these people, how eager they were to hear us speak God's word, what a sweet nature the children had, and how delighted they were to get these tiny Bibles we passed out. That change started that night, as I lay awake all night long, with tears pretty much my constant bedfellows. It would be the third night before I slept a minute, after the whole team prayed for sleep for me - and someone dug out a sleeping pill or two from their bag.

The next morning, we did craft things with the kids we had brought along, played and laughed a lot with them. They were totally delightful. A couple of young girls just could not accept the fact that I could not understand a lick of Spanish. "No Comprende" became my constant answer. The little girls felt that if they could just take my cheeks in their two hands, hold my face still so I was looking right into their eyes, then say the words very slowly and clearly, a light would just come on in my head, and I would understand. "No comprende."

One of the Indian boys stuck a piece of metal almost through his foot. A man picked him up. I asked the man if he would be OK. He looked at me, very seriously, and shook his head no. Seeing none of the Indians with any means of first aid, we dug our kit out, I dug out the metal, washed the mud out of it as best I could, covered it with disinfectant, then wrapped it up good. His mother was very appreciative, and carried him home. We prayed for him. I never saw him again.

One of the members of our team, slightly over college age and from a northern city, had brought a trunk filled with teddy bears and other soft toys. He started passing them out to the children, and they went totally wild with joy. Many ran to show their family. The word spread like wildfire. Many, many mothers came running with their children. Along about that time, someone brought us the word that the Mayor had been very, very drunk from the festival yesterday, but he was now awake and sending a truck to haul us across the village to "city hall," a large building that at least had wood floors for us to sleep on. Well, we were beginning to worry that the toys might run out, as more women and children, and now some men, showed up.

About that time, the truck arrived. We quickly loaded our gear on the back, and as we started loading the trunk, with very few toys now, the mothers were tearing at our arms. Pointing to their children, they screamed, "My baby! No toy!" The last of the toys were in sight, yet more and more Indians just poured out of their huts. We finally all got on the truck, and started out, with dozens of Indians running behind. The men were now at the front of the pack.

About half way to city hall, we saw we were going to meet another large truck on that very narrow street. The trucks just kept coming, and the mirrors on both trucks fell off into the road. The drivers just got out, looked at their mirrors lying in the road, shrugged their shoulders, got back in, and drove on. Now, in America, we would have soon had two police cars on the scene, and two lawsuits would have been in the works. Life is just more laid back and simple, with the Indians, at altitude.

We reached city hall, with a short lead on the Indians, got everything inside, and locked the door. But the back yard was a problem. There was a high mud fence around the compound, with a gate, no lock.

Alright. Now I am back in the jam I was in when I started this story. As luck, or more likely God, would have it, right about that time the late little Indian preacher from Cusco, Pastor Cirro, showed up. He talked to the parents a long time, then came and talked to us. He told us, through an interpreter, that we must never pass out gifts with abandon, like that, to people who have nothing. Gifts must be given to the church, and would be slowly passed out later in an orderly fashion. He also told us the people had settled down, and that he didn't think this was going to damage our mission here.

I've thought a lot about that situation, and knew that somehow, I should have had the wisdom to handle that situation before it got out of hand. After all, I *am* the one with gray hair here, now a little grayer. All I could figure was, to just prevent the toy "pass out" before it got started. Once it got going like it did, and without being able to talk to them, about the only option I could see on the table was what we did. Just run. Gray hair and wisdom don't *always* go hand in hand, you know. " Dumb young" usually transfers into "dumb old."

There were a lot of windows in that building, with no shades. The Indians, adults and children alike, just lined up at those windows, and watched every move we made, while we unpacked our stuff. When someone left, another Indian filled that spot, just staring. They kept that up whenever we were in there that day, but were nice enough to leave their posts as it got dark.

That night, The preacher was there, the church was full. Their little benches were about six inches high, and I couldn't hang with that, so I just hung out in the back, Agua Amigo at my side as usual, and leaned against the wall. The little preacher saw my situation, and sent me a stool, which I gratefully sat down on. I put my index finger tip on the end of my chopped off thumb, and flashed him the "OK" sign. His smile faded. Seems that little signal has a whole 'nother meaning in Peru.

The next day, the Indian Christians were to meet us at noon. We planned to go to every house, witnessing. They finally showed up, and hour late, and then said we needed to brew up and drink some coca tea first. Seems at altitude, things just move more slowly. A way of life. Things went well, talking to the people. Seems the people who were trying to tear my arms out of their sockets yesterday just loved us today.

It seems spousal abuse was rampant amoung the Indian families. Many of the Indian women had bruises on their faces. Pastor Cirro got right in the faces of the husbands, when he saw that, and they just stood there, head down, and took it.

Then we were about to head up on the hill overlooking the village, to talk to the people up there. Our college girls were hesitant to go, and they didn't want to talk about it. Finally, one told me that when they went to the toilet, just a few bushes remember, a group of little old men on the hill tended to gather and try to watch. They really did not want to talk to them face to face.

That night, the whole village showed up. We presented the Jesus movie, in their language. Agua Amigo held my hand the whole time. Then, we put on a little drama the college kids had worked up. They really didn't know what to do with me, so I was given the role of the soldier who beat on the Jesus actor while he carried the cross. I was told to just continue to lash the Jesus actor with an imaginary whip until the music stops. I started lashing; the music dragged on. More lashes, more music. The altitude was hitting me hard now. But that music just wouldn't stop. I think the Indians were making bets about who would get beaten down first, me or the Jesus actor.

The next morning, we walked a mile or two to a small village to talk to some more people. We split up. I followed my guides and interpreter up to the high country. I was to speak to a group of people up there, and they were getting their cattle ready to take out to graze. A young husband and wife team led us, and she had her 17 day old baby on her back. Well, that young woman, 17 days out of childbirth, just walked circles around me at that altitude. All the Indians must have developed very large lungs, because the altitude didn't seem to affect them like it did us. I think I did a pretty good job, for me, witnessing to that group, and we headed down.

They knew how I had struggled on the way up, and the husband guide ran ahead and found a donkey for me to ride down. Well, that was a major guilt trip, getting me a donkey to ride, just like they did for Jesus in the old day! Bad as I felt, they had the donkey, and there was just no way around it. I straddled the little donkey, my feet were touching the ground, and that pore' little donkey started swaying, then slowly falling over to one side! I had to walk down, but I felt better about it.

Our guide couple just really took a liking to me, and I could tell that they were putting a lot more stock in me than I deserved. At the bottom of the hill, they called the interpreter over, and made a long speech. The interpreter said they wanted me to be their children's-- she struggled for the right word-- Godfather. They wanted me to do a dedication ceremony with each of their four children. I thanked them, told them that was a very great honor for me, and that I could arrange it. We left them there and went back to our village.

It wasn't long before they and their children showed up. They were all dressed up in their very best. I told them I would go get the little preacher to do the ceremony. The dad waved that off. No, he wanted me to do it.

I had no idea what a dedication ceremony should be like, but the principals were all dressed up and lined up, waiting. I just turned slightly away from the interpreter, so she couldn't hear what I said. One at a time, I put my hand on their head, raised the other arm, and began. I remember I had the child's name, the lord's prayer, portions of the 23rd psalm, and some other biblical statements in there.

If you are old, and go on a mission trip, you best be prepared for anything, I learned.

We were leaving the next morning. Late that afternoon, we all gathered up our clothes we weren't wearing, and all our stuff we wouldn't need on the way home, and laid it out in a row, so the Indians could pick out what they needed. The little Indian preacher, way under five feet tall, took my long handled underwear. Said he was going up to very high altitudes next week, and he could sure use them there. I could only imagine what he looked like, wearing them.

I announced I had an extra pair of reading glasses, and did anyone need them? They all pointed to Lenore, the church mother. She ran to get a tiny bible that she had been given years before. She put on the glasses, and she screamed. She could read it – for the first time! She hugged me with tears in her eyes, and thanked me over and over. I had seen only one pair of glasses in the village, worn by the school teacher. I thought we had brought an over-supply of small bibles, but now they were all gone. And many Indians still wanted them.

The Indian ladies announced they were going to cook their best hens the next morning for us, before we left. I had been eating power bars, mostly, all week, trying to avoid the horrible stomach bug so many people got. But who could say no to their best hen?

We bedded down to sleep late that night. There was only one big room, so the girls had a sheet hanging up between them and us guys. I got to thinking back to my younger days. I remembered hearing stories on TV about a group of terrorists, the Shining Path, who terrorized these Indians in the Andes. 7000+ were killed.

The Shining Path was the brain child of Abimael Guzman Reynoso. He had spent years in China, and had become convinced that Mao's revolution could be replicated in Peru. It was the most scary and bloody group of terrorists of the 1980's. Years ago, I had nightmares about the Shining Path. I had heard more stories after we got here, how they would come into a church, line the people up in a row, and ask each one if they believed in God. Some admitted they did, some were afraid to. Those who were afraid to admit they believed in God, standing here in this church, were shot. The others were forced to join their group. They wanted only brave people in that group. Well, over the years, the leadership was caught and put in prison, and the terrorist group pretty much disbanded. But we had been warned. Remnants of this group were still hiding out in these Indian villages. Since Indians in these mountains never lived to be very old, I felt that some of them were dead by now. Just as that thought crossed my mind, around midnight I believe it was, I heard many, many soft footsteps going up the stairs outside, up to a big room above. My heart started to pound faster. Were they Shining Path remnants, and were they going to test this tiny group of believers tonight, our last night, at gun point? I stayed awake a long time, listening. But I never heard another sound, and they never came back down.

    I noticed as we sat down to eat the next morning, some of the college kids were faking their "best hen" eating as well as they could, not really taking in much at all. I ate my share, however, telling the ladies over and over how good it was, and it was good. Before dark that day, I set in to lose ten pounds the quick and hard way. I'm not sure why native food, well cooked, does that to us so often. But it does. But I have a theory. Water, in food, boils at a much lower temperature at high altitude, and stays at that temperature until the water boils away. This bad bug must be a tough one, who can handle that low temperature, and does its thing when we eat it. The Indians, over the years, have become resistant. We have not.

    After saying our goodbyes, during which Agua Amigo just seemed to not be able to let me go, (and I him) we headed out to Cusco. Tomorrow, our off day, we were headed for Machu Picchu!

    On the way back to Cusco, we passed a small pickup truck. It had just had a flat, and the back was loaded with Indians. Well, they just hopped out, and the driver changed the tire while they held the truck up. Never seen that before, or since.

I have to admit, I chew tobacco. A little habit I picked up during my construction days. That was a big no-no for this trip, so I had to swear off it for the duration. I was, truthfully, about to have a nicotine fit by now. I got to looking at all those little Coca leaves, lying around the hotel. I wadded up a small piece of one, and stuck it in my mouth. I found it made a pretty good replacement, and we weren't around the Indians any more, and besides, the piece was so small, no one knew. Well, it worked so good, I pretty well kept a small piece hidden in my mouth all the next day, and until we flew out the next day.

The ride to Machu Picchu was breathtaking. The train had to do a strange move to get out of the valley Cusco was located in that I had never seen before. It would start up the hill at an angle, then stop and back uphill at an angle on another track, then repeat this over and over until it was high enough to head out.

The Valley of the Incas was beautiful. We rode past many Inca ruins, and gradually headed down until we were in the tropical rain forest.

On the way down, we traveled along beside a river that dropped so fast through those rocky gorges that I knew no one could survive those waters. A fellow train rider who knows about such things told me it had a "seven" rating, with "five" being all a person, swimming, could survive. I didn't know it then, but I figured out later, this river was the upper reaches of the Amazon, and world class kayakers had survived it, traveling the Amazon from end to end.

Traveling through the rain forest, one could see

towering mountains in the background. Many reached into the clouds, but occasionally, we could see the snow capped peak in the top of our vision, yet the beautiful flowering tropics in the bottom. I quickly got out my camera, but that view was covered in clouds again. A rare sight. Cusco is technically in the tropics, map wise, but so high, it is very cool.

Machu Picchu is one of the wonders of the world. An Inca village was once built on the top of a very tall, very steep mountain. It was so steep, one would have to be a skilled mountain climber to reach the top. This location provided them a measure of protection from their enemies. The Incas were the most skilled rock builders of all time. I saw one large rock, in one of their structures, that had 27 different angles cut into it. All the adjoining rocks fit so perfectly to it, that one could not stick a toothpick into the joints. Narrow terraces were cut into the mountainside, for raising food.

One young Indian businessboy had it figured out. On the way back down that very steep mountain, the road consisted of a dozen or more very tricky, long, switchbacks. This little Indian boy kept waving at us all, on the bus, before we left. Then, the sure footed youngster ran straight down the mountain, in the middle of the switchbacks, waving at us all each time the bus passed. Again, again, and again. When the bus stopped at the bottom, finally, he climbed aboard, pulled his hat off, and walked down the aisle with a big smile, collecting a whole hat full of money from the passengers.

Those Inca ruins were lost to the world for centuries, until discovered by Hiram Bingham, an American archaeologist, in 1911. They were cleaned up, and made into one of the great destinations of the world. That was a breathtaking trip.

The Inca empire, one of the largest and most powerful civilizations ever, was brought down by less than 200 Spaniards. How this came about involves a number of factors. The Indians looked upon the Spanish, in their metal suits and hats, riding great animals, as Gods. Many of the Indians were disabled by various diseases the Spanish brought with them, which spread like wildfire because they had absolutely no resistance to them. The Inca empire was totally ruled from the top, with orders passed down by sub leaders.

The Spaniards marched to Cusco, containing 40,000 Indian warriors. The year was 1533. The Inca King went out to the Spaniards, in a gesture of welcoming these Gods. The Spanish captured him, and cut his head off right in front of the Indians. The Indians were like a snake without a head. Nobody was there, once the king was dead, to issue orders. The Spanish took over, and brought down the entire civilization. Once Cusco was occupied, the Spanish installed a compliant
young Inca prince, Manco, as a puppet ruler. After 3 years, after the Spanish had chained him up, called him a dog, urinated on him, Raped his wives, stole his gold and jewelry, Manco got mad. He fled, and he established an Inca city, Vitcabamba, and restored it to its former glory. It took the Spanish 35 years to capture this city, and by that time, Manco had died and Manco's son, Felipe Tupac Amaru ruled. Felipe was led to Cusco with a golden chain, and he was hanged and mutilated in Cusco's main plaza.

This closed out the final chapter of the Inca Empire.

The Spanish and other European explorers of the 1500's reported a great, advanced city in the lower Amazon valley. It was called El Dorado. Many great explorers searched for this great city, later in the 1800's and early 1900's. Many lost their lives there, such as Percy Harrison Fawcett, in the 1920's. He was one of the greatest British explorers of all time. He became so famous there, in those early days of modern communication, that many more lost their lives in search of him, or trying to determine what happened to him. Indians, disease, and starvation killed many of these men.

Later, faint signs of long gone, great civilizations were found by scientists, and it is generally assumed that diseases carried in by the early European explorers had so decimated the Indian populations that they now only existed as small, isolated tribes. Jungle cities consist mostly of plant material, which quickly disappears in the tropical jungle. El Dorado was no more. The Indians had learned how to build and maintain great civilizations in the Amazon jungle, a feat many early scientists thought impossible. But they were unable to deal with European diseases brought in by the early explorers.

Cusco is a mixture of Spanish and Indians, but there appeared to me to be very little mixing of the bloods over the centuries, because the Spanish one sees there look just like the Spanish one would see in Madrid. They are very beautiful people. I did see one tall, slim, very beautiful Spanish woman with a very short, heavy, Indian husband. The children varied. Some looked like her, some like him. It appeared to me that was the exception rather than the rule.

We flew home. I arrived 10 pounds lighter. Like I said before, I was changed, and that has been permanent. But there was something else going on with me, that puzzled me. If you have read my writing, I am sure you have picked up on the fact that I have been the insecure, shy, retiring type around most women, except Barbara. And she has brought a change in that aspect of me, to a certain extent. But I arrived home with different feelings. Something unexplainable.

We were headed out for a short vacation with Barbara's sister's family, upon my arrival home. As we toured around, I began to put my finger on it. I was feeling like I was a true chick magnet! I felt like every pretty woman we were around had eyes only for me. I even felt sorry for the young, muscular, handsome men they were with, because I knew their women were thinking only of me. This was a total and complete,180 degree change in my thinking. Barbara was so lucky to have me, and I was sure all the other women around were green with envy. How could I ever go back to Arkadelphia, and work on my rental properties in shorts, as I did before? I knew the young women would just never leave me alone, and let me work.

By the time we had gotten home, that feeling was beginning to fade. I looked up my chemist friend, and asked, "How far is the juice of the coca plant from being cocaine?"

He looked at me, puzzled, then said, "It's right there."

All I could figured out was, I was getting a super concentrated dose of coca juice by substituting it for chewing tobacco, nothing like the much watered down coca tea. I never felt like I could fly, but who wants to fly when you can be a full blown chick magnet!

I recently read a book about traveling on the upper Amazon river at great altitude. One of the explorers had been chewing on Coca leaves all day, and that night, he just suddenly ran out into the snow naked, thinking nothing could harm him, and ran around that way for a long time. Thankfully, I managed to keep all my symptoms inside me, and never put on a show. I'm glad about that.

Before Peru, Barbara has been working on me for a long time. My spiritual life was not what it should be. I had this problem, for many years. I looked at many fellow church attenders who seemed hypocritical to me. Some seemed to pray long, very elegant prayers. I didn't feel God required that kind of elegance in order to talk to him. If not God, then who were they trying to impress? Others were in their church position to further business interests, obviously. And some "strong Christians" appeared to be that only on Sunday. See them later in the week, and it was a different story.

Collectively, Barbara, Michael Holloway, my best friend who was killed in a motorcycle crash, and that trip to Peru affected me in such a way that I begin to realize that everyone around me, and I, was a sinner. My relationship with God had nothing to do with other people around me. They had their own spiritual life to work out.

I returned to Peru, a few years later. My motives, the second time were more pure. This time I was in a small village on the outskirts of Cusco.

When we arrived at the village, I discovered that my bag was not in the car. We finally figured out it went with another group, to another village, a long way off. The pastor who was with us at the time said he would take me to that village, so we started out in his car. Right after we left the church, we passed a house with a pretty girl, about 18, in the front yard. She looked at us, and she flushed. I saw a certain look pass between them, that look that passes between two people who share a dark secret. I saw that look many years ago, when we lived in another city, pass between a man leading the singing at our church and a lady in the front row. Barbara had seen it too, and later, we discussed it. We thought surely, we had misread it. Both of these church members had spouses and a family. A couple of weeks later, they ran off together.

I hope I misread this new look, too, but I doubt it. This pastor had a large family.

When we got to the village where my bag now resided, One of the mission trip members, also with grey hair, was leading a funeral procession up the mountain, about to preach a funeral. Like I said before, If you are old, and you go on a mission trip, you best be prepared for anything.

The people were much the same, except now we cooked a very large meal each day, the college kids went out in the poor neighborhoods and brought the kids in like pied pipers, each child with a bowl and a spoon, ready to eat. I was somewhat unofficially in charge of my group this time, and I was determined to prevent my kids and I from getting that horrible stomach bug. I treated all the water personally with chemicals, I watched over what we all ate, and all they did, like a hawk, and whe we were flying home, I had the satisfaction of realizing it was successful. No one in my group had gotten the bug. Pride goeth before the fall. When I stepped off the plane, it hit me, and hit me hard.

My gray hair, thinner and grayer now, still caused me some guilt attacks. A ceremony was set up one night at a small village, for me to officially present a soccer ball, one I had no role in bringing along in the first place, to the city fathers for the benefit of the children of the village. The main pastor's wife made a very long and elegant speech one night, thanking me for all the great work I had done for the children of Peru, over the years. I had been in Peru, in my life, maybe a total of a dozen days. But, I accepted her misplaced praise with great dignity, as one with hair such as mine should do.

The last day, with everyone else headed for Machu Picchu, I begged off. I hired a car and driver, an interpreter, and headed out to my old village, to see my friends and search for my God children – and Agua Amigo.

That did not cost as much as it sounds, probably about what a rental car alone would have cost me at home. The little Indian preacher, now my dear friend, Pastor Cirro, went along. He and I have never exchanged an understandable word between us, but we communicated easily with smiles, handshakes, gestures, laughter, and love. He told me, through the interpreter, that he had a picture of me hanging on his wall. Funny. I have a picture of him on my wall.

I had been trying to trace my God children all week. Seems the oldest girl, now nearly grown, was in Cusco for awhile, then the trail went cold. The rest of the family was harder to trace, but I hoped to find them at or near our old village. Turned out, when reaching the village, they had moved on. But I did find Lenore, the church mother, busily cooking corn over an open fire in her hut near the church. I gave her several more pair of reading glasses I had brought for her. Her father was there, now totally blind with cataracts. Where is my friend the eye surgeon, Frank Teed, when I need him? She sat us down to a meal of mostly corn on the cob.

The corn grains in Peru are huge, larger than a big marble. We just pull them off, and eat them one at a time. I now realize, that was the one place I messed up, in guarding against the bug. But what could I do? Just tell sweet Lenore I wouldn't eat her corn? Afterwords, I found several of my children, now nearly grown. I was wearing my trademark hat and the same white coat, and they recognized me. My family, with my four God children, Lenore told me, had moved to a village farther away, but she would see them at a festival later. I gave her an envelope containing all the money I could spare, and asked her to give it to them. Indians have nothing. That small amount would make them rich.

Lenore told me her son was working, some distance away, but he could be sent for. I really didn't know who her son was, and time was getting short, so I said, "No, we've got to go." We were nearly back to Cusco when it hit me. Her son was Agua Amigo! My "water friend!" I had missed my last chance to see Agua Amigo! My eyes filled with tears, and overflowed.

I knew I would never be back to Cusco. That altitude thing hit me hard this time, and I knew I would be pushing my luck going again. One of our OBU kids, who went on up to 14,000 feet or so, got extremely sick, and had to be quickly brought back down. There's only a couple of places in the world where people actually live at those altitudes, and there's a reason for that. My very last morning in Peru, our group decided to take the names of all those we worked with this week to the top of a mountain and pray for them. I carried the names, and we headed up. About halfway up, I handed the names off and told the group I would wait for them there. You young'uns go on. Nice to be young.

I sat down on a rock, and just looked. Far below, I saw a person working out in a field. The more I watched, the more I began to realize, I was watching a world class athlete of some description. He/she could raise one leg straight up, with the other standing on the ground, and put that body in all sorts of amazing positions.

I watched a plane take off in the valley far below. The runway was at least twice as long as an ordinary runway, even one designed for the large jets. It took every bit of it for that plane to get airborne. Thin air.

Goodbye Peru. I love you. Goodbye, Agua Amigo. I'll hold your hand again in Heaven.

For some reason, the other leaders had to fly back half a day early. I was given the job of making sure all the kids got home. At the airport, I was sorta nervous. Being a world traveler, I shouldn't be, but Barbara had always got me through the airports, and this was an awful lot of kids to get home. When my carry-on was X-rayed, they found something. They told me there was Leatherman tool in there, (with sharp blades) and why was that? Well, I did carry several of them down in my checked luggage, as gifts, but they were all gone. I emptied the bag, it was not there. They X-rayed it empty, and there it was. Showed me the x-ray. I dug around in the bottom, and found it under the first layer of the bottom. They were very concerned about me now, I could tell. I had no idea what they would do with me. They could make me stay in Peru. So, I told them how sorry I was, how it was just an accident. I gave up the *weapon*, I begged and pleaded until they let me off, then repacked the bag, and hurried down to rejoin the kids. A few minutes later, the same man came down to see me. Said someone left a hat up there, did we leave it? My hat was on my head, so I asked the kids. No response. I said, "Last chance! Did anyone leave a hat?" no response, so he left. In about 3 minutes, I remembered. I had bought a hat for Frank Teed, and that was it. I rushed back up to him, told him that was my hat.

He was about tired of messing with me now, and said, "But you said, last chance! Last chance!" A couple of my kids had to come up and rescue me. And the hat.

A strange, safe feeling has always enveloped me on mission trips. What better way or place to die, than out, doing God's work. Fulfilling the Great Commission? I guess I figured if I die here, St. Peter will just give me a pass straight through to Heaven. I won't even have to account for all my sins.

We flew into DFW, and I rode toward Arkadelphia with the "wild child." He had been on the other trip, too, and he was trouble. Once, in Lima, he followed some stranger off down a dark alley who told him he had a special deal for him, he said, and he got lost. Almost missed the plane. On the first trip, he wanted to carry only camo clothing. I told him that camo attracted unwanted attention in third world countries, told him how my camo hat had gotten a truck load of soldiers to point their guns at me once in southern Mexico. We argued awhile. He would always do the unexpected, kept a person nervous about what he would do next. Little did I know he was about to totally outdo himself.

Anyway, on the way back from Dallas, I was riding in "Wild child's" car. I went to sleep in the back seat, and woke up to the sound of our windshield breaking, "wild child" screaming, and screeching tires. When I opened my eyes, we were lodged under a 16 wheeler, crossways, right in front of the back tires, and being dragged down the road at 70 MPH. The side of our car had cut a "V" shaped, two inch gash in the bottom of the truck siding, and the car being lodged in that
gash was all that was keeping us from being rolled up like a tin can. The driver of the truck handled it perfectly, slowing down very slowly, and when he got down to about 40 MPH, our tires were gone and the metal rims were grinding away.

When we stopped, I looked up at the two boys in front. Other than shaking with convulsions and probably in shock, they seemed to be OK, and lots of people were already on the scene getting them out. I was worried that traffic would hit the car before the boys got out. The car was sticking out in the fast lane. I got out and started directing traffic. Strangely, I never got excited. Not one bit. Others in our group started arriving, found the two boys lying in the grass shaking with convulsions. They knew I was in that car, so they started walking the road ditches trying to find me. Finally, someone yelled, "There he is! He's the one directing traffic!"

I really just have no explanation for my reaction, or lack of one. I called Barbara two minutes after I got out, and she said later I was perfectly calm. Maybe, I've just ran out of adrenalin. Maybe being asleep when it happened caused it. Or, maybe, just maybe, that strange safe feeling was still surrounding me. The mission trip wasn't over yet.

As we rode on to Arkadelphia, in someone else's car, I asked "wild child" for an explanation about how he could *possibly* have gotten that car into the position it was in when I woke up.

"Well, I've had six other wrecks, and they were just barely my fault too, and -" That explained it all.

A perfect ending, I guess, for my adventures in Peru. To this day, I regularly converse with Edith, my interpreter in Lema. Her last adventure was leading a group of Christians to Cuba. She keeps me posted regarding the activities of Pastor Cirro. I guess I will never again see my four God children in Peru – or Agua Amigo. But they will always be in my heart. And it gives me some measure of satisfaction knowing that my children are probably still *rich,* by Peru Indian standards.

MY BEST FRIEND TOOTER

WHEN I FOUND TOOTER, he was an 8 week old, part German shepherd pup. He had a black and white cross on his chest. I carried him, resting on my forearm, the two miles back to our farm. As Tooter grew, he learned quickly. He became my constant companion as we hunted, fished, and trapped – or just roamed the bottoms and mountains for the fun of it. He quickly learned to "stand," "heel," and "back up." Once learned, he obeyed perfectly. If I needed help getting up a muddy creek bank after looking for mink signs, I had only to say, "back up." Tooter backed into position, waited until I grasped his tail, then pulled me up the bank. Tooter was a world class sprinter, by human standards. Using the "stand" command, I timed him at 7 seconds flat in the 100 yard dash, eclipsing the world record by two seconds or so – for a man.

Tooter saved me more than once. One hot summer day, walking barefoot down an overgrown lane to fish at Lily Pad Lake, Tooter was in the heel position. He suddenly stepped ahead of me, then jumped aside. Looking down, I saw a large moccasin, coiled and fangs bared, lying where my next step would have taken me.

Tooter became a good squirrel dog, though not in the normal sense of the term. He did not trail squirrels, but ran, crashing through the underbrush, scaring any self-respecting squirrel into movement. His sharp eyes caught the flash of fur, and another squirrel was treed. Once he had him in sight, he would follow him when he jumped from tree to tree. We worked well as a team. While I waited quietly on one side of the tree, Tooter crashed to the other side to turn the squirrel. They were an important source of meat for my family. The only meat we ate was either an occasional chicken, salt pork, which got old after awhile, or meat that I hunted or fished for.

One balmy autumn day, when I was in the eighth grade, I packed my tow sack hammock, food, water, and my .22 rifle, and Tooter and I set out to climb Main Mountain. This was the tallest of all the mountains around, seven or so ridges over from our farm. We followed Stowe creek up the holler, avoiding most of the climbing until we reached the big one. It was a hard, tiring climb up the mountain. We reached the summit at sundown. The trees on top were mostly knotty, gnarled oaks. Fox squirrels abounded here, but many trees were hollow. It was a real challenge, getting a mess of squirrels on top of Main Mountain. I set up camp, we shared the water and food, and I crawled into my hammock. Excited about our hunt tomorrow, I finally dozed off.

I awoke with a start. The moon was up, and an ominous wind blew through the tree branches. An owl hooted in the distance. Although it seemed I had been asleep a long time, the moon told me it was not yet midnight. My major concern, however, was Tooter. I had never run onto anything in the woods that frightened Tooter. But here he was, whining, crying softly, pressing against me, staring into the darkness. A faint rustling in the leaves came from the direction of his attention. I picked up the .22, releasing the safety. The rustling, about 100 yards out, slowly circled us. With Tooter following every move with his nose, whining, we strained to see through the darkness. The circling continued, at intervals, throughout the long night.

Tooter and I pressed closer and closer together. As a faint light appeared in the east, the rustling disappeared. We found no tracks in the freshly fallen leaves, never knowing what had stalked us throughout that long, fearful night.

The hunting was good, and with the sun heading toward the horizon, we headed down the mountain with a full pack of Fox squirrels and memories of a night that the passing decades have not erased.

The good hunting on Main Mountain set up yet another adventure to Wing Hollow. My buddy, Bob Rice, wanted to try his luck with those Main Mountain "foxies." One Saturday we set out up the holler. After a long hunt, we had a few, and the sun was dipping low, so we turned toward home. Tooter thundered through the underbrush, in his customary manner, a hundred yards to the right. Suddenly, a large gray shadow flashed across the trail in front of us. Bob and I both glimpsed the animal, a large wolf or coyote. I glanced at Bob, noticed his chill bumps were as big as mine, and we picked up the pace.

As we neared the last turn in the trail before Turner's Store came into view, I realized my hunting knife was missing. Remembering the last place we had used it was where we field dressed the squirrels, my concern for my Marine Combat Knife overcame my concern for the wolf. As Bob stretched out on the trail soaking up the last rays of the late evening sun, I started back up the trail. Tooter and I quickly found the knife. On the way back down, a sinister plan began to form in the dark recesses of my mind. Perhaps Tooter and I could use the wolf episode to have some fun with Bob. Just before we came into sight of Bob, I gave Tooter the "stand" command. I went around the curve, saw Bob stretched out on his back, hands behind his head, chewing on a weed. I softly called Tooter, then began running, screaming, "Bob! The Wolf!" I saw Bob glance up, just as Tooter, alias the great gray wolf, burst from the timber.

Under normal circumstances, there is a process to be followed in getting to one's feet from his position. I have never been able to explain or understand exactly what happened in this situation, although I have thought through it many times in the past 50+ years. One moment Bob was glancing up, the next he was leaning into the wind, fairly flying down the trail to Turner's store. His feet seemed to scarcely touch the ground. A small cloud of dust marked his disappearance around the bend. When I reached the bend, there was no sign of Bob. Tooter and I set off down the creek toward home. Moments later, a car came speeding up the trail, a large dust cloud boiling up behind it. As it approached me, I made out a wide-eyed Bob, Buell Turner, and some old men who often hung around the store, whittling and chewing tobacco. Guns bristled out the windows. I had some tall explaining to do.

Tooter was not always perfect. Late one summer afternoon, Mom sent me to herd her young chickens into the coop for the night. Any chickens not locked up securely at night would probably become a meal for a coon, or maybe a mink. A mink might eat part of one, but kill all of them, just for fun. The chickens kept circling the coop in front of me. Round and round we went, with no apparent signs of progress. Finally, in exasperation, I called Tooter into action. He quickly developed a liking for this new game, and he was good at it. We soon had every chicken in the coop.

Late the next afternoon, as I came in from the fields, what I saw beside the porch stopped me short. A dozen dead chickens were stacked in a row. Tooter, I soon found out, had so enjoyed the game that he continued it the next day. He had "herded" every chicken to death!

I dreaded facing Dad. I knew what was coming. Chicken-killing dogs could not be tolerated on the farm. Finally, the inevitable could be avoided no longer. "Son," Dad said slowly, "that many killings would get anyone a death sentence." My dad was a hard man. He had to be, scratching a living out of this hill farm. Hard living requires hard decisions. Dad, however, more than anyone else, understood the bond between Tooter and me. Tooter was spared, and I promised to teach him never to kill the chickens again. I guess Tooter understood, because he never did.

The time came for me to leave the farm. I was off to college. Tooter never did accept this well. He drooped around, his spirit gone, searching for me each day in all the old places. On the rare occasions when I got to hitchhike home for the weekend, Tooter always spotted me coming when I was still a speck in the distance. He would suddenly regain his "world class" speed, and a rough and joyous reunion resulted as we ran up the lane. One time, he jumped on me, our noses meeting none too gently. Mine was the one that was bloodied. Another time, a flying leap sent a tooth through my watch crystal. I still have that watch. That and memories of a happy time are his legacy. With long periods of depression and separation and short, joyous reunions, my freshman year passed. Then I was home for the summer, and all was well in our world.

One summer morning, I was awakened at dawn by a loud commotion in our yard. Wiping the sleep from my eyes, the sight before me sent a chill through me. Two large wolves had Tooter, one on each end, stretching him out. When I yelled, they dropped Tooter and ran. Tooter chased one, caught him, and grasping him by the throat, began to squeeze the life from it. I grabbed Tooter, pulling him back. The wolf shook loose, and quickly melted into the woods.

During the next few days, Tooter seemed to be slowly recovering. One morning as he leaped from a load of cattle feed in our truck, he yelped in pain. He moved slowly to the porch, lying down, and soon was unable to get up. I carried him to the cool cellar. He wouldn't eat. As I checked on him throughout the night, he became weaker. At daylight he was gone. That day I buried him in a grave under the persimmon tree overlooking the valley and the mountains we had roamed together so many times. I spent the afternoon cutting his name in a large flat rock that I placed at the head of his grave. Tooter had come to me when we were both very young. He had seen me through my growing up years as my constant companion and best friend. His job was done. Now I am a man. I must go on alone.

THE YELL COUNTY FREE FAIR

FROM MY VERY EARLIEST YEARS, MY SISTERS AND I were very excited when we saw the huge searchlight moving back and forth across the night sky each September. We knew that meant the Yell County Free Fair time had arrived, and we could hardly contain our excitement.

On School day, Dad would give us 30 cents each, or maybe fifty cents on a good year, and we would board the school bus to cross the mountain to Danville, thirteen miles away. The big parade, the only one I ever saw as a boy, was exciting. One year, I entered 10 ears of corn from my own acre in competition, and won first place! A blue ribbon, and even more importantly, some cash! The next year, I was really pumped. I went through the whole corn crib, ear by ear. I worked for days to find the very best ten ears on the farm. I didn't even place.

The Scramble, on Danville's football field, was a really exciting night. I had watched it every year since I was a small boy. Someday, I wanted to do that.

The girls were in the Chicken Scramble. One girl from each school. Chickens were released on the field. The girls chased them with abandon. If they caught one, it had money attached. The younger boys chased greased pigs. Catch it, and carry it off the field, and it was yours.

When I was in the 12th grade, my time finally arrived. I was entered in the Calf Scramble. I had watched these for years, and I realized this was hard. I had watched many boys, larger and stronger than I, try to out-muscle their calf they had their hands on, and just totally wore themselves out. They were never able to get their short lead rope they carried on it, eventually losing it.

 I stripped down to my jeans and track shoes at one end of the field, along with the other six boys. Two calves were released at the other end. The gun went off. I quickly shot out to a lead. When I neared the calves, I noticed one was small, as usual. The other was a nearly grown heifer. Figuring bigger is better, I grabbed the tail of the large one with both hands. I knew immediately I had made a mistake. This one looked almost like a grown cow, and I was a very skinny kid. I reasoned quickly that brute force would never work. I was very short on strength, longer on endurance. I figured that if I just held on, let the calf do most of the work, it would eventually wear itself out. So, around and around the football field we went. On about the third lap, the calf made a quick turn, and down I went. Now it was dragging me. I was determined to hold on, no matter what. This was a high dollar calf. As the calf finished one lap of dragging, I began to realize with horror; my jeans were slipping down. Farther and farther. Soon, they would pass the point of no return. The crowd, seems like everyone in Yell County, began to realize the drama that was being played out before them, and the noise level picked up. The moment came when I had to make a terrible decision between my modesty and my calf. In 50 years or so, most of these people would be dead, and most of the others will have forgotten. I gritted my teeth as I made my decision. Whatever happened here to me tonight, I was taking this calf home. Most of these people didn't even know me. I could just go home and pretend I was very sick, stay home from school awhile. Maybe my school mates would forget.

Right as the critical moment arrived, the calf hesitated. Just for a second or two. Just long enough for me to regain my feet, and pull up my pants. The crowd let out a disappointed "ooooooooooh!" Then we were off again, leaving the football field far behind as we ran through back yards, eventually reaching a big field. Right in the very middle of that field, the calf could go no more. When I, at long last, led MY calf back to the football field and over to our truck, the lights were off, and the crowd had gone home. My dad told me later that he had heard a spectator say, just at the peak of the action, "That skinny kid will never hold that calf!" The man next to him shook his head, and said, "That kid is a Gillum, and a Gillum would give up his life before he would give up a hundred dollar calf!" Those guys knew my Dad. Guess I'm just a chip off the old block.

Once I had this heifer home, on our farm, it did not act like a normal heifer. It followed me around all over our farm, just a big pet. I figured I had *broken* it, like breaking a horse. When it was grown, it never produced one calf. It was just a really big pet all its life. Oh well...

1968 TRIP

BARBARA AND I DECIDED to take our first long trip. It was absolutely, more so than all others, on a shoestring. This was a very long time ago, before man walked on the moon, when Barbara and I were footloose and fancy free, son Corey was yet just a few dozens cells, multiplying rapidly, daughter Kinley was yet only a distant but hopeful dream. When Walmart was still just a single store, gas was 28 cents per gallon, Barbara was still cold natured, thus our home was still warm and comfy in the wintertime (though that was soon to change forever.). The first, with many more to come.

Our funds were truly meager, yet we owned a nearly new Corvair, freshly paid off. Our available funds amounted to a few pennies one side or the other of $200.

My oldest brother lived in the outskirts of Los Angeles, while my youngest brother, 14 years on the downhill slide side of me, lived in the mountains of Montana. Could we visit them both, see the sights in between, and get back to Fayetteville on our tiny stash of cash? We decided to find out. Now, shoestring travel, in its purest form, (cheapest) is, stay with relatives as long as they will want to put up with us.

We estimated their probable time tolerance level, and headed out one day in June 1968, on what should be about a two week trip.

We drove hard the first day, and as the last rays of the setting sun melted away, we found a cute little park. No, not a camping park, but a roadside park. Right alongside I-40. We carried our tent back in the bushes a ways, out of sight, hopefully, from touring serial killers, and set it up. I shudder at the memory of that sort of travel in the old days, but back then, we were young, bold, and somewhat foolish.

The next day we planned to see the Painted Desert, the Petrified Forest, many other sights yet unseen by our virgin eyes, and wind up at the Grand Canyon. We arrived at the Grand Canyon late, about midnight, tired but happy. Unfortunately, all the campsites were taken, but we did manage to find a nice little spot, though a bit smelly, right between the garbage cans and the dumpster.

We saw the Grand Canyon in all its glory the next day. As we were about to get on the park tour bus, the woman behind us took her customary long, deep drag on her cigarette, and flipped it back out the door. The lady driver was livid. "You go right back out there and pick that up!" she said

"How can I ever find it out there in that mess?" the woman protested, pointing to the vast array of butts already there.

"You just get out there and pick up any one of them," the driver replied. The woman, totally embarassed and humiliated, complied.

Needless to say, that very large, colorful hole in the ground was breathtaking. At one stop, at the head of the seven mile trail to the bottom, hikers who had just walked out of the canyon were lying around, totally done in. As they say, "7 miles down, 77 miles back up."

By late morning, we were headed on west. Getting into the Rocky mountains, we just simply could not believe the majesty of what we were seeing. And, unbelievably to us, many were capped, still, by patches of snow.

Late in the afternoon, we looked for another roadside park. Each one was dry, almost treeless, with no place to hide our tent, and overrun with small groups of Indians, sitting about. Some of the men looked at Barbara long and hard. Were they thinking how good that long, beautiful hair would look, hanging from their belt, or did they have something else entirely in mind?

Either way, this was no place to be camping, and we got back in the car and kept pressing westward.

Arriving in Los Angeles in the middle of the night, we drove slowly along that mass of endless streets trying to follow Harry's directions, but with little luck. I started to change lanes, noticed lights coming up behind me, and jerked back into the lane. Immediately, his blue lights came on. Roadweary as I was, I pulled over to the left side of he road, the closest point. As I emerged from the car, his loudspeaker bellowed, "Get back in that car, and pull over to the curb!" I quickly complied. He walked up, still not in a friendly mode. "What do you think you're doing?" He demanded.

"Well, I really don't know. I guess I must be lost as a goose." Hearing my Arkansas talk, he sensed what the problem was, and changed to a friendly, helpful tone. He directed me to our destination.

Arriving at Harry's complex, it was around 1 AM. Not sure of his apartment number, but knowing I was very close, I took my best guess, and knocked loudly. After a while, a sleepy man's voice said, louldy, "Go away!" He was not in a neighborly mood, and was not Harry. As it turned out, Harry lived next door, and was much more welcoming to us. Asking if we had much trouble finding him, I told him we did fairly well until the man next door got a little upset with us. "No man lives next door. Only a woman," he said, grinning.

Harry treated us like royalty for several days. He even showed us some of his work sites. Harry travels all over Southern California daily, servicing large earthmoving machines, and he criss crosses the LA area daily in his large truck. Years later, when we finally got him back to Arkansas, he would never step foot into California again, for the rest of his life.

He showed us Hollywood, Disneyland, Knott's Berry Farm, and many other fantastic sights of LA. Sensing we were on a very thin shoestring, he almost never allowed me to pull my, also thin, wallet.We got to know, again, most all of my California aunts and cousins, some I had met, most I had not.

We headed for Montana, cutting across Nevada, into Utah, and camped somewhat short of the Grand Teton National Park. Some sort of furry little animals, a bit smaller than a barn rat, spent the entire night running up on our tent, then sliding back down. Hard to sleep, with all that mess going on.

Arriving at Jackson Hole, Wyoming, the jumping off point to the park, We saw, for the first time, the majesty of the Teton Range.The most beautiful view in America, I have always thought since then. My fascination with the Tetons has lasted a lifetime, and I have driven back up there on more that one occasion, alone, and camped in the shadow of those mountains. Just looking. If you ever need inspiration, that's the place.

We decided to hike around Jenny lake. It didn't take long to begin seeing lots of elk and deer. Barbara was just beginning to feel the effects of being pregnant, and she totally gave out three quarters of the way around. I found a campground I thought would be safe for her, left her there, and continued on around to collect the car. I stepped out into the highway, at just the wrong moment without looking behind, and a very fast car brushed my shirtsleeve, one of those "near death" moments. The first thought that flashed through my mind was, "What in the world would Barbara do, up here alone, with me dead on the roadside?" Nowadays, in foreign countries, the question is different. How would I get back home without Barbara? Very tired, we continued on into Yellowstone, and found a real campground.

The next day, we took a leisure day and drove around Yellowstone. The loop around was very different then. The traffic was light, in spite of the fact we were there during a peak vacation time. This was totally unlike my last summer trip through here, when this loop was one big dusty parking lot. Many large animals still roamed the roadsides on that first trip, not the least of which were the bears. We passed a cinnamon bear, trudging along the road. We parked and went back. He was surrounded by tourists, and seemed to pay no attention to them at all. At least, not until Barbara walked up. He stopped, looked at her and, growling, made a three or four step run at her. She screamed and made a couple of dozen step run for the car. Very fast. I don't know what it is about Barbara, but big animals just seem to single her out and do that. Some don't stop at four steps. An alpaca, a large ram, and countless others. She always bolts for the car. Some of them turned out to be big pets, but how do you know? Best to run first, ask questions later.

We passed a big black bear, walking slowly along the roadside. We pulled ahead, stopped, but stayed in the car this time. He walked up to my side of the car and stood up, putting his front paws on top of the car, and looked in at me. I was feverishly trying to roll up the windows and start the car, while Barbara was feverishly snapping pictures. Good grief! He probably was just begging for a snack, as he had become accustomed to. But in my mind, he was looking for a big meal. A very big meal.

We just drove by and pictured, after that, and kept our distance. Heading out of Yellowstone, starting our last leg into the mountains of Montana, a minor disaster struck. Our clutch cable broke. I finally managed to tie a piece of rope onto the cable, and secured it to the clutch. We were still a long way from any help. Driving very gingerly, and seldom clutching, we limped into Harold's town.

Harold was in the Air Force, a radar tech. He and Lou also treated us royally for a few days, while we waited for our new clutch cable to come in.

Deer were everywhere. We saw dozens every day. And, trout just fought each other to be the first on my hook. But it was cold. Seemed like winter almost, and it was still June. My legs, without any boots, just froze, wading those trout streams.

Wintertime was a very bad scene in Montana, they said. One of their neighbors went out to feed his cattle in a snowstorm, and just never came back.

Our new clutch cable arrived, and we nearly filled a

large ice chest with trout, covered it with dry ice, and headed out. I have few memories about the trip back, partly because we were in a going home mode now, partly because we were out on those endless plains quickly. We did drive by Little Big Horn, and paid our respects to General Custer. I'm sure we camped somewhere, nothing else was possible. No more family in between us and Fayetteville. I do know we scraped together our last few dollars and pennies to fill the car up that last time, which cost nearly five dollars. We did prove $200 was sufficient for a 5000 mile, two week+ trip, if you have family scattered around at intervals. At least, it was in the summer of 1968.

That was the first of many long trips on a shoestring, for Barbara and I. We did more, when the kids were larger, But it was never a quiet, leisurely trip. A constant battle. Pinches, pokes, gouges, and hitting, with "Mama! He's looking at me again!" ringing in our ears. That just seemed to dull our wanderlust, somewhat, for many years. But it would come back with a vengence, later. Kinley asked once, "When we were little, and we went on a trip, it was to the nearest lake, for a campout. After we were grown, you now go all over the world. Now, why is that?"

THE PORK AND BEANS TRIPS

"WHAT IN THE WORLD ARE YOU THINKING?" she was saying to Barbara. "Haven't you read *The Bridges of Madison County?*"

"No, actually, I haven't," Barbara replied, still smiling.

Her brow tightly knitted together, the lady just said, "Well, maybe you should!" and shaking her head, walked away.

Many years ago, in the early days of our marriage, when Barbara was still yet a teen, Barbara readily accompanied me on my "roughing it in the wilds" adventures, for a time. Two particular trips brought that to an end.

Once, when we still lived at Fayetteville, we drove over to War Eagle Mills. We opened the farmer's gate and drove down to that beautiful river, which the farmer allowed at that time. This was before the days of the big festival now held there. We found a beautiful spot, we fished, built a fire, cooked, ate, and just generally had a great day. That night, we rolled out our sleeping bags, and since Barbara was not really a "sleep out under the stars" type of person, as I was, I made the concession of stretching a tarp over us. I slept well, as I always do at such a place. As dawn broke, Barbara was awakened by a big, slobbery kiss – right on the lips. No, not by me, this is not that kind of story. A big old hound dog.

"We need a tent," Barbara stated firmly, "if we're going to keep doing this!" I went to Walmart, right behind our house, the next day. I found a perfect one. But I didn't buy it. A purchase that major, in those days, was something for us both to discuss long and hard. We were pore' folks.

Tommy Beard was one of my best friends and fishing buddy. He was a student majoring in business, and he was destined to become a financial wizard, managing and investing money for several large companies. But to me, then, he was just another kid, newly married to his wife Pat, and he loved to go along with me in search of the catfish. While Barbara and I were still agonizing over that tent purchase, Tommy said to me one day, after taking me aside, "You need to scrape together every penny you can. A company up the road is about to make their first stock offering. This is a once in a lifetime opportunity. This company is going to really, really go places."

"Tommy," I said, "We live in a trailer park. We don't have money!" He didn't say any more. Just walked away, shaking his head.

Barbara and I made our decision that night. We would buy that tent. The next day, I walked into Walmart, one of only a small handful in the world at that time, and bought a six million dollar tent. Maybe I should explain.

Several years later, I was reading the Sunday paper one day. I saw an article about a large company from Arkansas, detailing what the initial stock offering for that company was now worth. The $36 dollars I paid for that tent translated into six million dollars at that time. The company? Walmart. My grandson Christian, also a budding financial whiz, called me recently to tell me that figure now stretched into 9 figures. But let's not talk any more about that.

Several years later, when he knew I had decided to leave coaching, and was looking for a teaching job, Tommy again advised me. "Walmart has just started a new program, training up store managers. No telling how much you could wind up making, if you get in that program on the front end."

I chose teaching. The story of my life. A poor boy, destined to die a poor boy.

Anyway, let me get back to my story. Shortly after we bought that tent, we went back to the War Eagle River, camping once more. The river bank was pretty well grown up in bushes, but I did find one clear place. Kinda in a swag, but the sky was clear, no rain tonight. We now also had air mattresses; I had to make Barbara as comfortable as possible, to keep her roughing it with me.

About midnight, dark clouds rolled in. It came a "toad strangler." (That's hillbilly for "A major rain.") I slept through it. I always sleep my best, out in the wild.

Until Barbara elbowed me sharply in the ribs. "My air mattress is floating around!"

By daylight, Barbara had had all she wanted of "roughing it in the wild places," and she has never weakened or wavered from that position in 45 years. The next day she declared, "If you are going to keep doing this, you'll have to go alone!"

Well, that set the stage. Barbara knew I have to return to the wild places periodically, to recharge my batteries. It's as necessary for me as breathing. I grew up a loner, and I am far more at ease and at home in the wilderness. It would be many years before "roughing it" was not the only option for such trips.

We worked out a deal. I would do my thing, in the wilds, while she would do her thing. That often turned out to mean, she would visit her family, go on car trips with her sister's family, or, later, her and one of our kids or sisters went on a cruise.

The Pork and Beans Trips were born. I planned my trips very carefully. Wildlife photography was my main goal. Hunting and fishing lost its attraction before these trips began. Barbara didn't like wild meat, but the clincher was, she didn't want to cook it either. If we were not going to eat it, I didn't want to kill it.

Not spending much money was rule number one. I cooked every meal, I never ate out. I cooked only the least expensive foods, so pork and beans was a major staple, along with potatoes and spam, if I really wanted to live high. I could pull over to a park picnic table, whip out my little burner and skillet, and have a meal ready in five minutes. Barbara and I adopted, early on, a little but very effective rule to live our lives by: *Always live below our means.* That rule has been good to us, and enabled us to do many things that poor people like us usually never get to do. How many genuinely poor people have been to every state, every continent, (except Antarctica) and forty countries? I camped only in the least expensive places, usually National Forest Campgrounds, or maybe Walmart's parking lot.

I planned my first real Pork and Beans trip. Barbara's sister planned a car trip to New England, six days, and they wanted Barbara to go along. This situation was perfect. I slept as late as possible the day I left, ten AM. Then I headed out for Rocky Mountain National Park. Actually, I just wanted to get as close to it as I could that day, never intending to drive the whole way, but that's the way it turned out. Those Kansas plains just offered few camping spots while thunderstorms rolled through. Driving through a small town in Oklahoma late that afternoon, I pulled over to study my map. I noticed in my rear view mirror that a truck pulled up behind, and an angry looking man got out, walked up to my window. "Somebody driving a truck just like yours just shot out my front window," he said, looking me and my truck contents over good.

"Now look," I said, "Don't you think if I had just shot out your window, I would already have my getaway planned out? Do you see what I'm doing? I'm reading a map! And, do you see a gun in here? I'm shooting with these cameras." He looked my gear over good, but I guess my words settled him down a little, because he turned and left.

I went on up through Kansas to I-70, did a hard left, and began the long haul up toward Denver. Approaching a long grade near daylight, the lights of Denver began to appear. As I dropped into Denver, my need for sleep began to overtake me. I dozed off twice momentarily passing through Denver, but soon I was in the Rocky Mountains, and my excitement pushed the sleep urge back. I realize now, a sleepy driver can be as dangerous as a drunk driver, and I don't push my limits like that anymore. No more 24 hour drives for me. Well, maybe one. A couple of years later.

I headed north, fully enjoying the early morning views of the Rocky Mountains, no big rush now. I arrived at the west gate of Rocky Mountain National Park around 10

AM, a twenty four hour drive. I arrived at a campground, set up my tent. I was much too excited just to be there to sleep now, so I walked through a creek bottom, looking for wildlife. I got a good picture of an elk calf suckling, and saw lots of other elk. I drove slowly back toward the entrance and back, and saw a large wolf and a moose with two calves wading in a pond. When I got back to camp, I was at 8000 feet or so. I decided to drive on up to the Continental Divide, at about 12,000 feet. Climbing on up in my little red truck, I was beginning to feel the effects of altitude sickness, climbing so high in my exhausted state. I turned around. By the time I got back to the campground, it was hitting me hard. I crawled into my sleeping bag, really not caring whether I lived or died, at the moment, and was soon asleep.

   I awoke at dusk, and could hear some sort of program starting up at the pavilion, but I really didn't care. I went back to sleep, and slept the night through. When dawn broke, I awoke, feeling a little better, but I still had a major headache, and my eyes were totally red from the long drive with my windows down. Looking out, an elk was right beside my tent. That brought me fully awake, and I soon was headed back up to the Continental Divide.

   Exiting my truck standing right on the Continental Divide, I looked up to the tall peaks around me. The divide was at about 12,000 feet, and the peaks went up to around 14,000. I could see tiny white spots near the top, probably mountain goats. Could I climb that high? I decided to find out. The altitude was hitting me hard. I walked 30 steps, rested, and did 30 more. Finally, I knew I had to be nearing where I had seen the goats, but no sign of them now. Then

I looked up, and they were lined up on a ledge above me, all staring at me, 60 feet away. I got several good photos.

Traveling a little farther in my truck, I saw a narrow foot trail winding up the mountain. I decided to take it. Half way up, I met a huge bull elk, his beautiful rack in full velvet, heading down. He was used to tourists, did not fear me, and saw no reason to yield the trail to me. He kept coming, and I was about to take my chances down the steep slope, when he took the lead role and headed straight up the mountain. I did get several good photos.

Heading home, I decided to make a halfway stop at Witchita Mountains National Wildlife Refuge near Lawton, Oklahoma, and have used that as a good place to spend the first night out since then, several times. It was set up as a place to start somewhat of a comeback for the Buffalo, right after millions upon millions had been killed for their hides. It still has large herds of Buffalo roaming free, as well as many deer, elk, and smaller animals. It has a couple of good campgrounds, and it is a good spot for wildlife photography.

My next trip was toward Okefenokee Swamp on the Georgia-Florida border. It is simply a spot where the Sewanee River spreads out very, very wide, fifty miles or so, and is still one of the true remaining wild places in the United States. It was not successfully crossed by the white man until up in the 1930's. Alligators abound, by the thousands, and it takes three days or so to paddle across in a canoe. Raised platforms have been placed about a day's travel apart, to avoid having to sleep right down in among the gators. I had always wanted to paddle across it, but never could find anyone to go with me, and one can't do it alone. Against the rules.

I headed out, again in my little red truck. I got to Tallahassee the first day, it was raining hard, and that little bit of mud to put a tent up on was only $10 less than a cheap room, so I violated one of my rules that night. I arrived at Mark Twain State Park, on a peninsula well out in the swamp. Tons of wildlife to photograph. I rented a canoe the next day and paddled far out into the swamp and got some really good gator shots. If I knew then what I've since learned, I would not have gotten quite so close. I have heard they can outrun a horse for 30 feet, but I really didn't believe it until I saw one do it, going after a bird, at Aransas, on the Texas Gulf Coast. They can really come up on those toes and fly! I got one pic of a big mama gator sitting on her nest, and as I snapped the shot, I saw movement above her. When I got the pic back, there was a baby gator running over her head. I've been back to Okefenokee several times since, and I always see lots of wildlife, and called up many foxes.

On the way back, I found a pure white squirrel, totally beautiful. I dropped down to the Florida gulf coast to camp, and while I was cooking supper, sun still up, the raccoons were already coming in for supper. I set up a photo session after dark, heated some leftover soup up in a skillet, and they flogged me. I got eight of them in one photo. One particular coon constantly kept stalking me, coming real close. I was not sure exactly what his intentions were, but I finally got up off the ground, and ran him off.

For my next trip, I decided to drive totally around the border of Texas, with Big Bend National Park my main goal. I spent the first night, again, at the Witchita Mountains, then drove down the western edge of Texas the next day. My old trucks never seem to keep the A/C working, and this one was no exception. I about burned up. West Texas is different. I passed the opening gate to a ranch, with a dim trail going off across desert out of sight. The sign said, "so and so ranch, 38 miles." Distances are very great in west Texas. Telephone poles were about head high, consisting of little scraps of limbs. Just work with what you've got. I topped off my gasoline every time I passed a rare station. Distances were the same in Big Bend, 20 miles plus from the entrance to the Visitor's Center. When I started in the building, a big roadrunner was leaning up against the building, in a small bit of shade, tongue hanging out. It WAS hot that day. I started to go back for my camera, then I thought, I'll see lots more. I never saw another that close. There is a campground on the far south side of Big Bend, right along the Rio Grande, but it was deserted, and it didn't have a good feel about it, right on the border. The major campground is up in the mountains, so I chose it. Lots of desert wildlife around up in those mountains.

Javelinas, or Collared Peccaries, were plentiful. Stalking a large group, I came upon a large male, very close, and it made him mad. His hair went straight up, and I snapped a photo, not totally sharp, as I was getting out of there. Texans tell me, they will even attack a man on a horse, as well as on foot, and those sharp tusks can cut a man or a dog up real good.

Heading east along the Mexican border, I got to a large State Park just after they had closed down for the day, and I left early the next morning, so I never saw another human. The jackrabbits were plentiful, though, and I got my best close up jackrabbit photos at sundown.

If anyone ever asks you, how far it is around the border of Texas, it's about 2200 miles, including a few side trips.

I did several other Pork and Beans trips, mostly in the 1990's. I always scheduled these when Barbara was otherwise entertained, in some fashion. The most recent of these involved her going with her sisters Sugar and Frances, along with France's husband, Bill. They went on a cruise to Hawaii and on to Fanning Island, during which Barbara completely lost half her birthday. The ship anchored offshore on her birthday, the launch to the island carried her across the International Date Line into another day, then came back to what was left of her birthday that night. I went on a trip into the Grand Teton Range during that time, and spent several days mostly just looking at my favorite view in America. As always, in my cute little red truck.

When the cruising crew returned, the sisters told me right off, "Bill slept on top of Barbara every night while we were at sea." That caused a momentary wrinkling of my brow, until Bill said, "I prefer to say, I slept *above* Barbara." Bill had the top bunk.

Actually, I saved us a lot of money with my trips. I never spent as much as I would have had I went along on that cruise, nor did I gain as much weight. And, I was happy, in the wilderness, plus Barbara was always happy to see me when I got back, and likewise. A win-win situation. I finally decided, I had photographed, in some fashion, about every animal I was likely to find in America. But if one of those long, super strong digital lenses ever falls into my lap, I think I will start them all over again, if Barbara is agreeable to that. My limited lens at that time limited my photos, and, after all, I have always been only a "pretend photographer." I'm not like Barbara. But, I was out there, doing what I love to do, in the wilderness. My Pork and Beans photo album still lies on our coffee table. But, actually, I'm about the only one to ever look at it. But every picture, even the bad ones, bring about memories of a very special time in my life. I did sell one, a picture of the white squirrel. So, I guess actually, I am a professional wildlife photographer. That title and a dollar will buy me a burger at McDonald's. But of course, I never ate at a McDonald's on these trips. No fancy high-class eating for me - just finish off that can of pork and beans.

TOTALLY WONDERFUL, COMPLETELY HEARTBREAKING

BARBARA AND I ATTEND FELLOWSHIP CHURCH in Arkadelphia, Arkansas. We have been at Fellowship since 1999, Ever since we returned from a year on the road, seeing America. We were looking for a church. We attended the first corporate service of this church, at the Wesley Foundation at Henderson State University. We are the only members still in attendance who were here for that first corporate meeting.

We attended Calvary Baptist Church in Hannibal, Missouri for three years, but we lost that church when we moved back to Arkansas. It was our most wonderful church experience we had ever had, up to that point in our lives. The services were never really quiet. Churches like Calvary, who bus in a ton of disadvantaged people, especially children, and who have tons of outreach going on, local and abroad, and a church whose members are excited to be there for the right reasons, seem to often be that way, I guess.

When we left Hannibal and moved back to Arkansas, we searched for another church like Calvary for twenty three years. We attended several really good churches, met tons of wonderful people, had some really fantastic pastors during that twenty three years.

It's hard to really explain to you exactly what we were looking for, during all that time. Maybe it was that feeling of excitement just to be there. That certain feeling that makes us want to come to church just a little bit earlier, before the services actually start, just to be in the midst of that group of people. Or because we get well fed spiritually every Sunday. Or that feeling that makes us reluctant to leave when its over.

When we showed up for that first service at Fellowship, it didn't take long for us to realize, that feeling we had experienced so many years before was returning. And it's been there ever since.

We are fortunate enough to have two universities in our town. Along the way, a number of pastors who are associated with the universities came aboard. Many students followed. We now have hundreds of great college students attending Fellowship regularly. It seems that students who come to our universities are just the cream of the crop. Then, those who choose to attend church regularly, and become an active part of that congregation, on their own, are usually just the cream of *that* crop.

Instead of having Sunday night church services, we meet at homes in small groups. Like the first church. We meet, break bread, fellowship, study the word and pray for each other. Then we often have a campfire, roast marshmallows, and explode bamboo bombs, or the like. A few brave souls have even chosen to ride my zip line, sight unseen, down into the totally dark woods. Toward that big tree at the bottom nicknamed "splat." Then they go home.

This gives us the opportunity to really get to know and love these students. I cannot describe to you how great that is for us, and what a blessing this is to us. We have the opportunity to almost be substitute parents to these wonderful students for years. They become tightly woven into the fabric of our lives. But then, they graduate, and they often are gone, some forever, at least in this world.

Many are reluctant to leave Arkadelphia, and work at jobs related to the universities for a time, or whatever they can find. But Arkadelphia has few job opportunities of the type they can hang their hats on, and raise a family around. Sooner or later, we lose almost all of them. It breaks our hearts, again and again, to see them go. We like to think of them as young people we have had the opportunity know, love, have an impact on for several years, then send them out as Fellowship's missionaries to the world. Our loss is the world's gain. That's the wonderful side of it, but it does not stop the heartache.

But that is not the end of our story.

I'm almost certain Griffin and Stephanie fell in love in our living room, many years ago. They now have four wonderful boys. We not only correspond, but visit occasionally. Griffin called us on Christmas night. They were coming through Arkadelphia during one of our very rare snowstorms, the road was getting bad. They asked about spending the night, and I told him our home was always open to them. But in all honesty, I had to tell him. Barbara and I were both flat on our backs with a bad stomach bug. Your choice. After a short discussion, they sadly chose the slick highway, instead. But they will be back, and we will be there, from time to time.

Candi and Jeff had graduated, but they chose to stay around awhile. And, they were in love. Candi was a nurse at Hot Springs. Not just a very good nurse, but the one the hospital chose to deliver very bad news to the family about a patient, when those times arose. That kind of nurse. Jeff was temporarily training HSU students to be pilots, while waiting for a real job. Candi was ready to marry, start a family. Jeff seemed to have some reservations about being able to support a family, at that moment. I took Jeff aside after our group meeting, told him that if he missed out on *this* girl, he would never, in this lifetime, find another like her. He just smiled. Seems he had the ring in his pocket at the time. They have two wonderful youngsters now, and Jeff is a commercial airline pilot in Houston.

Lisa was our one connection between Calvary, the church we attended and loved in Hannibal, Missouri when we lived there, and OBU in Arkadelphia. She grew up in Calvary, and when she showed up in Arkadelphia, we took her under our wing. She worked for Barbara, on occasion. She was a photography assistant, cleaned our baseboards when Barbara was down in her back, and helped Barbara throw a tea party. Those kind of jobs are more plentiful in Arkadelphia, more so than the real jobs. She was training to be an athletic trainer, and had to transfer to continue that pretty quickly. Way too quickly. She just got married. This year.

Dayton graduated last year, and is currently getting a good, long look at some of the hard things in life, as well as some of the beautiful ones, as an African missionary. She's had dozens of marriage proposals while there, and took a young child, dying of Aids, in to live with her. She's there for a year.

Bethany is a Spanish major, and is currently studying in Spain for a year. We miss her. But we'll get her back, for a time.

Hillary and Annie have an even longer relationship with Fellowship Church than we do. Their parents, Michael and Shirleen, were some of the founders.

Michael, my best friend, was killed in a motorcycle accident, years ago.

In later years, I suddenly felt a need to call Hillary. Then later Annie. And finally, Shirleen. They later reported that each of those calls came during a major low point in their lives, and were a bit spooked by it. They wanted to know how I knew to call at that moment. I didn't know, but I have a strange feeling about how that came about. Michael was the strongest lay Christian I have ever known. I'll let you write your own ending to this little story. I already have mine.

Hillary graduated from HSU, Annie from OBU.

Hillary and John now live in Tennessee, Annie and Clayton in Texas. Fortunately, they both pass through Arkadelphia to visit each other. That gives us a chance to see those beautiful babies they are having.

I took Aaron catfishing several times, setting out sixty or so cane poles. Aaron says I taught him a good lifetime hobby. Aaron is a biology major, like I was. He soon hooked up with Cayla-Marie. They married, and have moved on to Fayetteville. Cayla-Marie is a distance runner, like I once was, sixty pounds and fifty years ago. They are a perfect match. Like two bookends. With emphasis on the word perfect. Africa became their next home.

Gobi was two weeks short of a master's degree when diagnosed with cancer. He was alone in this country, a student at HSU. Our church took him in, along with a lot of help from HSU. We drove him to Hot Springs to chemotherapy treatments regularly. When he became too weak to look after himself, Barbara and I took him home with us. Barbara often helped him dress to take him to yet another chemotherapy treatment. Barbara stood up in our small church one Sunday, said Gobi needed to go to MD Anderson Hospital at Houston. She needed $2000 by Friday. On Friday, she had $2000, a plane ticket, and paid motel reservations. He is now cancer free, a professor in Malaysia, has a beautiful wife and daughter. Our daughter put up a wonderful post on Facebook recently about her parent's love. A comment immediately popped up from a world away. "I know all about that love. It saved my life." Barbara and I had a good cry.

Joann graduated from OBU, sold everything she owned to raise money to go to China as a missionary. She stayed for years. When in this country recently, she came by and spent the night. I got out a truly weird thing I bought at a garage sale in Australia, to ask her if she knew what it was. She ran away screaming. Seems it was a Chinese idol or god of some sort. But it has been a totally well behaved weird thing in my closet for years now. Maybe she knows something about it I don't, but need to.

Daniel is one of the few who has not broken our hearts. He graduated from HSU, and found a real job in Arkadelphia. A rare thing. He still shows up regularly at our house on Sunday nights.

Another Daniel spent much of his time, while in Arkadelphia, wandering the poor neighborhoods, meeting children, bringing them to church, playing with them, as well as making them totally adore him. A local lady once saw what he was doing, called him over to her car, handed him several hundred dollars. She told him to spend it on the kids as he saw fit. He did. He also visited elderly, lonely ladies regularly, and drove them wherever they needed to go. We finally hired him to do his thing for the Church, and train others to do the same. But there was only one Daniel Graham, and when he and others he trained moved on, that work lessened. But others were inspired by him, as we all were, and are beginning to take up the slack. Before he left, Barbara asked him to be her Words with Friends (internet Scrabble) buddy. He told Barbara he would take it easy on her.

Barbara replied, "No! I want you to do your very best!" Soon Barbara was beating him like a drum. There's only one sixty something year old scrabble player like Barbara. I learned that long ago.

Kate hung around Arkadelphia after graduating, even ran her own business for a time. She worked tirelessly on the Kid's Festival for our church. Now she and Brian have moved on. Seems a seminary is now in their future.

Yet another Daniel, and Kathleen, are twins. They were both in our group. Daniel and Lauren fell in love. That romance, also, could have started in our living room, but maybe not. We now see their beautiful baby regularly. On Facebook. Kathleen is a gifted dancer, a talent best used in a larger city.

Most recently, Tim, our tireless power point and computer expert at our church, and his wife Kayla, who could always be found at our church working with the kids, left for Colorado, he for seminary and she for a university job.

Kylie was my best renter ever. An old soul, still in her twenties. She hung around for an advanced degree. Then, she had a chance to work with Neal Nelson, one of our pastors and director of HSU's Baptist Collegate Ministries. Who could pass up a chance to work with Neal? As a really big plus, she met and married Daniel, (We just love our large flock of Daniels!) still finishing up his own degree, a budding Sports Analyst or Sports Information Director. But, we fear he will soon carry her away from us, to a larger city, where his expertise will probably lead him. But we won't like it.

This is just a sampling. I could go on and on. My apology to all those equally loved students I didn't have room to include. Wherever our wonderful university kids/adults are in this world today, they will always be in our hearts. But we'll see them again. In this world or the next.

FATHER ANTHONY AND PHILOMINA

DURING OUR AUSTRALIAN ADVENTURE, Barbara and I stayed at a guest house in Sydney for several nights. We explored Sydney, and I worked up my nerve to rent a car, one with the steering wheel on the wrong side, drive across that huge city on the wrong side of the road, and figure out how to negotiate multi-lane roundabouts, and head out up the coast to points north, toward the Great Barrier Reef.

One night, at our dinner table, we met a great couple, Father Anthony and Philomena. We seemed to hit it right off, and after we told him we were about to head north toward Brisbane as soon as I got up my nerve to do that, they told us to call them when we arrived there, they would come get us, and we could spend a night with them.

A few days later, we did. They came to get us, and we soon arrived at their home. A great meal followed. While Barbara and Father Anthony washed and dried the dishes, Philomena and I pored over her road maps. We then spent a fun evening talking. He was royally insulted when Barbara told him they sounded British, informing us that Brits sounded like they "had a plum in their mouth, and were far more pompous." I, in turn, was offended when he indicated American football players were somewhat less that manly, having to wear head gear and padding, while Australian Footballers used none. He had to admit, however, that many of their young men got an awful lot of concussions.

He showed us a photo of him carrying the Olympic torch, and showed us their church. At that time, it was only a small building in their back yard. He said he was placing a photo of us over the altar, and they would pray for us daily.

Their church, he explained to us, was just like the Roman Catholic Church, except that the Priests were not celibate, an unnatural thing, and, since Jesus excluded no one, neither did they. Since that time, the church has grown very rapidly, with branches in many countries. There is an orphanage named after him in Africa, and he is now the Presiding Bishop. He was 65 at that time, she 70. We still stay in touch regularly. It was nice to sleep in a real house that night, and we awoke to many strange and beautiful bird sounds.

After breakfast, they drove us to the beach for a walk. They literally walked us both into the ground, several miles. They offered us the use of their beach house, half a day up the coast, but we had to decline, since we wanted to cover as much territory as possible during our stay. They led us out of town and got us started on the correct road, after giving us their official Catholic blessing.

Since we have returned home, we have stayed in regular contact with these friends. I told him once if they ever came to the US, we would come see them. Soon, he called, saying they were going to Hawaii for the official ceremony to make him a Bishop, wanted us to come. How does one explain to a Bishop that one can't keep his word? I had to start out by explaining how far Hawaii was from Arkansas. After he became Presiding Bishop, he once told Barbara that he was taking on the name of McCollip, in honor of a Saint. Then he said, "I personally believe, there are many living Saints in the world, today, like yourself." Well, that bothered me some. Even though it was an off-hand remark, it was, after all, said by the Presiding Bishop of the Independent Catholic Church of Australia. Just how official IS that? How does one live with a Saint? Can I still kiss her on the mouth? Can I sleep in the same bed? Must I always walk 5 steps behind? Just an awful lot I don't know about all that.

He once wrote to tell us their small dog, whom we knew, had got in a fight with a Cain toad and died. How could a toad kill a dog? I looked it up. A Cain toad has a poisonous skin. Bite it, and die. Australia is full of deadly creatures.

Only a few years ago, we got word that Bishop McCollip had gone to Heaven. Rest in peace, our dear friend. Though I know Jesus, in your casual conversation with him, refers to you as Bishop McCollip, you will always be Father Anthony to us. You enriched our six weeks in your wonderful country of Australia greatly.

J. R. TURNER

WHEN I WAS A YOUNG BOY, growing up in Wing, Arkansas, The Great Depression and World War Two were fresh on everybody's mind. Many of the adults I grew up around were tired, and somewhat beaten down by the hardships of life. But one man I knew in Wing was never beaten down. Never tired. I knew I could always count on him for a new, wonderful story about his latest adventure when he was in town. He always had new treasures in hand, such as nuggets of gold, found "1000 miles from the blacktop." And, he had a small eagle quill feather, shaped to be used by the Indians of Mexico to pick up gold dust.

My dad went to the post office each morning. If he happened to mention that J.R. Turner was back, I always quickly found a good reason to walk to Turner's store, knowing he would have another great adventure to tell me about, making this a big day in my life. I loved J.R. Turner.

Over the years, tales from J.R.'s wanderlust began to build a strong resolution in me. Someday, I would go to far away places. See new, exciting things and people. Just like J.R. Turner.

When my wife and I sold our business 14 years ago, I was overjoyed to find that my wife Barbara had the same wanderlust that J.R. planted in me many years ago. The first thing we did was lease our home out for a year, and start living out those dreams.

Visiting with J.R. when he was pushing 100, I knew his memories were fading fast. But when I mentioned King Leo, the prize Black Mammoth jack that was at the heart of the Gillum/Turner/ Compton super mule breeding enterprise in the early 1900's, his eyes lit up, and he began to excitedly tell me all about King Leo.

I mentioned the Lost Silver Mine story, supposedly right across the Fourche La Fave River from the Big Rock. His eyes lit up once again, and he became transformed; he excitedly told me of mobilizing 100 men, all walking the near side of Fourche Mountain, arm to arm, looking for it. He told me he's convinced it's right across the river from the Nancy Turner place. I truly believe, if his knees would but have allowed it, he and I would have quickly been on our way. One last, great search for the lost silver mine.

Knowing full well that some of the Old Gillums were solemn, serious men, I asked J.R., "What did you think about the Old Gillums?"

That question troubled him. He thought about it a long time. Finally, he said, "Well, the Gillums were not like other people." I knew instantly. J.R. had just named my book about the Gillums. Giving that book that name caused some grief for my brother Harold. Someone asked him, "Why does your brother think the Gillums were better than other folks?"

Harold answered, "Well, if you would just read the book, you would see being different does not always mean better..."

J.R. Turner was a true icon of Wing. He never lost his sense of humor, or his love of adventure and excitement. I think this, along with Effie Turner's genetics, helped to carry him beyond the century mark, which very few of us can ever hope to attain. Maybe we could all learn a thing or two from J.R. Turner's life.

This world is just not the same without J.R. Turner in

it. I will never forget him. He will always remain one of my heroes.

LIFE LESSONS

I ALWAYS GO TO THE FOUCHE VALLEY SCHOOL reunions. I always run on to a lot of old friends, and that gets memories going through my head that I thought I had forgotten. I saw Jim Roberson. He had such a strong handshake, it made me feel a little better about what happened to me 47 years ago. I was in the sixth grade, tallest boy in grade school, I could run longer, if not faster, than anyone else, Just generally, one of the big boys.

A couple of the younger, shorter guys, Jim happened to be one of them, got in a tussle at recess one day. I just sorta felt it was my obligation, as a big boy, to straighten these little guys out. I started pulling them apart. Well, Jim already had his adrenalin flowing, and he turned all his attention on me. It didn't take long to realize I should have minded my own business. Jim got me in some sort of hold that was just squeezing all the air out of me, and as a crowd gathered around us, he said, "Are you going to leave me alone?"

I didn't want anyone else to hear, and my wind was gone anyway, so I whispered, in his ear, "Yes." He let me up.

The next day, he brought a bunch of his friends around, pointed to me, and said, "There. That's the guy I whipped yesterday." I told them I didn't remember that at all.

Life lesson #1: Being older, and taller, does not necessarily mean you won't get your butt whupped. And being able to run farther is no help at all. Although it might help you put some distance between you and him, minimize the damage, and put some distance between you and all those kids laughing at you.

A funny thing about memory. I didn't remember a thing about that whippin' the next day, only to have it crop back up, 47 years later, when that strong hand started squeezing me again.

A REALLY young kid got really mad at me one day, I don't even remember why, but he just waded in on me with both fists flying, hitting me about the waist. He just kept on, wouldn't quit. Well, again a crowd was gathering, and I was not about to be seen hitting a really little kid. I was getting real embarrassed. Finally, Monty Dishongh said, "Pat, just get him in a wrestling hold." I did, and I had to hold him until recess was over.

Life lesson #2: Looking at the size of the kid tells you nothing about the size of his heart. And he may come after you tomorrow. And the next day.

I had a friend that was dirt pore', wore ragged, old patched clothes, the kind of guy a lot of kids shied away from. Lived over at Scrougeout. I went home with him one night. His mom was tickled, saying no one had ever done that before. She wrung the neck of her best hen, and we ate it for supper. All their beds were filled with hay, but they gave me the best one.

In the middle of the night, car lights hit the house. The whole family ran to the front window, yelling, "Company! Company!" Seemed to me like they had never had company before. Car was just turning around.

Life lesson #3: Buddy up with the down and out kid. Sometimes, they will just give you the best they've got.

That kid had needed glasses for a long, long time. One day he came to school with a brand new pair. We were wrestling, as kids do, at recess. I threw him down. As he got up, he reached into his pocket and pulled out his new, now broken, glasses. He just turned, put his head down, and headed back to the classroom.

When I went in, after the bell rang, he was at his desk, head down, looking at those broken glasses. His glasses were soaked with his tears.

After I got home, and off to myself, I shed some, too.

Life lesson #4: Go easy with the pore kid with glasses. They will have to last him a long, long time.

My buddies and I were playing ball one day at recess. The biggest, meanest kid in grade school grabbed our ball and threw it across the fence into a briar patch. He just laughed and walked away, and not a one of us said anything. A little later, that same recess, his ball rolled over our way. Without thinking it through, I just grabbed his ball and sent it sailing into the same briar patch. I immediately regretted that decision. He walked toward me, rolling up his sleeves. His arms looked like tree trunks, and his fists looked bigger than a softball.

We stood there, eye to eye. A crowd gathered. Rosemary Gilmore, trying to help me out of my pickle, stepped up right into his face and said, "Why don't you just leave him alone? I don't know about Pat, but I know Jack Larry can whip you." I was hoping Jack Larry would step up, but when I looked around, I couldn't see him anymore...

I remembered that one time Butch Garner had gotten the best of this big guy one day, by just making the first move and popping him right in the left eye, and that guy had walked off crying. I tried that. Didn't work. I now had knots all over my head. I tried the right eye. That didn't work either. Now I had more knots in between that first batch of knots.

Life lesson #5: Take a few more seconds, and think a little more before acting. And, just because it worked for Butch, didn't mean it will work for me. Plus, take advantage of the fact that Rosemary had him distracted, and put wings to the feet.

I hope I can pass one or two of these lessons along to my grandchildren someday. Maybe, just maybe, you can too.

This year's reunion is coming up, And, no matter how many guys Jim Roberson gets into a tussle with, I will totally be minding my own business.

LEARNING WHILE TEACHING

THE JOB STARTED IN THE MIDDLE OF THE YEAR. I had just graduated from college in January, and I felt very lucky to find a teaching job at that time of year. It was at Saint Paul, Arkansas, deep in the Ozark Mountains near Fayetteville. It wasn't until later that I realized it was because they had already lost so many teachers that year.

It paid two thousand dollars for the semester, big money to me. It was sort of a bits and pieces job, just fill in where a teacher had been destroyed and quit, where a senior sponsor had been run off, where another just couldn't take it anymore and walked. It didn't seem to matter that the subject didn't match my degree, my area of expertise. But really, at that point I had no area of expertise, although I was pretty well convinced I knew it all. I did get one physical education class, in my field, and that actually turned out to be my salvation at St. Paul.

I knew the coach, Billy Max, an old Arkansas A&M grad like me. He invited me to share his trailer. I went along with him to many of his games. His senior boys basketball team was very short, no good, and would pass up a layup any day for the glory of gunning a thirty foot shot. Just quite naturally, they won no games that year. The next year I was coaching, and my team of all sophomore boys won the first three games. I was suddenly the town hero. But that didn't last long. We lost most of the rest of them.

Teaching went pretty well, everything considered. I had a hard core group of senior hillbilly boys in my PE class, but I was a hard core hillbilly too. These guys, I knew, were at the forefront in running off teachers, so I put in a little segment on distance running right off. Since I had just came from being a college distance runner, I led them out on a three mile route. They were determined to not let a teacher outdo them in anything physical, and they kept up until they just, one by one, collapsed. They respected physical things much more than teaching ability, fortunately, and we got along pretty good. One of my boys collapsed to the point that I had to load him up in my car and take him to the doctor in Huntsville, twenty miles away. We were late getting back, he was still pretty much out of it, so I drove him home and milked his goats for him.

Time for the senior play was coming up, and, as the senior sponsor had already been run off, I was *the man.* When we started having practice at night, I soon realized I had my hands full. Sometimes, many of them would just not show up. Those that did had not been studying their lines. I knew a disaster was in the works, and I was right. When the big night came, I posted a good sized batch of prompters around behind the curtains. It really was not a matter of prompting, often they just had to read the whole line. And sometimes, the wrong actor grabbed onto a line and just ran with it. Halfway through, a very loud alarm clock that some junior had hidden in the couch on stage went off. I still have that clock. You just can't believe how loud that clock was.

Oh well, all's well that ends well. When it was over, they called me out on the stage, told me how much they appreciated my hard work, and presented me with a brand new fly rod.

I was returning from seeing my girl one Sunday night, well after dark. I cut through the mountains. When I passed a new Ozark National Forest sign, I saw it was on fire. I grabbed an old rag and was trying to put the fire out, when an old, beat up station wagon drove slowly by. I got the fire out and went on to St. Paul. The next day, a kid brought me a message from his grandpa. Grandpa said, "Don't be messing in my business again." This was along about when the Forest Service stopped allowing locals to run their cows up in the mountains. I guess grandpa had a grudge about that.

The end of the school year rolled around. Time for the senior trip. I was again *the man,* with a lady out of the community agreeing to go along to watch after the girls. She really didn't do much of anything, I think she was just on vacation. I drove the bus to Little Rock and booked us into a big hotel. These mountain kids were totally awestruck. I began to realize most of them had never been to a city before. Many of them just wanted to ride the elevator, up and down, as long as I would let them. Some of them were older than me, and a few of the girls were pretty and flirty. A twenty-one year old guy just really should not be responsible for them, that long. But my *do right mechanism* was turned on and kept me in good stead.

We went on to Hot Springs. We went for a ride on a party barge. I had never driven one before, but I was again *the man*. As I came into a dock, I tried gracefully to shift into reverse. It would not go. I tried again, desperate this time. No luck. I yelled to the kid up front. "Hold it off, Max! Don't let it hit!" Well, I was giving an impossible assignment to that little boy on that great big barge.

BOOM! Everyone came running out of cabins, and from everywhere. I had to cough up several bucks to get out of that.

Oh well..

That was not the end of it. My judgement was bad. I had made another big mistake. I passed out everyone's meal money for the whole trip the first day. Max, and some others, were big spenders – for about a day. Then they begged and starved the rest of the trip.

Coach Billy Max resigned, and they offered me the coaching job for the next year. I took it.

The most noteworthy thing about my coaching time at Saint Paul was getting a personalized insult from Frank Broyles himself. After a particularly bad practice by the Arkansas Razorbacks he told newsmen, "We looked like Saint Paul out there today." Well, I was the only coach Saint Paul had, and we didn't even have a football team. As I looked around to see if maybe he aimed that insult at somebody else, I didn't see anyone but me. Ironically, a couple of years later, I was coaching at Fayetteville, and two of his sons were on my football team. What goes around comes around...

I was good at not wasting money when I started to college. Can't waste what you don't have. College had honed that ability even more. I had three hundred ten dollars monthly take-home during that teaching semester, on which I lived, made new car payments, and still saved eight hundred dollars.

Soon after, I brought my new bride to St. Paul. It had taken me a year, almost to the day, to persuade her I was *the man*, even though I had known it the first time I saw her. I took her around, showing her the housing possibilities up there. The first was a small box, right in the middle of town. She said that just would *not* do. So, I took her way up in the mountains, five miles off the blacktop, to show her the second possibility, up close to the Orval Faubus birthplace. The only neighbors were in the graveyard next door. She quickly decided that box in town was not *so* bad, after all.

When I first arrived at Saint Paul it was midwinter. Those hardwood forests were drab and dreary. Now, spring had brought to me bright green leaves and a brand new bride, completely changing my world. We found a new, beautiful spot in those mountains to picnic almost every day. A wonderful start to our fifty years together.

SEDUCED BY PEARL WHITE

BARBARA JUST HAD TO HAVE A NEW CAR. Not *new* new, but new to us. We do not buy new cars. Bonnie, Barbara's cute little HHR was just way too hard on her bad back, to her way of thinking.

She had already decided which car she wanted, a Nissan Murano, a couple of years old. She had ridden in one before, belonging to our friend Judy, and she knew it rode well. I told her on the way to Little Rock, this was her buy, her car. I would just be watching.

We went to Lander's Toyota first, arriving about 10:00 AM. The nice young guy who came out to help us was a very good salesman. Barbara told him she was going to buy a Nissan Murano, today, one or two years old, and asked if he had one. He had three. After she had seen them all, she settled on the one she liked best. But she just could not make up her mind. Said she should probably go to the Nissan dealership, who had already described one they had, on the phone, just to compare. And, it's just right over there.

Now, I'll have to say this. That business of not being able to make up her mind was not a haggling technique. It's the way Barbara is. In a food line at a restaurant, I often get embarrassed, and the customers behind get impatient, waiting for her to decide between two seemingly minor items to put on her plate. Then, choosing a drink. She always seems to evaluate each and every plus or negative of each one. So, it's just Barbara. She never, all day long, mentioned the possibility of them lowering the price. "This car is silver. Well, my last two were silver. I had hoped to change colors." The nice young man dropped the price a few hundred. She considered that for a long time. "Well, It IS really nice, and I really like the cute hubcaps and the miles it has. But the inside is dark, and it will really be hot." The young man trimmed a few hundred more off the price. After a few more rounds of spotting possible drawbacks, accompanied by more trimming, the young man retreated inside and brought out the big gun, the little Lander's brother. After proper introductions, and Barbara going on about knowing his wife, how she knew her, etc., she went back to work on the car problem. "Well, I just can't decide this so quickly. I just should drive over and at least see that other one at the Nissan dealership, then it will be easier, and that way I can think awhile." The young salesman chipped in from time to time, in more of a begging tone now. Little Landers dropped a few more hundred. Barbara headed for our HHR, saying, "Well, before I buy, I'm just going to drive by that other one and look at it. I really like this car, but I've just got to be sure."

As we drove off, the young salesman was hollering, "Just drive by! It will be a lot quicker if you don't stop at all!"

As we drove in at Nissan, we saw Pearl White, though at this point, that was only her official color, not yet her name, right beside the entrance. Barb immediately liked her. A very nice young man came out to greet us. He was also an opera singer, as well as a car salesman.

"Hi! We're going to buy a Murano today, and I love this one!" Barbara said. We looked Pearl White over, and he took us inside to his desk to fix us a drink while our trade-in was evaluated. As she sat at his desk, she got a text. The little Landers brother said he'd drop off another thousand.

We went back out to look at Pearl again. "Oh goodness. Her seats are very light colored. That will get dirty so fast!" Opera man drops 500 off. "Are the seats automatic?"

"No ma'am." Opera man drops 500 more.

"That pearl white color is sooooo beautiful. But I just can't seem to get over those light colored seats."

"Let me get the manager over here." Said opera man.

When he arrived, the problem was explained to him by Barbara. "I just love this car, but the other one we're looking at has dark seats, won't get dirty so easily."

"Tell you what, ma'am, we'll take it and get a professional job of scotch guarding done on the whole inside before you leave."

Barbara was impressed. "What about that little spot on the seat?"

"We'll get it professionally cleaned, too." He took another few hundred off.

I have been listening to so much of this, I was beginning to get into it. "Will you fill up the tank"?

Barbara elbowed me in the ribs. "Stop being so picky over such tiny little money things! That's crude!"

"Yes, of course we will."

Barbara noticed that the tires seemed to have some wear on them. Opera man walked around showing the new tire tags, still showing on the bottom of each tire. Manager man left.

"Oh no! I just noticed this one does not have automatic lights! Maybe I should just real quickly run over to Lander's again. They're right over there, and I need to see if its lights are automatic. And it's much more sporty! I just can't make up my mind."

"Well, Ma'am, that other car IS a year older. And don't forget that 68 month power train warranty that a non-Nissan dealer can't give. But let me go talk to the manager again."

He returned. Finally, everyone involved was obviously about worn out, the two cars were about $100 apart in price, and a deal was struck. Barbara had been totally seduced by Pearl White, in only four hours or so. As we waited for the cleaning, scotch guarding, and filling up the tank, the manager walked over to Barbara, smiling, shaking his head and her hand. "That was the best job of negotiating I've seen in a very long time. Just look at how much you got our man to come down."

As we drove away. Barbara said, "I don't know why he said that. He sounded like I was a haggler! I never even mentioned money! Haggling is such a man thing! Oh, my! It's nearly five o'clock! And I was planning to eat lunch with Kinley, after we bought the car. This day has just FLOWN by!"

Barbara had her new car named before we got home; Pearl White. And a string of pearls now adorns the rear view mirror, but not until after Barbara had considered this move for a few hours.

"But do you think those pearls are not white enough to match the car? Do they look tacky up there? Do you think they block the view too much?"

I didn't say a thing. Sometimes, a little indecision can be a good thing, I had learned that day.

CATFISHING WITH TUCK HULL

WHEN I WAS YOUNG, ABOUT TEN OR SO, Earvin "Tuck" Hull was one of my next door neighbors, as the crow flies. But in Fourche Valley, next door could mean a mile away, which was the case here. Earvin was a big time hunter and fisherman; it seemed to be the main focus in his life. The Game Warden, Bob Campbell, seemed to try to shadow Earvin a lot, apparently convienced he would eventually catch Tuck in an illegal situation. I have heard that he once did, when they were both young, and he hauled him to the jail at Danville. Tuck's brother, PC, went to Danville, and bailed him out, as that story went. But both were old men now, during my youth. It was common knowledge during my youth that Bob still chased Earvin, though I don't know how successful he was. I never heard of Bob catching Tuck in an illegal situation again.

Tuck was fun to be around. He was very friendly to me, and told me lots of tales of his exploits. He often brought us a big batch of buffalo, a rough fish with nice white meat but very bony, taken on one of his night time gigging trips. We ate them like candy. Since I was so young, my sisters just picked out those fine, forked bones for me. When they got tired of that, they just handed me small bites of wadded up cornbread, and I didn't know the difference.

One day when we were talking, he told me, "If you will catch up a big jar of grasshoppers, and bring them over tomorrow morning, we'll go catfishing." Well, catfishing with Tuck was just about the most fun thing I could think of, so I got right on it. We arrived at the river just after lunch.

There is a two or three mile stretch of the river that is very shallow. Even when the river runs normally, The water there appears to be only two feet deep or so. So, it was not a place where people normally fished, to my knowledge.

That area was totally deserted, except during deer season. And deer hunting was not very productive in that valley in those days.They had all been pretty well chased down and eaten up. A few would be ran out of the mountains by deer dogs and killed each season, But when someone legally killed one, it was big news. During my entire youth, I saw only one deer in those bottoms, though I spent most all of my spare time of my youth hunting, wandering and fishing there. My brother Harold did kill one, just before he left Wing. He hid his gun under a log and carried it out. Harold went back to get his gun, and he couldn't find it. Dad went back with him later, and they looked again. Dad noticed a pile of leaves nearby, dug in it, and there it was. Harold must have been pretty excitd when he killed that deer. Charley Bill Stout claimed his dogs were chasing it, and ran it over Harold, so it was half his deer, he said. So, Harold carried him a big batch of the meat.

Tuck showed me that day that there was more to that stretch of river, fishing wise, than met the eye to one not familiar with it. At intervals, several deep holes occured. They were generally far apart, and the only practical way to find them was to wade the river for miles. But Tuck knew them all. And, he also knew that fishing there early or late in the day was not the thing to do, as I had always thought, where catfish were concerned. Early and late, the catfish ranged out in that shallow water, even in dry times, feeding. In the heat of the summer day, they came back to those few deep holes. And, since the river was low, food more scarce, they were still very hungry. Drop a big juicy grasshopper into the middle of one of those holes, and more often than not, a big cat was waiting.

Earvin was using a fly rod. I used a long cane pole. We caught all the catfish we could easily carry out that day, some longer than my arm, something that I was just not used to in my fishing experience. I normally caught sunfish, perch, goggleyes, and mud cats. I memorized the hole locations, and after that I fished them regularly, though I had to walk many miles to do it.

During years when grasshoppers were not readily available, my buddy and I discovered that if we rode to Danville with Dad when he went to buy cattle feed, or whatever, we could quietly sneak in the back door of the chicken processing plant, and we could usually pick up a gallon or two of the unusable chicken livers off the end of the conveyer belt before someone discovered us and ran us out. That worked even better. Those bad livers were destined for the garbage, anyway, so we never felt guilty about that.

Fifty Years Later -

The river bottom in that shallow area is just covered with big, slick rocks. So, I never get to fish many of those holes now. Getting there and back is too shallow for a boat, without getting out and pulling it most of the time. My knees just won't hold up to it. But one good hole is easy to get to, and I fish it regularly when the river runs low. Other people laugh at me when I head out catfishing around lunch time. But they just don't know, and where that hole is concerned, I just let them wallow in their ignorance. Lord knows, I spend more than my share of the time wallowing in that!

ON BEING CLASSY

SOME TIME AGO, I wrote a story about a friend of mine. When describing his wife, the first description that came to mind was *very classy*. Later, at his funeral, the pastor's first descriptive words about his wife was, *a very classy lady*.

What is it about some people that just seems to bring the word "classy" to mind? What is it about some people that lets us know they have it? That experience seems to have gotten that question rolling around in my head a good bit, while I'm thinking. I'm very good at thinking, especially when you just consider the sheer volume of it. Not necessarily quality thinking, not necessarily very productive thinking. Just thinking.

Are there descriptive words out there that are so anti-classy, that, if they truly apply to the person in question, rule out any possibility of being classy? To me, some of those words would be snobby, gossipy, unkind, rude, selfish, prideful, boastful, vengeful, vulgar, intentionally too loud, (physical limitations, such as not hearing well, do not count here) and shallow. Like I say, this is just my list. Yours may be very different, yet better. Or worse.

Are there single, descriptive words out there that, if accurately applied, would prove that classy fits? I seem to have a problem with this question. Perfect will not work, because none of us are perfect, yet some are classy. Flawless? That implies perfect. So it would follow that we may have a few minor flaws, yet still be classy. What type of flaws would be allowed? Could it be that only minor flaws that do no harm to others would work? I tend to think so. There seems to be so many factors out there that go into making up a classy person, that no single word or short description can work, alone.

Physical traits: While physical traits may be our first indicators, such as how we carry ourselves, how friendly we are, our posture, how we choose our clothes, how neat we are, how clean we are, etc. may get us tentatively in the right group initially, the core of it must come from within. We can't keep that hidden forever. And, our station in life we are born into can limit these outside appearances.

When we were in the middle of the second largest and worst slum in the world (Kibera, in Kenya), a little girl who I remember as being around ten years old ran out into our path. She smiled and said, "Hi! How are you?" Her clothes were rags, just hanging on her body, but class stood out all over that girl. Barbara and I both wanted to just take her hand and take her home with us, away from that place.

Can one learn to be classy? Some people say no. You have to be born with it. Many of us are so far away from being classy, it's hard to imagine ever climbing up that far, and we may try and try and never succeed. On the other hand, I'm repulsed by the idea that any of us can be born into a situation, so deep in any hole, that we cannot ever climb out of it, no matter how hard we work. I tend to think yes. With hard work, we can learn to be classy.

I think regional dialects have no place here. We learn to talk like people we live among. Many people tend to look down upon others who do not talk like they talk. I, for example, know a ton of classy hillbillies. Those who look down upon hillbilly slang are shallow people, to my way of thinking. Other shallow people may judge by body build, weight or height. I tend to think physical characteristics of the body one is born with is not a limiting factor. Or, a positive one.

A classy person, generally, just "has it together." We know they are not about to just lose it in the middle of a conversation, and say something stupid.

A classy person is a good listener. Never quick to interrupt, or talk over another person. This whole statement smacks me right in the face. I'm too busy thinking of my reply, or my next statement, to fully listen to another. I need to work on this one. The more I write on this subject, the more I begin to realize where I fit in. So, can thinking too much rule me out? Maybe so, If I can't climb out of that hole. And I'm an old man. Don't have a lot of time to waste.

The "smirk" is a habit that we should be very careful with, especially for a smart person. It can easily convey the message, "I'm smarter than you."

I have a friend who is very smart. He pretty well always has the correct answer. But he usually starts his correction with, "Well, it *could* be that…"

When he does that, I just automatically know he's about to tell me a truth I can count on, take to the bank. A humble preface to a truth conveyed by a very intelligent, classy person. Some people, however, do not respond well to his gentle approach. He and I were once in a van traveling from New Orleans. The driver seemed to think his sense of direction was superior to others. When the driver passed the proper exit, my friend softly stated, "It could be we should have taken that exit." The driver paid no attention. We passed another exit. "We may very well have missed our turnoff." No response. Approaching the next exit, "Turn this thing around!! You missed the road!" This time, the driver responded properly. He had just not had it explained to him in those terms before.

Some people enter a room, and everything about them says, "I'm here! Look at me!" While other people enter a room and everything about them says, "Hello. How are you?" Guess who fits where.

So what have I accomplished with this story? In the end, very little. Food for thought, and that's about it. I have never worried about being classy, myself, possibly because I normally do not occupy a position up at the top, looking down; I seem to spend a lot of time at the bottom, looking up. But I'm me, and I just love me, even if it turns out that, in the end, I'm in a small minority.

A classy person would be very hesitant to put others into a judgmental position in any conversation. So, if we meet on the street, and you ask, "What about me? Am I classy?" Chances are, I would just look at you, smirk, and answer, "I'm far too classy to answer that." Then you'll know.

ON LOOKING FOR A MATE...

MY WIFE BARBARA IS A PHOTOGRAPHER. After she did hundreds of weddings alone, and pretty well ruined her elbows by carrying that heavy suitcase around so much, we became a team. Though I was only a pretend photographer, having not a single creative bone in my body, I did have the mechanics of the camera down pretty well by then, so I took the pics, Barbara posed everyone and hobnobbed with everbody. We wound up doing hundreds of weddings together. (We once did four weddings in 24 hours) So, after being around so many people about to take that plunge, we both began to recognize traits each posessed that would make or break the marriage. Thought I'd pass some of them on to you.

 A guy who has never had a thought about hitting a woman just never speaks of it. If he has ever told you he would never hit you, he has that thought in his head, or he has done it before. If he tells you that regular-like, plan on being a human punching bag after the wedding. Bust outta there!
 Don't marry for looks; looks will fade. (Barbara's the exception!) Character is what lasts forever.
 Watching how he/she treats the family gives you a good idea how you will be treated.
 If you have gone over the top, helping him/her, and been shown little appreciation, he/she has just gotten into the habit of expecting that of you. He/she is taking you for granted already. It will get much worse, but never gets better.

If the wild, bad boy/girl is the only one who attracts you, your life will be one long, living nightmare.

A woman can never change a bad boy. It just gets worse.

If she expects her parents to go into debt, or steal from their retirement fund, to finance her big fancy wedding, she's selfish and self centered. Get away from her. She'll break you, too, and then you'll be history, anyway.

If he/she cheats on you before the wedding, it will increase tenfold after the wedding, when the hot passion with you settles down some. Forgiving can, at best, only buy you an insecure future. First, express your appreciation for having given you this little warning sign, then turn and run. Before its too late.

If you know he/she loves you more than you love him/her, you won't be doing any favors by settling for that. You *will* be doing everyone a big favor by easing out of it now. If the spark is not there now, it never will be. A gentle letdown is in order.

The dominant person will set the pace, and by now you know where you fit in. If the dominant one is not good with money, and goes through it like slicing hot butter, and if you're not that dominant one, get out fast. Hell on earth is headed your way. Best if both are good with money, but that might be a little too much to ask.

When all your friends and family say no, you'd do well to go - - fast! Remember, they're the ones who love you the most.

Watch out for the "Hollywood Syndrome." If he/she requires constant adoration, you won't be able to hold up to those standards very long. And they'll be looking for someone else who will.

Beware of the control freak. If he/she tells you they are the only one who loves you, and are always trying to get you away from family and friends, break the door down if you have to. But get away.

In our wedding photography career, Barbara and I saw a few little tell-tale signs that always prompted us to put a rush order on the pics!

If the bride gripes a lot at her bridesmaids on the wedding day, just remember. She picked them, like she picked you. Don't expect to fare any better after the wedding. You might want to consider sneaking out the back door.

If the bride's Mama is a good Mama who has worked hard to bring this thing together, and the bride gripes at *her* on that day, she's selfish and self-centered. These people don't stay married. Cut your losses and get outta there, however you can.

If you see, on the wedding day, that the wedding itself takes priority over the groom, plan on always playing second fiddle, at best. Start running, and never look back.

If your new husband and your father get into a fist fight at the reception, and yes, we have seen that, It's too late. But you might wish to check about an annulment.

ACCEPTANCE COMES SLOWLY
by JONNIE SUE GILLUM WILLIS

This story was written many years ago by my sister Jonnie, about her struggle with Polio.

MY PARENTS AND MY TWO OLDER BROTHERS and I lived with my Grandma Gillum until I was four and a half years old. From the start, I was the family weaklin'. They tell me that Grandma rocked me in her lap as long as she could hold me. Then I sat beside her as long as there was space. I remember rocking so hard in my own chair that I turned over. This girl might have been sickly, but determination led her to pick up the chair and ride it to many big towns which were foreign to my country environment.

It seems that I had tonsilitis very often. The doctor never considered me well enough to remove my tonsils, until I was grown. Because of my weaknesses, I had to take many medications. Many months of my fifth grade year were spent in bed. I had some problem with my heart, and the doctor advised complete bed rest. Santa Claus brought my gifts to my bedside table that year.

Because of my frailty, Mom insisted that I wear long handles and long stockings to school. My first grade picture reveals my rebellion. The stockings are rolled down and the long handles are rolled up.

Several months of my first grade year I had to stay home battling bronchitis and tonsilitis. By that time, I was so caught up in the magic of reading, writing, and arithmetic that I kept up with my school work at home.

School was such a joy.

As I reached those pre-teen years, I felt it necessary to play as rough as my brothers and sisters. We would ride homemade carts with blinding speed down hills, played in the creek, built playhouses around trees, played ball, rode bushes to the ground, swung on grapevines, and climbed every tree in our yard.

From a very young age, I struggled to get a squeaking sound from our worn-out pump organ. Then one day, I succeeded. That was it! I wanted to play the piano. Of course that was out of the question. We couldn't afford to buy a piano, and there was no piano teacher available in our small rural town of Wing. That didn't keep me from dreaming. I walked around playing the notes with my fingers in the air. One day I found an advertisement for music lessons by correspondence. I begged and pleaded and continued to play in the air until my Dad finally found an old piano that he could afford. Then he agreed to order 12 of the 96 lesson correspondence course. After he saw how faithfully I practiced, how hard I worked, he ordered the remaining lessons. I could picture myself as a famous musician, music teacher, or at least a church pianist. (*This was a major, major concession for Dad, coming at about the time the sharecroppers notes were being paid off after the Depression.*)

In January of 1946, I accepted Christ as my Savior. I was on top of the world. I just knew I'd outgrown the health problems and live happily ever after. Ours was a very busy life, and I always enjoyed my part in our many jobs to be done. When a new brother, Pat, arrived I learned to help with the cooking, housework, food preservation, gardening, etc. I continued to make time for those all-important piano lessons for one year. Thats when my world came tumbling down.

The pain in my neck began on a hot, dry August day in 1946 when I was 13. My right arm was weak. Mom insisted that I rest while she, Jan, and Barbara continued to carry water from the creek, bringing it up the hill to water the flowers. (*Mom always kept a variety of pretty flowers around the house, and always made time to care for them.*) I insisted on carrying a bucket after they got it in the yard. I never realized that this would be the last thing my right arm and hand would ever do.

The next day, I was in bed, in pain, with total paralysis in this arm and hand. My entire body grew weaker as I lay in bed for three days. The country doctor had never seen a case, but he suspected polio. (*That country doctor was uncle Arthur.*) My parents hired a neighbor to take us to a doctor in Russellville. In a short time, he headed us to the University Hospital in Little Rock. After the painful spinal tap, my diagnosis of polio was confirmed. My memory left me after I was rolled through a door with a sign which read, "Isolation Ward - No Admittance." I was put to bed, unconscious, on a Saturday afternoon.

By Tuesday morning, the doctor felt sure that I'd never survive, so he allowed Mom to put on a mask, a gown, and gloves to visit me. Evidently this was the turning point, because I remember the tears flowing as I opened my eyes and saw her. I couldn't talk because of a tube through my nose to my stomach. Also, my entire body except my head was in an iron lung. I can still hear the laborous sound as it forced my lungs to breathe. Since I am a very modest person, I still remember the embarassment as the doctor came to check on me daily, housed in this respirator for a week, no gown or covering was placed over my naked body. The pain in my neck had intensified because of the rubber collar surrounding it. I still have a scar from the irritation of that collar.

Gradually, I learned to breathe without help. Then I was placed on a firm bed with no pillow. My left hand, eyes and mouth were all that moved above my waist. Both arms were tied above my head at night. Later, I learned this was to help my lungs expand.

Two weeks after the initial attack, I was moved to Children's hospital. There was my Dad outside that isolation ward. He had spent many hours there the past two weeks. Tears of joy flowed from my eyes as he rode in the ambulance across town with me. During all this time to save my life, no brush or comb had ever touched my hair. It was matted, tangled, and dirty. I felt like a mess, but I was alive! As soon as they had me in bed one nurse shampooed and brushed my hair. After a bath I began to feel much better.

Now the real workout began. The heat packs felt good to my sore, stiff muscles. Slowly, the physical therapy began to loosen my limbs. Strength gradually returned, and I couldn't wait to be on my feet again. I can still see the frightened shock on the nurse's face the first day I put one foot against the side of my bed and raised myself up. She was afraid I would fall flat on my face, but I didn't! From that day on, I began to experiment to see what I could do. Many days, planning creative ways to do simple daily tasks was half the challenge. There was no time to say "I can't". The act of sitting up in a wheelchair one afternoon was one of the hardest tasks I ever accomplished. I gradually relearned to walk, feed myself, and to write in manuscript with my left hand (before polio, I was right handed.) Soon I was able to help other girls, and I felt like the most blessed girl in the ward.

After three months I was fitted with brace around my body which held my right arm out and up. "Oh please, don't make me wear this out in public," were my thoughts as the nurse strapped it on. The Barnum and Baily Circus had come to Little Rock and the nurse was taking some of us. "You might as well wear this and start getting used to the public," she said as we left the hospital. After I began to enjoy my first circus, I soon forgot how I looked.

Just before Thanksgiving the doctor said I could go home. My dreams of going home and starting to school in the 8th grade had kept me going all those sleepless nights in the hospital. Dad came on the bus to get me. Normally the bus didn't come by our house. However, the driver made an exception and took us to our driveway. Seeing my home again and my family running to meet us brought tears of joy. I was a survivor, and I was home!"

After struggling many months, Jonnie eventually learned to do about anything others could do. She married, raised two girls, and taught school for thirty years. She found a way to cook, can food, and work in their garden. Her right arm and hand was always paralyzed, and her left arm was very weak. She played the church paino, with her left hand. I was shocked once when I heard her say she was the weakest person she ever knew. I always felt she was the strongest person I ever knew.

THE POINT OF NO RETURN

SPORT DUNNAHOE, BARBARA'S FATHER, WAS ONE OF A KIND. A man I will never forget. He was always ready for a fishing, hunting, or camping trip when we got to Watson. Even as an old man, it never bothered him a bit to sleep on the hard ground. If a catfishing trip was in the offing, he hooked up the middle buster, plowed up a strip across the old hog pen, and we picked up a gallon or two of huge buckshot worms. Then we headed for the river.

If there were games to be played by the children, Sport was always the ringleader. Even in his older years, with arthritis in his knees from so many years of following a mule and a plow, he could always keep up. Once, when he was about 65, we were playing touch football. I was just a few years from running college track, and I thought I was a runner. I went out for a pass. Sport was covering me. I just could not shake him! He stuck to me like glue.

When the children and grandchildren got rowdy in the house, Sport just looked at the rowdiest one, stuck out his hand, and said, "Come round' by me, boy!" (Boys and girls alike were "boy" to Sport) They never "came round" by him," they knew the danger in that. But they all exited the room pronto. Mission accomplished. There were always plenty of rowdy kids. I've seen 10 crawling babies on the floor at once in his house. And that was just in the living room.

Once, when Barbara and I were in California, we visited her cousin who grew up near Watson. He said, "When I was a child, every weekend, all us kids showed up at Sport's house. Our own fathers were too tired to play, but Sport never was. He demonstrated to us all how a father should play with his children, and I am a much better father myself because of Sport. He influenced an entire generation of boys, and they are all better fathers because of it."

Although Sport was always loving and protective of his girls, he also taught them to take care of their own problems. Once, just after Barbara started driving, she ran out of gas a quarter mile from home. She walked home, saw Sport in the yard, and told him the truck was out of gas, and started walking in the house. Sport said, "Hey, wait a minute! Go out to the tank, get some gas, and go get the truck. You ran out of gas, not me. Next time, be sure there's plenty of gas in the truck before you head to town."

The one time Barbara remembers disobeying Sport, he had told her she could take the truck to Watson. Well, when she got together with her girl friends, they wanted to go to Dumas, so she took them. The next day, she was torn by guilt, and she told him. He said, "Well, you shouldn't have." That was the end of that.

Sport was endlessly curious. If I showed up at Watson with some minor car problem, the first thing Sport would say would be, "I wonder why a feller couldn't -" and then, he would proceed to tear into the motor to see, stopping when he found out. Or maybe, when the car wouldn't run at all. I soon learned to keep my car problems to myself at Watson.

Watson, in the old days, not that long ago, was a lot like the old west. A man had to look out for himself, and his family. Nobody else would. Sport had a side to him that I never saw, or heard about, until after his death. Sport protected his six girls from the ugly things in life. They never knew about most of what I'm about to tell.

His only son, J.D., was right in the middle of everything with him. And, J.D. carries his genes. He's a lot like him. Once, Sport had loaned Albert, his nephew, his shotgun to hunt with. He handed Sport his gun back just as a Game Warden pulled into the yard behind him. He started ragging Sport pretty good about loaning his gun to that kid. Sport had enough. "Did he hurt anybody with it? Did he damage anyone's property with it?"

"No, but - "

"Then get in your truck and get off my property." The shotgun, still in Sport's hands, added emphasis. He left.

Barbara, as a little girl, witnessed this exchange, a rare event. She was scared they were just going to come and arrest the lot of them.

Sport would just not allow any man to take anything from him. Or push him. If you pushed Sport, there would only be a small number of possible outcomes. Sport would get hurt, you would get hurt, or he would stop you. And Sport always handled that option in such a way that it never happened again. The humiliation prevented that. That is best illustrated by this little example...

Once, a very cranky old neighbor had two large dogs. They were very bad at chasing and killing livestock. They struck Sport's livestock, and Sport went to visit the man. "That has to stop."

The old man said, "You mess with my dogs, and there will be some killing going on."

A few days later, they struck again. Sport had J.D. bring the gun. Sport gave the word as the dog ran by, chasing a calf. J.D, a dead shot like his father, took him out. Soon the other was dead too. Sport loaded them up, and they went to visit the neighbor. Sport threw both the dogs up on the porch, and pounded on the porch with his shotgun. When the old man emerged, saying, "What's going on here?"

Sport said, "You told me, if I messed with your dogs, there would be some killin'. I'm here to start it."

Well, the old man wilted. "Now, don't you worry none about those dogs!" They left.

J.D. was puzzled. "Why did we not just take the dogs down and throw them in the Bayou? He would never have found them."

Sport answered, " If we had done that, that old man would have been bad mouthing us all over the country. This way, there will never be another word said about it." And there wasn't.

One of Sport's cows wandered off into a neighbor's pasture. He sent J.D., a young boy, to get it. The neighbor man told J.D., "It's in my pasture now. It's mine."

When J.D. told Sport, Sport said, "Let's go get it." Sport started up toward the man's house.

J.D. said, "We could cut the fence in the back and get it out."

Sport shook his head. "I'll get it." He walked up by his front door, into the pasture, got behind it, and drove it through the man's front yard. Nothing was ever said.

The road grader man started making his turn through Sport's bean field, taking out more and more of Sport's beans. Sport stopped the man, told him to stop doing that. Well, before long, he did it again. Sport ran him off, this time with a shotgun. A short while later, the County Judge found the road grader man a new place to turn around.

A rich, big landowner bought up some land next to Sport. Told Sport, "The old survey is wrong. You'll have to move your fence back 50 feet."

Sport replied, "That fence has been there since 1927. It stays there."

Well, a while later a couple of surveyors showed up, started setting up their equipment. Sport and J.D. walked down. Sport: "Nothing is going to be changed down here."

The surveyor started explaining, "We're doing the job we were hired to do, check these old lines."

Sport said, "I've got a shotgun here that says you're not going to survey anything here."

The younger man wanted to get bad, but JD stopped him. "You just really don't understand the situation. If that old man says you don't, you don't. For your own sake, you best go home."

The older man toned the younger one down, and they went home. They never came back.

The girls, for the most part, never knew about any of this. Their sweet Daddy could just never have said any of those words. And that fits right in with my daughter Kinley's memories of sitting in his lap, putting rollers in his hair, and painting his fingernails. But in the "wild west" of the early Delta country, a man had to stand his ground or just move. Sport never moved.

I fully believe all of this for two very good reasons. First, J.D. is just like him. Second, I've seen those strong genes of Sport's in every one of those girls, cropping up from time to time. They call it "Dunnahoe Nerve." They are all very strong women, always ready to stand up to whatever life throws at them. All us inlaws were very fortunate to find a member of this family to scoop up and marry.

Sport just had that unique ability to be a fun loving, lovable person, always loved dearly by all those around him. But he had rather die than allow himself to be pushed. If Sport Dunnahoe had been my father, I could never have loved or respected him more. When I fished with Sport's grandsons, and great grandsons, I came to realize, some of them only know Sport Dunnahoe by his name. I hope, in writing this, they will come to realize what a great man he was. On my "Great men I have known" list, Sport Dunnahoe stands right up there with the best of em'. An ancestor to be proud of.

Later in life, Sport was diagnosed with dementia, but he never lost his sense of humor. A doctor was interviewing him in his office to determine the extent. "Mr. Dunnahoe, what is today's date?"

"Thursday, August 4."

"Very good, Mr. Dunnahoe. How did you do that so easily?"

With a little grin on his lips, Sport replied. "Its on the calendar, right behind you." Another time, he was in another doctor's office with a daughter. The doctor came in. She immediately started giving instructions to the daughter, ignoring him. She was saying, "Take one tablet, four times a day, and --"

Sport was pulling on the daughter's sleeve, with that little grin. "What is it, Mr. Dunnahoe?"

"Well, that just looks like it would be sorta hard – taking the same pill, 4 times a day."

"Point well taken, Mr. Dunnahoe. The next time I will talk to *you* about your medicine."

Barbara was taking Sport home from the hospital. At the door, she instructed, "Stay right here while I go get the car. Don't move."

Sport was getting around pretty slow by now, and said, "I could start right now and not get outta' sight by the time you get back."

Sport left us all with a vast array of "Sport-isms.". My favorite is, "Bein' right won't help yore' old haid' none."

After Verla Mae died, Sport just couldn't go on without her. He gently explained to all his girls, "I just can't live without her." Just a few months later, Phyllis found him dead in his bed one morning. The paramedics said it must have been a heart attack, there was a blue spot on his chest. But we all knew. A broken heart is just one kind of heart attack. Verla Mae's death had pushed Sport to the point of no tomorrow.

THE THING ABOUT THE RIVER

THE THING ABOUT THE RIVER IS, it has held a lifelong fascination for me, whether it be fishing, frog hunting, or just floating along, watching and listening to the wildlife that lives in, on, or along it. The river is a wonderful place. The pursuit of several animals that prowl below and near its surface has pushed me to travel to the far corners of Arkansas (wow!) and even beyond.

Now take the catfish. They reside in almost all significant rivers of Arkansas, but the concentration in the far southeast corner of Arkansas surpasses all. To my way of thinking, the entire Delta, excluding the people I love who live there, is a bit bland. Until you get near or inside the river levees. Then it becomes transformed into one of the most wonderful places on earth. The concentration of all wildlife is greater. They have been crowded out of the farmed portion of the Delta, and concentrated into these long crooked stretches of natural perfection. The lure of these whiskered monsters of the deep in the river delta has brought about so many of the memorable occasions in my life that this story has to be told.

Like my three very close approaches to death, all at Wargo. Wargo is simply one of the many oxbow lakes off the lower Arkansas River. I was once camped on a high bluff on Wargo. My partner in this adventure, as so often was the case in the old days, was Sport Dunnahoe, my father in law. I loved him like a father. An eighty foot tree was leaning far out over the water at the top of the bluff upon our arrival. Soon it would fall into the lake and disappear along with a good portion of the bluff around it.

Naturally, we moved our campsite well back from it as a precaution. Our catfish lines were set and baited. We went to sleep. In the middle of the night, we awoke to an earthquake, or so we thought. We peeked out of the tent. The entire bluff, pulled by the falling tree, had caved off, leaving our tent, and us, perched on the very edge of the bluff. The tree had totally disappeared, buried under many tons of river sand.

On another occasion, JD Dunnahoe, my brother in law, and I had just finished baiting our catfish lines on the far side of the lake, when a major thunderstorm struck right at dark. We started back across the lake in our small boat. The thing about the river is, when the waves are pushed by heavy winds, rain, and lots of lightning and thunder, it can transform quickly into a place one does not wish to be. We made it across without incident. I dropped JD off at his truck, then I turned into the teeth of the storm to head for the boatramp. The thing about a small, light boat, with most of the weight now concentrated in the back is, the front end sticks up high into the howling wind. I had just gotten started when a strong gust of wind picked up the boat – and I was airborne! Time slows down, up in the air. I had time to ask myself, "Where's my life vest?" and "Can I swim a lick with this rain gear on?" Then, I was dropped back to the water, the boat turned 180 degrees. I forgot about the ramp and struggled toward the shore, and for survival.

The thing about Wargo is – you have two choices: You can fish it and be cold, or you can fish it and be swarmed by hoards of mosquitoes. There is a very small window in between. I often chose the early spring.

Camped alone, I struggled out of my tent on a cold morning. My fire from the previous night was completely out, or so I thought. I picked up a gallon can of gasoline, stood back, and sloshed a long stream onto the remaining wood.

The thing about fire is – it can come to life from a single small spark, and run up a long slosh instantly. I found myself standing, with a giant flamethrower in my hand. I slung it – far. It may be a while before I fish Wargo again, but when I do, I will be sure all my affairs are in order first.

Not all my memorable experiences at Wargo were life threatning. Once Sport and I were asleep in our tent with only a very small hole in our almost-zipped-up doorway. The thing about small holes, though, is - it sorta negates being enclosed in a tent in the first place. In the middle of the night, Sport roused me from my dreams with an elbow to the ribs. "Pat," he said, " We are not alone." I switched on my light. The prettiest, most bushy tailed skunk I've ever seen was sitting on Sport's sleeping bag. We quietly enlarged that hole, and slid outside in our whitey-tighties, and waited, shivering. Fifteen minutes later, the skunk strolled out and off, never having left his calling card.

The thing about a family chock full of pretty daughters, like the Dunnahoes, is – sooner or later a whole herd of son-in-laws will fill that old home place on holidays, especially Verla Mae Dunnahoe's house. She seldom spoke, but when she did, it was law. We were all there for Christmas. The thing about men, especially young men, is – they are chock full of testosterone. They are driven to seek excitement, in one or more of its forms daily. It's a requirement of life.

We men were once sitting around relaxing after a big Christmas dinner at the Dunnahoe farm. Someone mentioned the river, and I woke up. I always slept through all those long discussions about farming. They bored me to death. The river is really rolling right now, someone was saying. "Let's go see it"! someone else chimed in. "Why don't we take the boat?" We loaded up the boat and headed for the river. As I think about it, forty some-odd years removed, only an irrational craving for excitement or extremely poor judgement could have brought about what happened on that cold winter day.

So, I and my in-laws loaded into that small boat and headed up river. The boat was far too small for that crowd, and not a life jacket was in sight. Sport was the only one old enough to have better sense, but there was no way, I mean no way, Sport would let himself be left out when a river adventure beckoned. Not even up to the day he died. The twenty horse motor pushed us up the rolling river. A rock levee extended well out into the river ahead. JD pushed the boat toward the end of the levee. The thing about rolling river water is – when it hits the end of a rock levee, a huge whirlpool can develop, and suck down anything that enters it. JD steered the boat around the levee. Suddenly we went down – down into the heart of the whirlpool. All around us was a whirlpool of water. Time to say our prayers.

JD opened up the motor full throttle. The motor strained. We whirled with the water. Ever so slowly, the motor pushed the boat to the side of the whirlpool; then, even more slowly, we climbed. As we pulled out, finally, we were all ready to go back to that warm living room, ready to be bored the rest of the day. Talking about farming didn't seem quite so bad. Our appetites were sated, for that day.

Once I was floating with my brother-in-law, Delton, down the White River to the Mighty Mississippi, then floated past the mouth of the Arkansas River to Arkansas City. We reached the mouth of the White River about sundown, and camped on a sandbar. The mosquitoes were beyond the edge of comprehension. In pioneer times, nobody could live here long, with malaria running rampant. The grave yard at Napoleon, Arkansas, a town there that no longer exists but was here in pioneer days, left lots of tombstones. Few, if any, died here that were older than 26. Anyway, we set up our tent, sprayed the doorway down good with mosquito repellent, dashed in and zipped it up quick. Then we spent the next hour picking off the mosquitoes inside, one at a time. Then, we could sleep. Or we would have, had it not been for the buck deer who resented our presence so much, he spent the night dashing up and down behind our tent, stomping and snorting. Anyway, now we can get down to the scientific work. By morning, my body was stopped up tighter than a drum. I took a good dose of castor oil, the most horrible tasting stuff God ever created, but one of the most effective. We then shoved off from the mouth of the White, down the mighty Mississippi. By the time we reached the mouth of the Arkansas River, I was rushing ashore to the bushes.

The thing about floating a major river is – you have lots of time to think. By the time we had reached Arkansas City, I had finished my calculations. It is six miles, 31,680 feet, from one river mouth to the next. The Big Muddy rolls along at approximately six MPH. The human digestive tract is 23 feet long. Using that raw data, castor oil must run through the human body at a rate of .0007 MPH. Something I had always wondered about.

The thing about the river is – some creatures can live both in and near it. They normally breathe air with their lungs and have to surface regularly when active. But with the coming of winter, they can bury up in the mud of the river bottom, get real still, and take in enough oxygen through their skin to live.

Such is the bullfrog, which is in the process of disappearing from this earth as I speak. Their numbers have dropped alarmingly in my lifetime. Now let's move our focus to the far northwest corner of Arkansas, to Fayetteville. My friend Bob and I decided to try our hand at catching bullfrogs on the west fork of the upper White River near Fayetteville. It had rained quite a bit, but it looked doable on the wide stretch of the river where we put in.

The thing about the river is – it can flow slowly in a wide eddy, even when up. When a narrow chute comes up, it can pick up the pace drastically. We were downriver half a mile before such a chute appeared, past the point of no return. We came around a bend, and our lights picked up a log, stretching from side to side, right at water level. Too late. We hit it, the boat turned sideways, we took on water on the backside, and our boat was swamped. We were held tightly against the log in the swift current. I looked downriver. Our gear was headed to Beaver Lake, accompanied by our lights, their beams swinging back and forth like searchlights at an airport. We tied the boat to the log, (I don't know why, it was going nowhere.) I floated downstream, gathering up what gear I could find. When I got back, Bob had salvaged what he could. He was now walking across the log, gear in hand. He had my large landing net in one hand, which should not have been in the boat at all on a frog hunting trip. Bob slipped slightly at mid stream, slowly sat down on the log, then even more slowly was pulled off and under the log by the current. When he surfaced downstream, he shouted, "My glasses! I've lost my glasses!"

You must understand. Bob's glasses were as thick as coke bottles, and he couldn't see a lick without them. And, they cost a pretty penny. Like me, he was dirt pore. This was a big deal. I looked up. Bob's glasses were perfectly balanced on the rim of my landing net, which was still in his hand. "Hold very still, Bob!" I shouted, as I swam over and grabbed them.

We finally righted the boat, sloshed most of the water out, and continued on. We had never floated this section of the river in the daylight, a big mistake. We soon entered a long hole that was filled with logs from end to end. We had to swim, pulling the boat over, under, around, and through. When the river merged with the main White River, it grew much wilder.

The thing about chill bumps - they start on one's lower back, slowly spreading upwards. They finally come across the top of the head, and stop, right above the eyes. Such was the case with me, as I sat listening. Listening to the wild rapids below, between us and my truck. It proved to be a long night, productive only in everlasting memories.

The thing about poor schoolteachers-the family has to eat. During the summer, I worked at whatever job I could find. I once worked for a plumbing outfit in Fayetteville. When they discovered I was a good, hard worker, they stopped renting a backhoe. I became a human backhoe, at thirty dollars a week. I told my working buddies about my frog hunting trips. One could float a five mile stretch on one of the pretty, clean rivers around there, and pick up as many bullfrogs as a family could eat in a while, in those days. The loud, deep bellow of a large bullfrog is seldom heard on the river nowadays. Then, one could hear a dozen at a time. There is no sound quite like it.

One very large guy wanted to go with me. He was not a nice person – big, tough, and rowdy. I finally agreed. We placed my truck on the War Eagle River, drove five miles up and put my boat in. As we sat around waiting for it to get dark, we were joined by an old timer, who talked our ears off. Sensing my partner was a true greenhorn who had never been on the river at night, he proceeded to tell a string of water moccasin horror stories. After a few, my partner got up, went to his truck, and got two rolls of duct tape. He proceeded to wrap a whole roll around one leg, right up to his hip. Then he did the other leg. I was beginning to have misgivings about this expedition. But we were there, committed. When it got dark, we headed down river.

The thing about the river in those days was – the old timer's stories were true. In the space of time that I now see one moccasin on the river today, I would see 10 then. They are disappearing too. Far too many people beating on their heads with a chunk. For every two bullfrogs we picked up, we saw one snake. Those rivers are so clean, and weed free, we had no need for a gig. Just keep the light in their eyes, slowly ease up on them, look around to make sure it is not also a target for a nearby snake, then pick it up. After I had picked up several frogs, and we had seen several snakes, my partner had lost all his bluster. He was shaking like a leaf. After another mile, tears were rolling down his face, and he simply would not get out of the boat. The thing about pulling a light boat over a shoal is; empty, it was easy. But add a whimpering 280 pounder, and it was back-killing work. It didn't help the bottom of the boat any, either. We were nearing halfway, over two miles to my truck. I could balk, and hope he was anxious enough to get home to get out of the boat, or I could just pull him the rest of the way. I just bowed up and did it.

The only other noteworthy experience on the rest of that trip was passing through a giant, new hatch of mayflies. They were so thick, one could not inhale without taking one in. When we did pass on through, the boat had an inch of mayflies in the bottom.

The thing about the river at night is, it just does that to some people. I once had a big, tough football coach in the front of my boat at night. We passed under a low hanging limb, a roost of birds thundered out, and he just ran to my end of the boat, sat in my lap, and sank the boat. Farther down, a large beaver, for some reason, went against his naturally mild, shy nature, planted himself in the middle of a riffle, and made it plain that he had no intentions of letting us pass. I had to get out and do battle with him with a boat paddle, while my partner hung in the back of the boat. The wild river at night is not for everybody.

It took two people, and two trucks, to do this right. I became more selective in my partners, and they became harder to find. I had to hunt less. I have only been snake bitten once in all my frog hunting days. The telltale two fang marks of a poisonous snake were on my ankle, and we headed for the hospital. On the way, we passed a farm where two men, an midnight, were gathering sweet corn from someone's patch. When we got to the emergency room, I felt a bit silly, because it never swelled up or discolored. I guess I was sorta wishing it would when the doc came in. All I could figure was, the snake had already used up his venom on another victim.

Frog legs, properly cooked, are the best of wild eating. But they do move around in the skillet, when cooked fresh.

The thing about me is, there have been two distinct periods in my life when the pull of catfishing the river has been really strong. I have related to you some of the high and low times of the first period, when young blood coursed through my veins. During the early years of our marriage, that was the single largest problem Barbara had with me. I was gone too much at night, on the river. Most of those times, I was gone all night. That period tapered off and ended many years ago, though all the reasons are hard to put my finger on. As a young boy, we truly needed the wild meat for food. It was that or eat salt pork, period. And the salt pork did not keep into the summer. When Barbara and I married , that need lessened, because Barbara didn't like to cook it. Then the need for wild meat disappeared. But I still loved the river, and my attraction for the river was transferred more toward wildlife photography, float trips, etc. Then, thirty years later, after I retired, I began thinking more and more about my catfishing days, and I missed them. I have not yet caught the big one, three 25 pounders about topped it out. After much soul searching, I made a deal with my soul. I would not kill it if it was not to be eaten or for bait. I often, especially around my grand children, use the Indian custom of thanking the fish for giving its life for our food. I have been more successful in my second period. I went through the learning curve a lifetime ago. For the last three years, I caught enough in one trip to feed the church catfish fry, seventy people or so. Several times. Up to 400 pounds per two-day trip.

I started writing my stories about my second catfishing period; then I realized they were all about me being clumsy, stumbling about, falling in the river, ruining one cell phone after another. Or about the boat getting away from me, having to swim for it. Or, being caught down river in a huge thunderstorm, and having to hunker down while it rained two inches, lightening striking the river around me. All because my outdoor senses are now dull. Or about how much my knees ache after a day in a small boat. Nobody wants to read that mess. I threw the stories away. Lots of catfish, but no good stories. And the only really BIG catfish got away trying to load it in the boat. But he's still out there, just waiting for me. We will meet again.

The thing about me, though - I just keep going to the wild places, until a pretty good story comes of it. The thing about Neal Nelson is – he just keeps letting me tag along until a good story is created. Such was the case last April.

Neal invited me along on his fishing/floating/turkey hunting trip with him, his dad Travis, and Scott Jackson. Neal and Scott are my pastors. Travis is retired, as am I. We planned a five day trip to float the last 17 miles of the river. The thing about the lower Buffalo is – it is relatively calm. It kinda gets a couple of old guys overly confident.

Neal sent out instructions telling us all what we could and could not take. But nobody took it seriously enough. We wound up at Rush with enough food and gear to keep an army comfortable for five days.

I was traveling with Travis. We loaded our flatbottom boat down good. Too good. Hardly had room for us to get in. The thing about Neal is, he is an all – around outdoorsman of the first order. The best I've seen. Neal scouted the first rapids. He shouted, "Stay hard left" on the L shaped rapids. Travis and I went first, he in front, me in back. I was hugging left. Travis said, "Pull right! We have to go right of that bush!" I did. When we got to the turn, I knew we were too close to the middle.

The thing about many rapids is, the largest waves are thrown up at the end. In the middle. We hit the big waves, expecting the front of the boat to ride the top of them. The heavy front end went under them. Neal was watching from above. "Hey, they made it!" Then, a moment later, "But they sure look awfully short!" Our boat floated, just under the water. Our gear was washing out. Our motor was under water. Fortunately for us, though I would not have wished it on them, two boatloads of turkey hunters were ahead of us. One of them swamped also. They were in position, gathering up their gear, and they started picking up ours also. Neal and Scott quickly crossed the rapids uneventfully, and started helping. One of the other boats approached us, and started giving us our gear. One said, "I've also got a garbage bag with a backpack in it." "Not mine," I said. We weren't planning any backpacking.

We pulled over to a gravel bar, and began spreading out stuff out to dry. The other group picked out a bar on down river. They finished first and went on. They had lost a valuable gun. Travis had lost very valuable rods. I lost two rods, myself, but they were garage sale specials, as is most of my stuff. We decided to spend the night there. Later, I realized all my clothes, including my coat, were gone. All the clothes I had left was the wet ones I had on, still wet, and we were looking at a cold spring night.

The river took all my clothes. Three days later, the river gave them all back to me, all dried and neatly packed.

I always pause here, in telling this story, for effect – to see if anyone will react to that last statement. No one normally does. WHAT WERE THEY THINKING? Does that seem like the natural course of events here? Does the river just normally take all your clothes, then spit them out, at your feet, three days later? Good grief! Are they thinking we have some sort of Jonah thing going on, since we have two preachers along? Or, more likely, have they not been listening to a thing I said. I vote for Jonah, but suspect the latter.

Actually, I remembered later. They were all in a daypack, the "backpack" the other hunters found. As it turned out, they were camped far down the river. We finally met one of their boats coming back up river, told the guys they were ours, and when we got there three days later, the clothes were all dried, re-packed nicely, left lying on a gravel bar for us. I was so tired of those filthy, wet clothes I had been wearing three days. Travis and I had to wait awhile for Neal and Scott there anyway, the other hunters weren't home, so we just stripped and took a bath, right in front of their camp. Other boats going upriver ran us into the bushes a couple of times, though.

After Travis and I had swamped a perfectly good boat in the first fifteen minutes of our trip, I think Neal and Scott feared we had gone senile. Just taken these guys along one year too many. When another fairly large rapids came up, Neal kept coming up with, "How about Scott or I take your boat across?" or, "Why don't we just tie a rope on your boat and ease it over?"

Travis and I would have died first. Our manhood was being called into question. "I was taking boats through worse places when you two pipsqueaks were still sucking a bottle," I was thinking. I felt sure Travis was too, though we never spoke of it.

The thing about Scott Jackson is – he has an outfit called Outdoor Discipleship Ministries, and he takes groups of young people to the deepest, highest, darkest parts of the world, seeking unreached people for Christ. He is the perfectly organized camper. He had every kind of condiment we could have found at home: every kind of coffee, additives, everything – all perfectly organized in a cute little box.

A few days into our trip, Scott and Neal were scouting for turkeys. Travis and I, not hunting, were in our usual position – in our chairs on a gravel bar. When they returned, Scott noticed a biological phenomenon. Dozens of beautiful butterflies, both Zebra and Swallowtail, were swarming around a wet spot in the sand. Scott was determined to get to the bottom of this. Why this wet spot, why not others? Maybe a strange spring bringing exotic chemicals to the surface. He dug in the sand there. He examined it very closely. The true, latent biologist was awakening in him. Finally, fearing he was about to taste it, I could stand it no longer. "Uh, Scott, that's where I peed."

Neal's true nature was revealed to us on that trip, though it was no surprise to any of us. Neal is the expert turkey hunter, Scott the novice. In the last place they hunted, and in the most likely, they sat side by side, full camo. Scott held the only gun. Neal called; a gobbler answered. This went back and forth a long time. Finally, Neal saw the gobbler. It was hidden from Scott. They waited for it to walk into Scott's vision; it just would not. Turkey hunters know. If you move, he's gone. Finally, the turkey was in the position for a perfect shot for Neal. Scott insistently scooted the gun over to Neal. Neal reluctantly drew a bead on the big gobbler. He had him dead to rights. His finger would just not pull the trigger. Neal's nature would not allow it. He spends his life, doing things for others before himself. That servant nature would not allow him to call a turkey in for Scott, then shoot it himself. At long last, the turkey strolled away.... Scott free, so to speak.

The thing about my second catfishing career is – the good stories, and the 40 pound cat, are still out there, waiting somewhere beyond the next bend in the river. Actually, in case you have not yet suspected it, my lifelong love for the river is not really primarily centered on how many, or how large the catch is. Rather, it is all about just being out there.

If you slide a 14 foot flatbottom boat into the gentle waves of the river at daybreak, maybe a family of beaver will be swimming around, slapping their tails. Possibly, an otter will be floating on his back, a shellfish on his chest, using a stone to try to open it. You may see a pair of wood ducks take flight through the mist rising off the river. Perhaps a big cottonmouth will swim by, floating like a long balloon on top of the water. You might, hopefully, hear a big bullfrog roar, like his namesake, in the distance. Sometimes, a doe and newborn fawn will come down for a drink.

Paddle along quietly for awhile, then just drift. And look. And listen. Then, you will know why I love the river.

UNCLE FRANZ

I WAS BORN WHEN MY DAD was 52, my mom 40. The youngest of the Gillum Wing generation. My cousins were grown and gone, all my siblings were gone by the time I was 12. So, I pretty well grew up with all the old folks. The Gillums mostly lived side by side, or about as close to side by side as we got in Wing. A mile apart.

Most of my uncles and my dad were pretty serious, no nonsense, hard men. At least, they were by the time I came along. I never knew any of them when young blood flowed through their veins.

But Uncle Franz was different. He still laughed a lot, and he found things in life to enjoy. He was very, very, smart. He spent much of his working life teaching, as an administrator, or as a Civilian Conservation Corps director after the depression. He had retired by the time my memories of him began. He came back to Wing, built a house, a big fishing pond, got land and cattle. His girls were still finishing up school, so Aunt Grace hung out at Conway until they were grown. He was so sick of dressing up every day, he came back living and dressing like a sure enough hillbilly.

He taught at Fountain Hill awhile. He told me once they lived in a pretty rough part of town, and when they came back to Wing for a visit, (Everybody from Wing comes back as often as they can. Wing is just about the perfect place to be. Just about. The one thing missing is a lot of options about what to do for a living. So he, like me, had to scramble around in other, lesser parts of the world to make a living and raise a family.) He was a little worried about his house and his stuff while he was gone. So, he found the biggest, roughest, meanest man in the neighborhood, took him his house key, and asked him to watch his stuff while he was gone. That worked perfectly. Nobody ever messed with his stuff. I told you he was smart. It was a hard day's drive from Southeast Arkansas in those days, what with all the mud holes to get through.

Uncle Franz seemed to go to bed about the time the chickens went to roost. But he was up by the middle of the night, and a whole lot of that time, he was pounding on his old, beat up typewriter. I saw him doing that many times, but never knew what he was doing in those days. It was not until recently, when I began to see some of his work, that I realized he was a world-class poet. But his work seems to be pretty much lost to the world. The copies of his poems that I have been able to get my hands on are pretty dim, probably copies of copies of copies from an old typewriter not much good to begin with. But I'm going to do the best I can to figure out some of them, and share them with you. Hope you like them too.

Three Shots Rang Out

A man was riding on parade
A great good man who fervently prayed
For peace and freedom the wide world O'er
When three shots rang out and he's no more.

A man so young and sincere too
Ambition spurred to drive him through
A fearless man with wisdom's store
But three shots rang out and he's no more.

A speechless world rose quick and fast
To honor him whose soul had passed
From life through death to live once more
For in hearts those shots closed not the door.

A mortal form lies lifeless now
No wicked worry to fret his brow
Yet he's greater now than e'er before
Since three shots rang out and he's no more.
**

No Sparkles Show

Sometimes the dew on blades of grass
That crowd in over the padded path
And hide the footprints in the dirt
Goes by unnoticed as I work.

No sparkling diamond hue I see
Because my eyes are so busy
Searching for another sight
A little spot of red and white.

It's hidden somewhere in the grass
I must not miss it as I pass
Of course it probably would be
As well that I did not see.

Yet something inside me tells me "no"
And that's the reason no sparkles show
On blades of grass when wet with dew
At early day when morn is new.

Dew sparkling grass is just as wet
And sparkles just as bright, still yet
It bothers me not as much by half
When looking for a newborn calf.
**

Oh my gosh what was that
That weird sound out yonder?
Sounds just like a squalling cat
followed then by rolling thunder.
Curiosity got the best of me
Out the window I looked to see.

Then quick as lightning's flash
I rushed over to the window
Pulling up the bottom sash
I saw kids on the biggest bender
No, not drunk, I didn't say
Just a frolicking group at prankster's play.

On they came so thick and fast
Noisy costumed witches leading.
Followed behind by lad and lass
Street decorum knew no heeding.
Turned the corner down my street
And at the door yelled "trick or treat!"

Treat. The choice was made post haste.
What was left for me to do?
I knew I had no time to waste
When I viewed closely this weird crew
Dressed so spooky from head to feet
Playing innocently "trick or treat."
**

Uncle Franz drove his Farmall Cub tractor by our house just about every morning. I knew he was going to check his cows. But I also knew that before lunch, he would be down at the lake or the river, fishing. If I was able to get loose, I grabbed my pole and headed down that way. Sitting on the river bank with Uncle Franz, catching one bream after another, was always time very well spent. I always rode out on the back of his tractor.

In his later days, a doctor discovered he had an aneurism in his stomach. He was told that if it burst, he would die before he could get to a hospital. Uncle Franz said, "That sounds like a good way to go." He had no operation. A while later, he did go. Just that way.

COACH

I FIRST MET BILL MAYO at my church, a couple of years ago. He, and his wonderful wife Margie, had just moved to Arkadelphia. I liked him immediately. He was one of the nicest guys I had ever met. He was humble. He apologized at the least provocation. I saw right off that he never took any credit for anything he or anybody around him had ever done. All that credit automatically went to God or somebody else. He knew more about football than anybody I had ever run onto, and he talked more about sports than anybody I had ever talked to. After our discussions that day, I started calling him *Coach,* and it has pretty well stuck ever since. Becoming one of my best friends ever seems to have pretty much stuck for always, also.

Bill was born in Blytheville, Arkansas, the only child of William Bert and Lillian Mayo. Bill attended Blytheville High School, where he played football and participated in track and field. The home Bill grew up in was eventually given to the city of Blytheville, (by Bill,) designated for a place for poor people to live. Who woulda guessed.

He attended Arkansas State, where he, of course, played football. He was a guard. According to people around Bill, he was very good, playing above his physical stature. Later, he was a graduate assistant.

Bill coached one year at Osceola, where he also taught science, world history, and math.

He was called for active duty Army. He was assigned to Fort Sill in Lawton, Oklahoma. He and Margie decided to get married first, so they did, then took off to Lawton as a sort of substitute honeymoon. Soon, his general realized he was a full-fledged football man, and he was assigned as the line coach for the Second Battle Group, 39th Infantry. Bill was active duty two years, in the reserves for six years, and on standby for eight years.

In 1959-60, Bill was the assistant football and track coach at Blytheville. Bevo, a ninth grader at Blytheville who was too old to play for the junior team, came over to play with the senior team. (His nickname came from the University of Texas mascot.) Bevo's junior high coach came by. He was down on one knee, chewing bubble gum and filming. Bevo's junior coach watched – Bill was working them hard – "Bevo, are these coaches tough?"

"Don't know, Coach."

"Why don't you know, Bevo?"

"Haven't fought them yet."

In 1961, Bill's first head coaching job took him to Trezevant High School in Memphis, a brand new high school. He was using all sophomore players against full high school teams. The team was not expected to win any games for three years. Bill had to start out teaching the very basic fundamentals to these players. His first step, the summer before, was to visit the families of all his prospective players. He went to the home of the Talley boys, Phil and Steve. He thought it a bit odd that they were sitting in the car, reading funny books. Come to find out, they had no air conditioner in the house.

There were lots of ups and downs that first year. One positive thing, his quarterback completed 31 out of 35 passes in one game.

Many of Bill's players were interviewed by me for this story. Almost to a man, they showed great emotion and respect when speaking of Bill.

After four years, his original beginners moved on. Bill could not stand the idea of staying there without them, so he moved to Amarillo as first assistant football coach at Caprock High School.

In 1965, the opportunity he had always wanted came along – coaching at the college level, at Southwestern-at-Memphis. During his time there, he was offensive and defensive line coach, and head track coach. I interviewed several of Bill's fellow coaches. One fact kept coming up in their comments – although Bill was primarily a football coach, he worked equally hard in all the sports he coached. And, he was equally concerned that they would all succeed.

In 1970, he coached at Emory and Henry College in Virginia. He called one coach to schedule a game, and the coach informed him that he would not play against him, even if Bill brought Emory and left Henry behind.

In 1971, he was called as athletic director back home in Blytheville. The school board was determined to hire the best athletic director they could find, to rebuild a program that was very far down. They had won very few football games in the last ten years. They had not won a homecoming game in all that time.

Bill called on a number of men in the community to help rebuild the facilities. Bill stressed to his coaches "Never brag about what *we* have done. Always give credit to others, the town."

An indoor field house (with indoor football practice field) was built. New nets for baseball, as well as soccer, were installed. Cheerleading, baseball workout, and weight rooms were built. A new girl's gym was constructed. A coaches conference room and coaches offices were added.

New weight facilities were added. The football stadium, along with new lights, was upgraded. Separate gymnastics facilities were built to prevent crowding. All this was done with very little expense to the school.

The best football coach he could find was hired, even though he had to go against the wishes of many in the community to do so, because Blytheville was primarily a basketball power at that time.

The first year he was there, the football team won two

games. The second year, five were won. The third year, they were undefeated in the regular season. They lost to Texarkana in the state finals.

When Bill looks back at what was accomplished he realized that, in some way or another, God led the way for all this to happen. In his heart he realized that in all that had been done, God had prepared him to be a good athletic director, so that much could be accomplished.

When Bill retired as an athletic director in 1996, he rejoiced. He had accomplished much, mentoring new coaches and providing them with great facilities. The coaches were given what they needed to be successful. Bill is very thankful for the close personal relationships he has established through the years.

When asked once if he realized he was a legend in Arkansas, he replied, "I don't know why – after all, coaches coach, and athletic directors sit." Par for the course for Bill Mayo – the credit must be passed on to others. God had given him the secret for getting things done, empowering others. During all the time I have known Bill, if anyone ever mentions to others all Bill has accomplished, he immediately says, "I did nothing. God did it all."

Part Two

Much of what I have written in this story, up to this point, is "About Bill, according to Bill." I soon realized that Bill will not brag about himself. To tell you a full story about Bill, I must write part two, "About Bill, according to others." This includes interviews with men he coached, men who were team mates, and people who had simply known Bill for a long time. I would love to include many coaches of Bill's during his playing days. But, Bill is around 85 or so. 'Nuff said. These men spoke with great emotion when talking about Bill Mayo.

Harris Warbington, Bill's quarterback at Trezevant High School – *"Twenty came out for football the first year. Eighteen remained after the first week. Nine never left the field. We worked very hard. Later, army basic training and football in college was a cakewalk by comparison. We never lost a football game because of conditioning. Bill was always one of my heroes. He still is. He taught us that heart is more important than anything else. If you care enough, you can accomplish most anything.*

When I came out to practice the first day, I was finishing off a scrambled egg sandwich. He got all over me. Coach told me to never show up for practice not ready to play. He told me I was the quarterback, the leader. He knew I would not quit, no matter what.

Bill's yard was rolled with toilet paper. I had nothing to do with it. He called me up, told me to be at his house in fifteen minutes, ready to clean up that mess. And, bring help. After that, we players put the word out at school. Nobody was to bother his yard. We knew who would end up cleaning it all up.

Bill's main thing was his honesty, and how detail oriented he was. I survived many things later in life because of the toughness he instilled in me. Now, nearly fifty years later, Bill calls me two or three times a year, and talks for over an hour. When I played in college, years later, I realized other coaches were not like Bill Mayo. We learned from Bill: surround yourselves with like-minded hearts, and you can get things done."

George Roberts, running back at Trezevant – "In three years under Bill's leadership, I never heard a bad word. Bill stood up for his players with other teachers. He would listen to a player's feelings, trust our judgement. He taught us to never let a bad situation get us rattled. He was primarily a football coach, but he cared greatly about other sports. Track, basketball, etc. We never talked on the bus before a game. Coach added ten or so plays each game, new to the other coaches. (Bill commented that some were the same plays from a different set.) We were completely prepared for each game. Each week, the two who played the best/hardest were the captains the next week.

One thing Bill Mayo never learned – how to have a short practice."

Larry Wright, Bill's first football coach he hired as athletic director at Blytheville – "Bill was a hard worker. A smart, hard worker. A fine gentleman who really hustled. I learned a lot from Bill about strategy. Bill worked very hard to get new equipment for his team and coaches. Bill would do anything for his coaches. He worked so well with me. Blytheville football had been way down for many years when Bill took over. After just a few years, we were undefeated."

Doug Quinn was the last football coach ever hired by Bill. He was from Mena, but was hired from the University of Georgia. He remained at Blytheville for 22 years. He was very articulate and a good coach.

Bruce Hay played football while Bill was athletic director at Blytheville, then went on to play football at Arkansas. He then returned to Blytheville where he lived (and knew Bill a long time.)– "Bill was a good player himself. It was difficult for Bill to hire a top notch football coach, because Blytheville was big on basketball. But he got it done, and the results unified the town. Everybody loved Bill. His wife, Margie, may well have been my best teacher. She taught me typing, and I know what a great teacher she was.

There were far more of Blytheville's athletes placed on college scholarships during Bill's tenure than at any other time, before or since."

From Gary Briley, a good football player for Larry Wright while Bill was athletic director at Blytheville - "Coach Mayo was a fine gentleman. A good man. He was totally instrumental in everything done to help the program at Blytheville. Coach Wright was loud, Coach Mayo was the buffer. He always had a positive attitude.

Both men came to Blytheville after many lean seasons. The two bonded and caused a change in the program. We went from the outhouse to the penthouse in three years."

The facts are, dozens of state and regional championships were won by many different sports teams by Blytheville under Bill's watch.

In 1967, Southwestern-at-Memphis won the conference in football. They were undefeated in the conference and won the Collegiate Athletic Conference championship in track, along with the Tennessee Intercollegiate Championship. That year, 13 of the 16 existing records in track that had stood for 29 years were broken.

Once, when coaching at Emory-Henry, the team Bookkeeper did not show up for the bus home. Bill waited two hours, but he never showed. When the team arrived at home, the opposing coach called, said he had put the lost boy on a plane home. Seems the lost boy had gotten distracted. He and coach had a long discussion later.

On a Blytheville bus trip home from a game in 1949, the bus stopped on the roadside. Six or eight players wound up doing exercises in a road ditch for some time. That was necessary only once.

Once when coach was a sophomore playing in a game at Hot Springs, Russell Mosley was Blytheville's coach. Joe Dilde was the Hot Springs coach. Both coaches had played at Alabama under Frank Thomas. Each coach had two conference championships at Blytheville; Dilde in 1932 and1933, Mosley in 1948 and 1950.

Bill Mayo has left a tremendous impact on the shape of interscholastic athletics in the state, as well as the nation. One of his greatest honors was when he was inducted in 1998 into the National High School Sports Hall of Fame. In 2007, Bill was inducted into the Arkansas High School Athletic Administrators Hall of Fame. In 2012, Bill was inducted to the National Interscholastic Administrators Hall of Fame. Bill gained national prominence when President Reagan appointed him to the White House Conference for a Drug Free America.

A leader in his field, Mayo has occupied several prominent positions. In 1988, Bill was selected as president of the National Interscholastic Athletic Administrators Association. He has served as chairman of the NIAAA Hall of Fame selection committee.

Bill has served two Lions Clubs as president, winning awards from each.

Bill Mayo was president of seven different organizations. He has so many distinguished accolades, I could go on and on. But you get the idea. Nobody has worked harder in his chosen field than Bill Mayo. But to me, He's COACH, a great guy to hang out with, and a wonderful friend.

This story is written by my grandson Jordan Barksdale.

CAMPING TRIP

WHEN I WAS YOUNG, I JUST LOVED getting in the car and going and camping with my dad. We used to camp all the time. Trekking all across Arkansas and beyond. But we fell out of that habit about five years ago. You see in the past few years, I haven't been so adventurous. I normally stay in the house and play video games or have some indoor fun, but deep down I missed those days of outdoor fun that my dad and I used to share. So let me tell you about my last hiking experience.

It was a Saturday morning, and my dad and I had been preparing for a five to six mile hike. I reluctantly told him I was down to do it, even though I really didn't want to do it. So we left around 5:00 AM, got in our cars and started heading to Albert Pike Recreation Area. Now when I say I was out of shape, I mean it. I couldn't run up the stairs without being out of breath and feeling that knife stick into my side. So yeah, as you can tell, I wasn't prepared. We drove for a good hour or two and we are driving on a dirt road on the side of the mountain. I drive a 1996 Ford Explorer, and I'll tell you what, driving on the side of a mountain with a car in front of you kicking up dust to the point where you can't see is super terrifying. I was gripping the wheel so hard I left hand imprints on it.

So, we were off to a good start. Once we got there we parked and put our packs on and started off on the trail. It was around 6:45 at night once we started so the sun was about to go down and the only flashlights we had were our headlamps. Around thirty minutes later, the sun was just about down, so I decided to take my head lamp out. I put the straps around my head and switched it on, and within fifteen seconds, I was swarmed with literally every type of bug that lived in that dang forest. Every step I took, at least six huge bugs would smack me in the cheek or fly up my nose. It was a nightmare, but I pushed on.

We walked for another thirty minutes, and then decided to stop and set up camp. We also decided to bring hammocks instead of a tent. So while Dad was putting up the hammocks, I went for fire wood. We made a fire, ate some food, then laid down and went to sleep. The next morning I awoke to rain drops hitting me in the face. I jumped up, startled, and threw my tarp over me, the one I brought just in case it rained. I kind of dozed for thirty minutes or so, then decided to get out. I saw my dad sitting in the river drinking some coffee so I decided to get in the water also. I slowly made my way into the water, and sat next to Dad. It was then, that he told me something I did not want to hear, whatsoever.

He said, "Jordan, I'm sorry I didn't tell you sooner, but we are actually hiking twenty six miles, not six." As I sat there in the freezing cold river, with freezing cold rain droplets smacking the top of my head with still twenty four miles to go, I got to tell you; I really wanted to quit, right then and there. But I decided to man up and see it through till the end. Big mistake. We got out of the water, packed everything up and went back to it. Oh and by the way, there were six mountains we had to go over, but I didn't know this at the time. After about a mile, it started to rain again, except this time a lot harder. We walked and walked through the rain for hours, till it got to the point where we really couldn't stand being rained on any longer. We stopped and hung our tarp over two trees and sat down in the mud. Everything was soaking wet. There literally wasn't one single thing that wasn't soaked in my pack. So much water collected in my bag that it was 30 pounds heavier. So, as I was sitting there in the freezing cold mud with a soaking wet tee shirt I had pulled over me as a blanket, I began once again to question going on. I really wanted to just turn around.

But finally it stopped raining, so we pressed on. A half a mile later we got to the base of the first mountain, and I'm not talking about a hill or anything like that. I'm talking about a mountain. We started up and boy was it hard. About half way up I started cramping all over and my side was hurting incredibly bad. We got to the stop, and decided to set up camp. We made another fire, sat down, and started eating some freeze dried lasagna. Then we got in our hammocks. I wasn't going to make the same mistake I had made the day before, so I hung my tarp over my hammock. Thirty minutes passed and it started to pour down once again. The rain was making it humid in the hammock, so my skin was sticking to material all over. And, I remember just hearing my dad snore. It was making me mad that he could just sleep through all of the terrible things that were going on.

The next day, we ate breakfast, pulled on our soaking wet clothes, and started heading down the first mountain. I remember thinking how much better it was going to be to walk down the mountain instead of up. But somehow, it might have been even worse. Every step I took forced my toes into the end of my shoes and hurt very badly. It was really painful. Once we made it to the bottom of the mountain, we filled up our filter bottle with some water out of a stream and started heading up the second mountain. We got about half way up and the weirdest thing happened, all of a sudden I had this huge rush of energy and I felt like I could've run a marathon. It was my second wind. So we got to the top, went down and started up the third mountain, then the fourth, and then the fifth and so on.

So, Dad and I were making our way down the last mountain with four miles to go, when we started thinking about stopping and setting up for the night. We were both chaffed and tired, so we sat down by the side of the road and started setting up our hammocks. While we were setting them up, I heard a car coming down the road. We both took off running down the road waving our hands like crazy. The car came around the corner, stopped, and the men inside agreed to give us a ride back to our car. Boy, were we relieved to be done with all of that. Even though the hike was very miserable at times, it was very empowering for me, and showed me what I am capable of doing, if I push myself. Now, I'm not saying I'll ever hike some dang mountains again. But, all of this has helped me not to give up. And, I am really grateful for the whole experience.

Made in the USA
Columbia, SC
21 February 2020